Immanuel Wallerstein

and the Problem of the World

Immanuel Wallerstein
and the Problem of the World

SYSTEM, SCALE, CULTURE

David Palumbo-Liu, Bruce Robbins,
and Nirvana Tanoukhi, editors

DUKE UNIVERSITY PRESS
Durham and London
2011

© 2011 Duke University Press

All rights reserved

Printed in the United States

of America on acid-free paper ∞

Typeset in Carter & Cone Galliard by

Tseng Information Systems, Inc.

Library of Congress Cataloging-in-

Publication Data and republication

acknowledgments appear on the last

printed page of this book.

Contents

Acknowledgments

This volume is derived from a conference convened and organized by Nirvana Tanoukhi at Stanford and sponsored by the Program in Modern Thought and Literature. The initial set of questions that guided the participants emerged from this statement:

> "Globalization" has recently replaced "postcolonialism" and "diaspora" as the buzzword in the humanities and humanistic social sciences, presenting the disciplines with the challenge of describing "world-scale" phenomena. However, this challenge has triggered a varied and uneven response across the disciplines. For example, while history has moved away from Braudelian historiography towards "comparative," "migration," and "border" studies, comparative literature has undergone a shift away from traditional "influence" studies to most recently witness a revival of the question of "world literature." Each discipline has conducted its own experiment with analytical frameworks espousing world-scale ambitions, among which has been Wallerstein's influential world-systems analysis. Are these experiments relevant to current methodological debates? Does the globalization debate warrant a reconsideration of world-scale analysis for the study of subjects like world literature, global environmental ethics, or post-national governance? And if, in this enterprise of "global" knowledge, "the world" cannot be taken as a tractable unit of analysis, what can?

The essays that were originally presented addressed such questions, and raised their own in turn, which has led to the reshaping and reconsideration of our starting point, as was intended and hoped for.

Besides these participants, Tani Barlow, Gopal Balakrishnan, Neil Brenner, Helen Stacy, and Kären Wigen kindly agreed to add their thoughts to our conversation. Along with the authors of the essays contained here, we would like to thank the following individuals who presented their thoughts at the conference: Liisa Malkki, Aihwa Ong, Anna Tsing, Michael Watts, Akhil Gupta, and the late Richard Rorty. We would also like to thank Monica Moore and Jan Hafner for their hard work in staffing the conference.

—David Palumbo-Liu, Bruce Robbins, Nirvana Tanoukhi

Introduction

The Most Important Thing Happening

"I had a gut feeling in the 1950s," Immanuel Wallerstein writes fifty years later, "that the most important thing happening in the twentieth century was the struggle to overcome the control by the West of the rest of the world."[1]

In the 1950s Wallerstein (born in 1930) was in his twenties. The gut feelings thinkers have in their twenties tend to be self-formative. In deciding what is "the most important thing happening" in your century, you also decide, if you are ambitious enough, what the largest thing will be in your intellectual life, which is to say what you need to figure out, or whom you want to be as a thinker. In Wallerstein's case, what gave him that gut feeling turned out to be large enough to guide him through a half-century and more of extraordinary intellectual achievement. In this sense, among others, it seems appropriate to say that large is beautiful.

As moments of self-orientation about the most important thing happening, gut feelings organize what will be visible to us, impatiently sorting out what doesn't matter all that much from what really does. In recent years Wallerstein has turned his attention to academic disciplines and the ordering of knowledge—again, a large view of large subjects, and subjects to which the chapters gathered here will return. But the single most consistent thread running through his lengthy career is that visceral perception of the 1950s. What has mattered to him most often has been evidence that could be brought to bear on "the control by the West of the rest of the world," on the unequal distribution of resources and life chances that has resulted from it, on how global inequality can be understood and eventually, hopefully, undone. Anything else has mattered less. It is the brilliant single-mindedness of his concern with this very large issue that is the main source of his intellectual influence and the main reason for this existence of this volume.

This is not always how others have taken Wallerstein, nor is it how he himself has explained his work. Why did the unit of analysis have to be the world rather than, say, a tribe or a class or a nation? In *The Modern World-System* (1974), the first volume of his monumental trilogy, Wallerstein says that he chose the world as the appropriate unit because it was only at this scale that he could see "system" (7). His analogy was with astronomy—the physical laws determining the orbits of the planets around the sun. His sole criterion appears to be formal coherence. But the solar system analogy, of course, hints at a hierarchical social content (sun and planets, core and periphery) that it does not openly declare. Factoring this content back in, one would say that there is a system only if there is an answer to the question that matters most: how is the present system of global hierarchy held together? At the same time, the analogy between world-system and solar system makes considerable trouble for Wallerstein. The solar system is unlikely to be affected by any conceivable human intervention, unless you decide to count the re-naming of Pluto. Might the same be true for the world-system? The suggestion is politically inconvenient, to say the least. It warns us not to take on faith the proposition that social injustice can and must be described as systemic at the world scale.

Wallerstein did not pause to note this problem. Nor did he argue the priority of the global hierarchy issue over all others. He simply took it for granted. He had some grounds for doing so. Before writing *The Modern World-System*, he had spent almost twenty years doing sociological research on Africa. His work as an Africanist in the period of decolonization convinced him that in order to make sense of what was happening before his eyes, he could not continue to look only at Africa. The misery and violence he saw there, which did not seem to be disappearing with the end of colonial rule, were not determined wholly or even preponderantly by local actors or realities on the ground. "The decision about the meat lacking in the kitchen," as Brecht says, "is not taken in the kitchen."[2] The pertinent lines of causality stretched out of sight across the globe. As his dependency theory friends had already begun to argue, the Third World and the First World were interconnected in the strongest, causal sense. There was in fact only one world, Wallerstein now proposed, though the world was divided into three main zones: core, periphery, and semi-periphery. You could understand the structural differences between the zones only if you looked at the logic that held the whole world together: that is, the world-system. To understand the inequalities that persisted beyond the conquest of political independence, you had to move to the largest scale.

This preference for world scale could of course be seen as the arbitrary and eminently contestable selection of one sociological perspective from a range of plausible perspectives, one unit of analysis or conception of the world (the world as system) rather than any number of equally desirable alternatives. Wallerstein could be accused of taking for granted, in time-honored Hegelian-Marxist fashion, that the truth is always the whole. But Wallerstein departed in major ways from Marxist orthodoxy. (Crucially, he redefined capitalism in terms of trade rather than in terms of free wage labor, thereby allowing slavery and other forms of physical coercion to count as typical capitalist phenomena.[3]) Thus it makes more sense to think of Wallerstein's choice not as unthinkingly doctrinaire, but rather as existential—as a judgment summing up the state of the world at a given time and shaping the analytic perspective that seemed best suited to deal with it. This is not to say that the inclination to the world scale was merely personal or innocently spontaneous. Nor is it to say that, as the intellectual representation of a gut feeling, the unit-of-analysis selection is epistemologically unassailable. But in the face of the blatant injustice and suffering that defined his existential starting point, epistemological critique may well look like quibbling. At the higher level of seriousness that is forced on us by the subject matter, this choice cannot really be refuted. A gut feeling can only be displaced by some other gut feeling. Any alternative methodology, any smaller unit of analysis, any other conception of the world that tried to displace it without coming to terms in some equally visceral way with global inequality would risk looking trivial.

The editors of this book would like to help organize a debate about these matters that will not be trivial. Is such a debate already under way? Both the recognition of the impact of colonialism, on the left, and the imperative to adapt the disciplines to economic globalization, on the right, can by now of course be considered old news. Since at least the early 1990s, much of the excitement in the cultural disciplines has been generated by work that, without necessarily clarifying the political impulses it was obeying, showed us ways in which the move to the world scale could be productively managed. Arjun Appadurai's "Disjuncture and Difference in the Global Cultural Economy" came out in 1990, helping replace anthropology's focus on "discrete, terri-torialized cultures" (in the words of Gupta and Ferguson) with attention to global cultural flows and "the ways in which dominant cultural forms may be picked up" by the dominated and infused with very different meanings.[4] Paul Gilroy's *The Black Atlantic* came out in 1993, further encouraging the hunt for large transnational configurations that a focus on the local or national scale had left invisible. Pascale Casanova's *La République mondiale des lettres* appeared in 1999 and Franco Moretti's "Conjectures on World Literature" in 2000, laying out attractive but quite distinct models for the conceptualizing of literature at the global scale. It would be futile even to try to number the many disciplinary manifestoes of the last two or three decades that have offered promising blueprints for a globalizing or transnationalizing of knowledge.

Viscerally speaking, however, scholars in the cultural disciplines have remained somewhat ambivalent about the process of their, or our, globalization. In one sense, ratcheting up our work to the world scale has been a chance to satisfy our own most fervent inclinations. We Euro-American cultural critics tell ourselves, and rightly, that we have committed an ethical and political injustice in excluding so much of the rest of the world from, say, the setting up and interpreting of canons, the choice of categories we apply when we compare cultural forms and social realities, and so on. The principle of democracy cries out for greater inclusiveness and conceptual reform. In any case, we are interested in the most vital and vibrant cultural expressions, and these increasingly emerge outside the old metropolitan centers. We are more or less happy to comply with the globalizing imperative, then, for these reasons and others, even if we are not quite sure what form the compliance should take, whether subtle or not so subtle varieties of exploitation may be built into it, whether non-European writers and thinkers will see themselves as benefitting or not, and so on. The uncertainties of literary critics are at least matched by those of historians. If history is to be written beyond the scale of the nation, as historians seem to agree that it must, should the result be called world history? global history? international history? transnational history? The competing names point toward disciplinary visions of planetarity that are perhaps not quite ready to compete, not yet having come into focus. A similar compound of confusion and expectancy can be detected in anthropology, ethnic studies, and other disciplines. Mixed feelings? Yes. Gut feelings that can be confidently acted on? Perhaps not quite yet. The gravitational pull of the world scale is clear. What that scale ought to mean to us remains a conundrum.

At this moment of eager and expectant confusion, world-systems analysis is especially good for humanists to reflect on, we would suggest, precisely because it is somewhat unfriendly to the humanities. Wallerstein's original argument was that the control by the West of the rest of the world worked by means of unequal exchange. Unlike an empire, therefore, the modern world-system did not require a single political hegemony. Nor did it require cultural homogeneity. It could happily accept both political and cultural differentiation. This implied that the hypothetical achievement of political emancipation or cultural self-expression on the part of some non-Western collectivity would not necessarily have any effect on the system as a whole. This is not a promising implication from the perspective of the humanities, which take for their object of knowledge cultural self-expression (and its eventual pay-off in terms of political consequences). Humanists could logically conclude that what the humanities do is not very important. Wallerstein has not always discouraged that conclusion. When he tells the story of how the current disciplinary division of labor evolved, he suggests that the social sciences were born out of a nineteenth- and twentieth-century struggle between the humanities (on the whole politically reactionary) and the natural sciences (on the whole politically progressive). This scenario gives the juiciest role today to the social sciences. Having dialectically absorbed and transcended their predecessors, including the traditional humanities, the social sciences must continue the struggle by overcoming their own internal divisions. They are the unmistakable hero of Wallerstein's story, the agent of humanity's struggle to understand and escape the social reality in which it is caught up, a disciplinary hegemon that (unlike the global hegemon) its subordinates ought eagerly to welcome. If you are a social scientist, it's an inspiring narrative. But it leaves nothing valuable for the traditional humanities to accomplish. Or, to be more precise, it suggests that there would have to be a major change in the humanities in order for what they accomplish to acquire political significance.[5]

Still, cultural critics ought to cherish this lack of enthusiasm. We ought to take it as a sort of tough love. At a moment when we are in any case trying on various world-scale identities, it offers us both a well-developed vision of what the world scale means and the challenge of re-inspecting our customary interpretive practices in its harsh but revealing light. We may end up re-affirming our loyalty to those practices. In the end we may agree, as humanist critics of Wallerstein have frequently concluded, that analysis in terms of the world-system entails a fatal disrespect for culture, or subjectivity, or difference, or agency, or the local, or any of the other objects of knowledge and the positive values that humanists ordinarily and sometimes unconsciously take as their own. But if so, these objects and values will have been exposed and argued through in a new way, and they will no longer be quite the same.

One example of a familiar object that looks new and strange at the world scale is class. In the humanities, even champions of cultural particularity tend to respect class, if only as a category of victimhood assumed to resemble other, already-respected categories. Critics of culture do not seem very bothered by the status of class as a cross-cultural universal. Yet the perverse effect of world-systems analysis is to throw any universal, world-scale conception of class into question. This conclusion follows not, of course, from deference to cultural particularity, which world-systems analysis has very little of, but from its defining premise: unequal exchange across the international division of labor. If there is an unequal exchange between periphery and core, as Wallerstein insists, the meaning of class cannot remain the same across this line. It simply will not mean the same thing to be a "worker," say, in Denmark and in Togo. For the system that guarantees a flow of surplus from the Togos of the periphery to the Denmarks of the core allows for a certain percentage of that surplus to be distributed among Danish (or American) workers. The recipients in the core nations—let us not enter now into the question of how many they are, or how much of that surplus they receive—will still be "workers" in the eyes of those around them. They will often struggle with various sorts of deprivation, indignity, and insecurity. But structurally speaking, from the point of view of the system as a whole, it is an obvious mistake to put them in the same category as the people at the periphery whose surplus flows into their pockets. Moreover, it would be foolish to expect that the world-system's gravitational pull on class identity would not show up in one way or another at the level of worker subjectivity. As Wallerstein puts it, "At a certain level of expansion of income and 'rights,' the 'proletarian' becomes in reality a 'bourgeois,' *living off the surplus-value of others*, and the most immediate effect of this is on class consciousness."[6] This is a structural fact of some importance if one is trying to understand, say, the proven vulnerability of large sections of the American electorate to bellicose nationalism, including economically disadvantaged sections. Wallerstein may be wrong in his predictions of the imminent collapse of American hegemony. But as the U.S. cedes some of its accustomed privileges and the Lou Dobbsian political temptations of xenophobia aimed at immigrants and East Asian economic competitors grow stronger and stronger, this world-scale relativizing of class consciousness grows ever more peremptory.

Notice that in this instance the logic of global interrelatedness does not produce a politically correct result. Nor is it by any means identical with some of the more familiar logics that tend to get instinctive nods of agreement from humanist audiences. It is quite different, for example, from the common assumption that the effects of the metropolis on the colony will always be marked by some reciprocal imprint that the colony (or colonialism) can be discovered to have left on the culture of the metropolis. That interesting if questionable hypothesis derives from Freud's notion of the return of the repressed and perhaps ultimately from the Hegelian dialectic.[7] There is much evidence that, ethically and disciplinarily appealing as it may be, it is contrary to fact. Did the Irish Famine of the 1840s leave any significant trace on the Victorian novel? If it did not, then can culture be understood on the model of the unconscious? Are we sure this is really how the world is connected? The sort of reflex assent that the proposition of reciprocal cultural influence tends to receive, most often without anyone even thinking to pose such questions, suggests that certain paradigms of world interconnectedness now in wide circulation repose upon an unexamined ethical a priori ("our culture must reflect the harms we have done" or "all cultures are equal"), rather than upon genuine curiosity to know how the world actually is and is not interrelated. This volume seeks to stimulate such curiosity and the discussion about competing conceptions of the world that will necessarily follow from it.

With that end in view, we offer Immanuel Wallerstein not as the inevitably correct answer (indeed, world-systems analysis is strenuously interrogated below), but as a tool to think with, a machine that can shake up established or rapidly congealing assumptions about the shape of the world. That includes Wallerstein's own assumptions. Consider the first sentence of Eric Wolf's *Europe and the People Without History* (1982): "The central assertion of this book is that the world of humankind constitutes a manifold, a totality of interconnected processes, and inquiries that disassemble this totality into bits and pieces and then fail to reassemble it falsify reality" (3).[8] This is a brief against disciplinary specialization as such. Judged by the substantive criterion we have attributed to Wallerstein—can this knowledge be used to understand global inequality or not?—Wolf seems prepared to throw overboard perfectly useful knowledge, and to do so on the purely formal grounds that such knowledge is specialized. Wallerstein, himself a passionate critic of specialization, might well agree. But if so, his gut feeling would have to be invoked against his account of disciplinarity. (Or vice versa.) As you jump from one scale to another, all your theoretical or epistemological or political commitments cannot be expected to line up perfectly with each other. The topic of scale demands that you put your ultimate commitments in play, and leave them there.

It demands, for example, that some of those who take a "small is beautiful" line on cultural particularity recognize that they are still in the grip of a very large meta-narrative. A few pages after his protest against disciplinary specialization, Wolf offers an explicit critique of Wallerstein. Wallerstein's aim, he writes, "was to understand how the core subjugated the periphery, and not to study the reactions of the micro-populations habitually investigated by the anthropologists" (23). Wolf does not want to choose between these two options; he wants to think "simultaneously on the level of the encompassing system and on the micro-level" (23). But his phrasing allows for an easy slide from "reactions of the micro-populations" to the *subjectivity* of those micro-populations; this is one sense of "reactions." There is no guarantee whatsoever that the study of such "reactions" would seek out causal linkages to system, though Wolf himself does seek out those linkages. Local subjectivity could well be studied, in other words, for its presumed inherent value, and not for how it might change the story of expansion, subjugation, and continuing inequality. This would mean losing sight of "the most important thing happening." Or it would be to assert that the most important thing happening is a story of cultural democratization in which new voices break free of their old silencing or marginalization, make themselves heard, attain the dignity of self-expression. This is of course another meta-narrative, though one that rarely dares or cares to speak that name.

The alternative story of coming to dignity by coming to self-expression has a fatal attractiveness to those whose disciplines take culture as their object, perhaps because it is much easier to find examples of. When Lowe and Lloyd insist on attention to the "excavation and connection of alternative histories and their different temporalities that cannot be contained by the progressive narrative of Western developmentalism" and "adamantly emphasize[d] diversely localized projects and struggles," they illustrate the way even the best intentions can be short-circuited.[9] The fact that "localized projects and struggles" exist does not mean that such projects and struggles are aimed at disputing "the control by the West of the rest of the world." Sometimes that's their aim, and sometimes it isn't. People struggle with each other over many other things. A great deal of what they struggle over, and perhaps most of it, cannot be assumed to have any political coherence whatsoever, subjectively compelling as the struggle may be at the moment to those involved. We need to ask, then, whether there is a real connection between struggle and system. Anyone who thinks there is takes on the obligation to show how the connection works. It may work, but the case has to be made. When Lowe and Lloyd disconnect "alternative histories" and "different temporalities" from "the progressive narrative of Western developmentalism," they seem to celebrate the simple fact that these histories and temporalities are there. The question of whether they have had any impact on global inequalities of power or even threaten to have any has not been canceled, but it has been postponed.

In the hands of other, less politically engaged thinkers, this postponement risks becoming permanent. One sign of this risk is the pervasiveness of the notion of "alternative modernities," which properly rejects the stigma of cultural inferiority imposed by developmentalism, but also disguises the severe political, social, and economic hierarchies that continue to structure the world. If every society has achieved the distinctive modernity that expresses it, then what's the complaint? In getting rid of the opprobrious epithet "traditional," haven't you also gotten rid of the description of damage inflicted that any complaint against social injustice requires? Should we be overjoyed to think of the world's cultures as equal and equally modern if so much else in the world remains so unequal? There may be satisfying answers to these questions, but in order to discover them the questions will first have to be asked.

Asking them will involve renewing our tolerance of what Lyotard called "grands récits." Many of the objects of interest these days—not just global inequality, but Tani Barlow's "modern girl," the place of racism both inside and outside of European culture, and any number of others—call on us to learn once again to tell large stories, and to tell them better. The horrified recoil from any hint of panopticism has clearly had its day. Here for once we can take our cue from the market. Readers hunger for large stories that (like Foucault's own very large story of modernity, which never acknowledged its own scale) offer them some sort of large-scale vision.

"Large-scale vision" is the phrase Wallerstein uses, in the dedication of *The Decline of American Power*, to indicate his common ground with the dedicatee, historian William McNeill. As the "X is a construct" paradigm comes to seem more and more dated, it becomes less and less plausible to keep nonhuman actors (like the germs and rodents of McNeill's *Plagues and Peoples*) out of our accounts, however anxious we may be to preserve the relative autonomy of the cultural. Wallerstein's insistence that the world cannot be understood without bridging the "two cultures" divide is likely to seem more and more prophetic. In the coming renegotiations between the humanities and the social and natural sciences, it seems likely that the cool, even inhuman, visions of both McNeill and Wallerstein will be increasingly appealed to.

But they are of course different visions. To see the value of the larger scale as such does not necessarily involve suspending disbelief in the particular large story that Wallerstein tells. Nor need it entail accepting the overwhelming causal powers that he ascribes to his unit of analysis—in other words, the assumption that the world does indeed form a system and that the system explains all major historical events within it. "Auschwitz, Gulags, and ethnic purification," Wallerstein writes, "all occurred within the framework of a historical social system, the capitalist world-economy. We have to ask what it is about this system that produced such phenomena and allowed them to flourish in the twentieth century, in ways and to a degree that hadn't occurred before."[10] He insists "that the explanation must be found in the functioning of the system" (42). This certainty that the functioning of the system can explain anything and everything, even Auschwitz, does not inspire confidence. Here the causal powers of the system are granted an almost theological omnipotence. This is what gives system a bad name.

Some will want to assert the reverse position: the programmatic impossibility of explaining Auschwitz. But that would be equally theological, for it would seek to wall off a sacred domain of irreducible mystery. Surely it is better to remain agnostic on the point of when, where, and how much of what is presently unknown or unexplained must necessarily remain unknown or unexplained. And to remain agnostic, for that matter, on whether in any given case system indeed exists.

What after all *is* system? "Globalization is not just some economic fad, and it is not just a passing trend. It is an international system–the dominant international system that replaced the Cold War system after the fall of the Berlin Wall. We need to understand it as such . . . We are now in the new, international system of globalization."[11] The speaker here is Thomas L. Friedman, cheerleader of globalization. Friedman compares globalization now to the Cold War before 1989. Each, he insists, is a system with its own unique logic and rules. But the Cold War was a political system; it was defined by state actors, by diplomacy, by the use or the threat of military force. What Friedman desires to say about globalization is that it is a system that works without politics. In this desire, though of course not in their own politics, Wallerstein and Friedman come together. Yet it's not clear that either of them can sustain the notion of a system that works by itself, like the solar system, independent of the contingencies of social action. In Friedman's case this notion is undercut by the parallel with the Cold War. In Wallerstein's it is undercut by the history of how the modern world-system came about. Voluntary acts cannot be kept out of this history. Indeed, if one considers the system-founding actions of the strong European states in the Early Modern period (or for that matter the actions of the Chinese state in launching the P.R.C. on the road to world-scale economic power), they are arguably decisive to it. Just as physical force cannot be excluded from the logic of capitalism—this was Wallerstein's own revisionist point about slavery—so action cannot be excluded from the definition of the system.

One of two conclusions would seem to follow. First, that what Wallerstein offers is not a theory of global capitalism or a system, but rather a *history*. And that like all histories his too contains—indeed, makes excellent use of—a great deal of messy contingency. This would involve scaling back somewhat our sense of his ambition. But it would still leave us free to applaud an immense accomplishment. Second, it might also be argued that this contingency-filled account is what a system *is*—in other words, that Wallerstein has indeed described the modern world-system—but that this system, like all systems, is much more open to contingency than he tends to recognize. This would avoid the trap of rejecting all system as such, thereby giving up on even the possibility of guidance as to how closely any given projects or struggles or sufferings might indeed be linked, or not, to the maintenance of global inequality.[12] In both cases—and they may simply say the same thing in slightly different words—there would be an obligation not to take a purely theoretical position vis-à-vis contingency, but rather to look and see, in any given instance, how much contingency there actually is or was. It would involve seeing the degree of contingency as itself contingent.

This may sound like quibbling, but it is intended as the exact opposite: to guarantee that the study of culture, to which all of the contributors here are committed in one way or another, can enjoy a justified sense of its place within the gut feelings of its practitioners. The emphasis falls on "justified." A defensive insistence on the value of my object of study or field simply because it is mine or because it is distinct from others (objects of knowledge usually are, more or less) will not constitute justification in the mind of a hypothetical objective observer. If culture is going to feel confident about its importance in the age of so-called globalization, it will have to earn that confidence. The premise here is that this is not too much to ask. Re-imagining culture as one contingency among others within the world-system does not mean lowering its relative value if it is accompanied by a raising of the value of contingency as such within the conceptualization of the world-system. Both culture and system stand to benefit from the conversation staged here between them.

The Chapters

These chapters are grouped under four headings. First, the chapters included in "System and Responsibility" look at the motivations and consequences for the humanities of both adapting, and rejecting, systematic thinking. They ask, most critically, whether thinking systematically on the world scale enables us to assign responsibility more efficiently or on the contrary blocks or disables ethical practice. How can one judge the effects the world scale has had or may yet have on responsible action? The second section, "Literature: Restructured, Rehistoricized, Rescaled," looks at two different models that adapt, in different ways, world-systems analysis to literary texts. They examine how different spatial and temporal schemata and structures, and the issue of scale and the ethical relations, each lends new definition to the "world" literary object. With the third group of chapters, gathered under the rubric "Re-spatializing, Remapping, Recognizing," our focus moves from literary studies to geography, area studies, and gender studies. Each of these chapters moves beyond world-systems analysis and is committed in one way or another to understanding how "globalization" should be read as a specifically historical dynamic that reconfigures geopolitical space particularly and unevenly. Finally, the chapters in "Ethics, Otherness, System" argue that seemingly universal notions of human rights law and rationality, seeking to discipline and adjudicate "the human" in its diverse behaviors and actions, derive from historically specific encounters with different cultures, religions, and races. They ask where the historical particularity of its origins leaves the liberal ambition to speak for justice and equality at the world scale. The collection ends with a short afterword in which Immanuel Wallerstein situates world-systems analysis vis-à-vis the humanities, and Gopal Balakrishnan's reassessment of Wallerstein's work.

System and Responsibility

Taking up the rough dichotomy between scientific and humanistic discourse, each seeking to survey and scale the world in newly global terms,
this cluster reflects upon Wallerstein's provocative conjunction of "world"
and "system" and considers the utility of his analytical model beyond pure
social science. How does its way of mapping the world compare and contrast with those of the cultural disciplines? What do the humanities stand to
gain or lose from the kind of systematic thinking evinced in world-systems
analysis? Can emergent forms of global scholarship learn from the frictions
between the disciplines and their distinctive points of emphasis? In "The
Modern World-System: Its Structures, Its Geoculture, Its Crisis and Transformation," Richard E. Lee both provides a useful account of the genesis of
world-systems analysis and comments on how it may be particularly enlisted
in the next phase of historical thinking. Lee traces world-systems analysis to
a particular moment in intellectual, cultural, political, and economic history.
Both a "protest or resistance movement within the structures of knowledge,
intimately connected to the social movements of 1968" and "an outgrowth
of the secular crisis of the processes reproducing historical capitalism in the
long term," world-systems analysis has been, Lee argues, a "forward-looking
movement during a period of transition." Critically, he sees our current historical situation precisely as such a period of transition, and therefore insists
on the continuing usefulness of world-systems analysis, both in terms of
knowledge and in terms of social justice. "Over the past three decades, the
crisis in the processes reproducing the organizational patterns of the modern world-system in all three structural arenas [the economic, the political,
the epistemological], despite neoliberal efforts bolstered by the rhetoric of
globalization (the idea that there is no other choice) to extend them, has become apparent. . . . Within the structures of knowledge . . . rationalization
has entered into crisis and the attendant transformation is already changing
the way we view the world, and it will eventually alter the possibilities for
human action that we are able to imagine."

How does the study of culture enter into this picture? According to Lee,
world-systems analysis intervened in a "third set of structures that were just
as constitutive of the modern world-system as those in the arenas of production and distribution, the economic, and coercion and decision making,
the political." Along with the economic and political was "the arena of cognition and intentionality, the structures of knowledge." Particularly critical

for our volume are the implications of locating cultural knowledge within this last arena. Lee sees all three arenas working in tandem: "These processes of knowledge formation, in articulation with those sets of processes associated with the 'economic' and 'political' spheres, account for the dominant relational setting 'disciplining' human cognition and intentionality, the 'cultural' parameters of possible action." However, this conjoining of the three arenas does not take place without friction, indeed, this schematization has perpetually generated a question that lies at the heart of any interdisciplinary ambition between the humanities and world-systems analysis—"if the 'broadly "cultural" aspect' of the world-system were just as constitutive as the economic and political realms, then ad-hoc, particularistic conceptualizations had to give way to a specification of the *longue durée* structures of this 'third arena,' including the cyclical rhythms and secular trends of their reproduction." Thus we see a specific fissure in the disciplinary production of knowledge, produced doubly: as world-systems analysis insisted on blasting apart the conventional methods of defining the unit of analysis, calling on investigators to turn their eyes to longer and irregular spans of periodization and a logic based on the division of labor rather than by discrete nation-states or nation-based consortia, the admission of the "cultural" proved an object resistant to such systematization. While this is seen by some as a debilitating impasse, or even a negation of the value of world-systems analysis, Lee sees this as a potentially enabling and indeed transformative tension.

As does the next chapter. In "Blaming the System," Bruce Robbins probes both Wallerstein's commitment to "system" as privileged unit of analysis and those habits of thinking in the humanities that appear to discourage such a commitment. Long before the 1960s indictment of "the System" as the source of social ills, there has been a tradition of counterposing "system," and specifically the economic system, to life-enhancing "culture": "As Raymond Williams tells the story in *Culture and Society* (1958), the division of labor names the characteristic disease of social and individual fragmentation that, in the decades following the Industrial Revolution, first calls the compensatory wholeness of the culture concept into being. As an antidote to society's modern divisiveness, culture is anti-system, at least in Wallerstein's sense, from its very origins in the romantic movement." Yet Robbins reminds us that the humanists' faith in culture as a potent antidote to economic inhumanity might be wishful thinking, and their rejection out of hand of a mode of analysis that would indeed see as a large part of its task the righting of economic injustice might well be self-defeating. He points to "the lack of clarity that results when scholars in the humanities, reacting against systematicity, refuse to ask . . . the question of whether or how far culture really does make a difference to inequality at the world scale."

By the same token, Robbins critiques Wallerstein's displacement of "culture" to the periphery, and his faith that this segmentation settles the question of culture's location. Ultimately, he offers a double indictment, which more positively can be read as a double challenge: "Wallerstein's belief in system (as definitive and exclusive object to be blamed) seems the very antithesis of the humanist's disbelief in system. For the humanist, what must be blamed is, precisely, thinking systematically. Yet as I've suggested, these apparent opposites have similar and disquieting (that is, quietist) political effects. And the counterintuitive symmetry goes further. If I have shown that Wallerstein has more in common with the humanities than he appears to, I hope I have also managed to suggest that the humanities need more of Wallerstein's sense of system than they admit."

Literature: Restructured, Rehistoricized, Rescaled

Weighing the relevance of world-systems analysis for a particular branch of the humanities, these chapters take as their focal point the invention, circulation, evolution, and capitalization of literature on a world scale. What, they ask, are the structural and systemic assumptions undergirding modern attempts to reach literary texts globally? Engaging world-systems analysis, they critique standing models of "world literature" while at the same time setting forth adjustments, advancements, and reinterpretations of these models. Franco Moretti's chapter demonstrates the usefulness of world-systems analysis to literary studies while also clarifying and qualifying that usefulness and proposing a complementary mode of analysis. In "World-Systems Analysis, Evolutionary Theory, *Weltliteratur*," Moretti argues that the literary world-system is best understood through an analytical model that accounts for the relation between modes of diversification and integration. In order to map the totality of what critics have called "literary history," he proposes a more scale-sensitive approach that would combine world-systems analysis with evolutionary theory. For Moretti, this means that instead of describing the integration of a single *Weltliteratur*, or a single "world *of* literature," it may be more accurate to differentiate two "world literatures," two distinct epochs of literary exchange. The "first" *Weltliteratur* precedes the eighteenth century. Best explained by an adapted version of evolutionary theory, it is a mosaic of separate "local" cultures characterized by strong internal diversity and the production of new literary forms by further divergence. The "second" *Weltliteratur*, which follows the eighteenth century, is, however, better explained by a modified version of world-systems analysis. It can truly be called a "world literary system" because, as a unified market, it displays a remarkable drive toward homogenization and (re)produces literary forms by processes of convergence.

For Moretti the problem of world literature hinges on the question of temporality, a political question that nonetheless must preclude normative assumptions about literary value:

> What are we to make of these two world literatures? They offer us a great chance to rethink the place of history in literary studies. A generation ago, only the literature of the past was considered "worth" studying; today, the only "relevant" literature is that of the present. In a sense, everything has changed; in another, nothing has, because both positions are profoundly *normative* ones, much more concerned with value judgments than with actual knowledge. And instead, the past and the present of literature . . . should be seen, not as "superior" or "inferior" to each other, but as two epochs that are structurally so different that they require two independent theoretical approaches. Learning to study *the past as past*, then, with the help of evolutionary theory, and *the present as present*, with the help of world-systems analysis: here is a possible research program for *Weltliteratur* in the twenty-first century.

In "The Scale of World Literature," Nirvana Tanoukhi reconceives the problem of "literary space" outside the framework of the "hard" structures of influence described by Moretti. Instead, Tanoukhi calls for "a literary critique of the geographic concept of scale" which would reveal the dynamics of context-dependency that underpins the practice of literary comparison. In the comparative study of the novel, as Tanoukki sees it, the African novel's specificity is produced in or as a cultural landscape which circumscribes both the mobility of the African hero and the meanings of his journey. In this Tanoukhi recognizes a literary equivalent to the dynamic of "emplacement by differentiation," which human geographers have come to associate with "the production of scale." The chapter explores the tension between the act of placing a text in historical context and the act of placing it in geographical context, using this tension to account for unexpected points of affinity between progressive modes of comparative literary analysis and more conser-

vative models of history by analogy. In order to reinvent comparative literature for our time, Tanoukhi suggests, it is necessary to reassess the concept
of scale, especially its performative dimension.

Respatializing, Remapping, Recognizing

Turning from literary and cultural studies to geography and history, these
chapters begin by considering how world-systems analysis influenced their
disciplines and then point out certain lacunae and problematics that it has
not addressed. Each considers the profound structural and systemic effects
of adding new elements to their discipline's methodological formulae—
scale, region, gender. They explain how such data disrupt and at the same
time illuminate the functioning of world-systems analysis. The authors propose new possibilities that point toward nothing less than a methodological
reconstitution of each of their disciplines.

In "The Space of the World: Beyond State-Centrism?," the urbanist
and sociospatial theorist Neil Brenner elucidates the stakes of "the scale-
problem" as it is represented within geography, describes its mounting significance in the context of globalization studies, and offers an assessment
of Wallerstein's conceptualization of scale: "Although Wallerstein defines
the capitalist world-system on multiple levels—for instance, in terms of the
drive toward ceaseless accumulation; the commodification of production,
distribution and investment processes; and the antagonistic class relation
between capitalists and wage-laborers—he argues repeatedly that its unique
scalar form is one of its constitutive features." To what extent, asks Brenner,
does Wallerstein's insistence on the vastness or interconnection of the world-
system move beyond an earlier conception of space as territory? In other
words, how robust is Wallerstein's conceptualization of geographic scale?

Brenner argues that one of the central intellectual barriers to a more adequate understanding of contemporary global transformations is the lack of
appropriately historical and dynamic conceptualizations of social space, and
develops this claim in three steps: first, by summarizing the conceptualization of sociospatial restructuring under capital; second, by developing an
interpretation of the epistemology of state-centrism, and finally, by differentiating two major strands of contemporary globalization research, "global
territorialist" approaches (such as Wallerstein's) and "deterritorialist" approaches. Brenner concludes by sketching an alternative interpretation of
contemporary global restructuring, a contradictory process of reterritorial-

ization and rescaling in which state institutions play crucial mediating and facilitating roles.

After Brenner's sociospatial critique of world-systems analysis, the historian Kären Wigen's "Cartographies of Connection: Ocean Maps as Metaphors for Inter-Area History" finds in the differentiated spaces of oceanic regions and Asia points of productive resistance to standing world-scale analytic enterprises. Wigen takes a guarded, pragmatic approach to the ambition of enlarging the unit of analysis. She notes that "by the 1990s, a countervailing turn toward micro-history, a widespread linguistic turn, and the rise of identity, meaning, and cultural logic to the forefront of American historians' analytical concerns combined to pull the field away from macro-history altogether. Yet the past two decades have witnessed a slow sea-change in the practice of history in the United States: one that has gradually forced attention back on large-scale movements and processes, albeit in more plastic and pluralistic ways."

Specifically, Wigen describes "the spatial turn" in history as an attempt to grapple with phenomena that are characterized by "an elusive, expansive geography" and which cannot be "satisfactorily investigated within the bounds of a single state [because they] spill across even the macro-regions of area studies." To historians, macro-history can be professionally and conceptually daunting. If the preferred unit of analysis continues to be the nation, which is taken as the inevitable basis of historical pedagogy and training, then macro-history will necessarily remain marginal. Nonetheless, Wigen acknowledges that even specialists who are skeptical of inter-area histories nonetheless "reveal local evidence of hybridity and multiculturalism" because of their continued commitment to the micro-scale. In the final analysis, she is inclined to see macro- and micro-historians converging on the same processes from "different scales of resolution."

Another historian, Tani Barlow, takes a different approach. In "What is a Poem? The Event of Women and the Modern Girl as Problems in Global or World History," Barlow suggests that the historian's critique of scale must re-examine the premises of "context-dependency." Adapting Badiou's concepts of "event" and "poem," Barlow brings to our attention "an event in history that is both not regional, since it is a universal, and yet launched in a region, Asia, that has not generally been considered an origin point in the story of globalization or capitalism." The choice of a methodological scale is not merely a practical preference, she argues, but already carries the political and ideological biases of an intellectual tradition. Barlow describes a debate between regional and world-systems analysts of Asia in which "prominent Asia historians . . . have repeatedly criticized and rewritten Wallersteinian world-systems theory through the prism of regional history." She complicates the terms of this debate by proposing that "the modern girl phenomenon is one programmatic instance of a world-scale event of woman, an event which has not been fully thought through in world-systems theory and which, by its absence and again in its presence, opens a useful lacuna in the systematics of globalist theories."

Neither containable by regionalist methodologies (as "Asian"), nor broadly and universally mappable in the sense that "class" or "labor" are, the modern girl phenomenon is best read as an "event" that shuttles in between these two analytic categories. It "exceeds the surplus of local (or 'regional,' in the language of the new regional histories) signification that the term 'women' calls up. . . . The 'global' phenomenon of women as a category of modernity was constructed precisely with world-scale ambitions at the same time it had to acknowledge (if not submit to) the protocols of the 'global' to even be articulated." This singular phenomenon was "launched from the multiple," that is, from various incommensurate spaces within Asia, and subsequently integrated into capitalist modernity. Using iconic advertising and other images of "the modern girl," Barlow maps the invention and circulation of this figure from multiple sites. The "modern girl" is thus marked by both its local inflection and its global legibility.

Ethics, Otherness, System

Blending the previous chapters' attention both to attempts at arriving at a world-scale system or structure capable of accommodating difference, and to the concrete resistance to such aspirations, the chapters by Helen Stacy and David Palumbo-Liu look at, respectively, law and rationality, with specific concerns about their ethical ramifications. They show how two "universal" notions at the heart of the definition of what it means to be human and act in the world—the notion of "universal" human rights and the universal endowment of rationality to all humans—were and are deeply embedded in the particularities of culture, religion, and race. The chapters demonstrate how the emergence and practice of human rights law and "reason" have had to cover over the traces of these particulars, and how these specificities come back to haunt and trouble the actual implementation of law and reason on the world scale. In "The Legal System of International Rights," Stacy sketches a comprehensive structural and historical account of the rise of International Human Rights law. Her *longue durée* account evokes explicitly the language of world-systems, arguing for a more capacious understanding of the evolution of the concept from the outset. Stacy asserts that "the picture of international human rights as a new post–Second World War world-scale movement ignores the longer-term historical, intellectual, economic and political forces that preceded it. . . . I argue that international human rights today are better seen as the most recent version of several prior world-scale phases, phases that have radiated outwards from Europe." With that larger perspective, the author is able to address the issue of ethics: "It is crucial to understand how inherent historical assumptions of inferiority and superiority, of religious, civilizational, and national difference found in these early phases have stayed with the development of international human rights discourse and troubled its world-scale ambitions."

Stacy demonstrates how the very notion of "rights," along with subsequent historical expressions of rights in terms of "universal rights," "internal rights," and "human rights," is embedded in distinct stages of the exportation, dispersion, and reinterpretation of a most elusive Western commodity, namely "analytical jurisprudence and the justification of law as 'positive law.'" She takes us through various phases of the articulation, institutionalization, and finally the professionalization of human rights in order to dispel the misconception that human rights are a recent product of the postwar period. However, Stacy also shows how, for better or worse, human rights today serve a different systemic function than they did before the world wars or during the various stages of colonial conquest and decolonization. What we now recognize as the discourse of human rights is an advanced stage of the unification of an ideological sphere of legality. In her view, human rights are far from "a turning-point of post-Holocaust European-American humanist ideas." Rather, they are an outgrowth of mature ideological instruments that catalyzed economic integration by conquest and trade, typically in the name of liberal rationality and progress.

In "Rationality and World-Systems Analysis: Fanon and the Impact of the Ethico-Historical," David Palumbo-Liu tackles more directly the liberal concept of rationality and its place in Wallerstein's attack on scientism. Palumbo-Liu argues that if there is indeed a keyword that organizes Wallerstein's theoretical framework, it is his revised notion of rationality, which entails a political and ethically informed rethinking of the disciplines: "Coterminous with the expansion of the unit of analysis in world-systems analysis was a moral and ethical rationale—the endeavor to view historical, political, and more recently, cultural phenomena in both spatially and temporally broader and differently systematized manners brought with it an ethical question as to how knowledge was produced about Others who were now drawn into a different epistemological frame. What could world-systems analysis bring to disciplinary knowledge that would differ qualitatively, and politically, from its predecessors in the social sciences? World-systems analysis found that certain methodologies, models, and assumptions—founded on a notion of rationality—obfuscated issues of morality and politics, of being with Others in a substantively rational way." World-systems analysis, according to Palumbo-Liu, is especially attentive to the contradictions of liberalism, particularly when liberalism is applied to those deemed to be specifically "minor" or "particular." For Wallerstein, as Palumbo-Liu reads him, Franz Fanon's wrestling with the notion of rationality rehearses key questions about the attempt to affect social justice globally. How can one do so when the Other is variously portrayed as beyond reason? How can one do so when the adoption of the reason of the colonizer both facilitates and disempowers at the same time? Fanon's linkage of rationality, race, and revolution is crucial not just to us, but to Wallerstein as well. Palumbo-Liu credits Wallerstein with defamiliarizing a notion of rationality that otherwise obfuscates the question of morality in politics, and with productively complicating the prospect of coexisting with Others in a rational way. We must be ready to follow. Like Fanon, we must be able to see the heavily political and racialized elements hiding in the concept of rationality, Palumbo-Liu concludes, while maintaining a vexed, contingent, suspicious relationship with it. Fanon's final statements point toward a hopeful, even utopian poetics that works through the gridlock of reason and difference.

Reflecting on his work and the reflections on it gathered here, Immanuel Wallerstein uses the example of religious studies as a discipline that can exemplify social science in a way legible to humanists. Perhaps, he suggests, history can serve as a common ground between humanistic and social scientific disciplines, between generalization and the appreciation of particularity or uniqueness. While "no statement about literature, religion, or world-systems is ever irreducibly unique," each statement emanating from these disciplines is aimed at naming a particular historical reality: "Literature, religions, and world-systems constantly evolve and change. And all statements are statements about a specific historical moment, holding true at best for that moment and not necessarily for others." Does this mean that "the world" is better conceived as a history than as a system? If so, how much planetary systematicity would be forfeited? If not, how much system can the world's history make room for? To what extent can history and system co-exist without contradiction? The collection ends with an evocative piece by Gopal Balakrishnan, who reflects back upon the various historical receptions of Wallerstein, and recasts both those modes of understanding Wallerstein and Wallerstein's own work in terms of the contemporary situation of capital as it relates to the notion of "civilization," addressing Wallerstein's pair of studies, *Historical Capitalism* and *Capitalist Civilization*. He isolates a particular point of tension between what he deems the abiding potential of Wallerstein's theory over and against a cultural, subjective will that may no longer be found: "Wallerstein's remorseless insistence that even the most anti-systemic states remained wholly subject to its multi-level compulsion to accumulate was qualified by the claim that the system's centuries-old power to englobe was in the midst of a long-term crisis. Perhaps we are now entering into a period in which the power of these compulsions, ever more dependent on debt and public subsidy, will begin to wane, opening up new parameters for 'de-linking,' more favorable conditions for break-throughs in self-determination. But the cultural, 'subjective' inclination and capacity for such political experiments may have also waned in many regions of the world-system." In particular, Balakrishnan queries the linkages between "capitalist civilization," the university system and its disciplinary structures, and the current economic meltdown.

The chapters collected here, from multiple social sciences and the humanities, raise precisely the questions raised in these two reflective chapters, as well as others, and in so doing put extreme pressure on the working assumptions that their various disciplines bring to the study of the world and the world scale. The question raised by Wallerstein at the start of this chapter, regarding his "gut feeling," has prompted our own reactions, visceral and otherwise, about the "biggest thing" happening in the early twenty-first century, and the ways world-systems analysis fits in the understanding of our times.

Notes

1. Wallerstein, *The Essential Wallerstein*, xvii.
2. Benjamin, *Understanding Brecht*, 34.
3. Robert Brenner's charge against Wallerstein is that he equates "capitalism with

a trade-based division of labor" (38), thereby imitating not Marx but Adam Smith. The key to this "neo-Smithian Marxism" is its subsumption of "class relations within the broader . . . development of a trade-based division of labor" (39). "The dynamic of development clearly resides in trade, not in . . . class relations" (56). Brenner, "The Origins of Capitalist Development." Wallerstein does not accept this charge; he insists that forms of labor control lie at the heart of his conceptualization of capitalism. He deals with this issue in *Historical Capitalism*.

4. Gupta and Ferguson, eds., *Culture, Power, Place*, 3.

5. For those humanists who take Wallerstein seriously, one option is to re-conceptualize and re-locate their work in a new classification of the branches of knowledge. Much of what we do could for example fall within a blurry but exciting interdisciplinary area where the humanities and the social sciences cohabit and interact. One name for this area is cultural studies. Another, though it has fallen out of favor since the era of high theory, is the human sciences. It's possible that the latter will return to fashion now that a purely defensive posture toward science, however ingrained in the traditional humanities, has come to seem something of an intellectual liability.

6. Wallerstein, "Class Conflict in the Capitalist World-Economy," 122.

7. See Ahmad, *In Theory*, 181–82.

8. Wolf, *Europe and the People Without History*.

9. Lowe and Lloyd, eds., *The Politics of Culture in the Shadow of Capital*, 5, 6.

10. Wallerstein, *The Decline of American Power*, 41.

11. Friedman, *The Lexus and the Olive Tree*, 7.

12. This argument is made with great eloquence in Ann Cvetkovich's *Mixed Feelings*. The secret unveiled by Marx in *Capital*, Cvetkovich observes, is not the suffering body on the factory floor, as one might expect. The secret is surplus value, a non-empirical abstraction. The body in pain is everywhere in history. By itself, however, it explains nothing. No amount of attentiveness to suffering as such will explain surplus value, which can also work without bodily suffering and yet is what makes capitalism a distinctive system.

PART ONE

System and Responsiblity

The Modern World-System

Its Structures, Its Geoculture, Its Crisis

and Transformation

RICHARD E. LEE

World-systems analysis emerged in the 1970s,[1] closely related to the medium-term decline of the world economic expansion that had been operative over the preceding quarter century and the end of the period of hegemony in the interstate system over the same period, which had been marked by the post–Second World War dominance of the United States. On the one hand, world-systems analysis was a product of the system that it sought to understand. On the other hand, it was a protest or resistance movement within the structures of knowledge—in articulation with the social movements associated with the upheavals of 1968—to the ways the world and its functioning had been portrayed, and thus it framed what actions, and in whose interests, were deemed possible and legitimate. As an outgrowth of the processes reproducing historical capitalism in the long term and their secular crisis, world-systems analysis has been and is a forward-looking movement during the contemporary period of crisis, and arguably transition.

The basic premise of world-systems analysis is that historical social systems have lives. They come into being as a unique and indivisible set of singular, *longue durée* structures. The processes of reproduction of these structures exhibit secular trends and cyclical rhythms that may be observed over the life of the system. Eventually, however, these processes run up against asymptotes, or limitations, in overcoming the contradictions of the system and the system ceases to exist. The structures of the modern world-system, or capitalist world-economy, emerged in Europe at the beginning of the long sixteenth century, the period known as the transition from feudalism to capitalism. By the end of the Hundred Years' War, an axial division of labor was developing between a western European core where high-wage, skilled workers produced low-bulk, high value-added manufactures, and an eastern European periphery where high-bulk, low value-added necessities were produced by a lower cost work force. The long-distance trade in these commodities resulted in the accumulation (concentration and centralization) of capital in the core.

The processes reproducing this relationship over the long term—the "accumulation of accumulation" or profit making for reinvestment and thus more profit making—underwent periodic fluctuations. The expansion of the system to incorporate new pools of low-cost labor provided the solutions that turned periods of world economic downturn into periods of upturn. A principal characteristic of the world today is that there no longer exist significant pools of labor outside the system to be incorporated at the bottom of the wage hierarchy to take the place of previously incorporated workers who have militated for and succeeded in negotiating higher remuneration. The result constitutes a challenge to capital in maintaining the world-scale rate of profit.

The "endless" accumulation resulting from the extraction and appropriation of surplus produced by labor could only take place within the context of what developed as an interstate system. Unlike "parcellized sovereignty"[2] (the overlapping geographic jurisdictions of feudal "realms") the multiple states of which this new system was composed were formally "sovereign," with reciprocal rights and obligations, at least to the extent that their territorial extensions, and the monopoly on the use of force within them, were recognized by other states. Fluctuating flows of goods, capital, and labor could thus be controlled across semi-permeable borders throughout the system. In practice, strong states worked to loosen controls during periods of world economic upturn and tighten controls during periods of downturn to favor accumulation (along with its concentration and centralization) and contain and defuse class conflict.

Like its economic processes, the geopolitics of this system also underwent periodic fluctuations. Competition among elites resulted in "world wars," the outcomes of which were short-lived states of "hegemony," a status of the system (not an attribute of a single state) during which one strong state exercised military, commercial, financial, and cultural ascendancy, before other parts of the world-system "caught up" to become once more competitive and the cycle repeated. Three such periods may be observed: the period of Dutch hegemony after the Thirty Years' War, the period of British hegemony following the French Revolutionary/Napoleonic Wars, and the most recent, the period of U.S. hegemony after the thirty-years-long First-Second World War. Significantly, over the past five hundred years, no power has been able to totally dominate the system and thus to turn it into a world-empire and today no seemingly credible scenario for establishing a new state of hegemony has emerged.

There was a third set of structures that were just as constitutive of the modern world-system as those in the arenas of production and distribution (the economic), and coercion and decision-making (the political). Indeed, in 1982, Terence K. Hopkins discussed the first two sets of processes: "The *processes* of the world-scale division and integration of labor and *processes* of state-formation and deformation . . . that constitute the system's formation and provide an account, at the most general level, for the patterns and features of its development."[3] In the same volume, however, Hopkins and Wallerstein et al. also claimed that there was "a third fundamental aspect to the modern world-system . . . the broadly 'cultural' aspect . . . even though little is systematically known about it as an integral aspect of world-historical development . . . [and] much preliminary conceptual work needs to be done."[4] This third arena has come to be conceptualized as that of cognition and intentionality, the structures of knowledge.[5]

The conceptual work necessary to the grounding of this third arena proved particularly difficult. It was not as though no one had been working on the problem; indeed, not only had questions in the cultural realm long offered rich subjects for study even at the macro level, culture had long been a central explanatory category of social analysis as well. Furthermore, the category *culture* had given rise to an important knowledge movement beginning in the mid-1950s.[6] However, if the "broadly 'cultural' aspect" of the modern world-system was just as constitutive as the economic and political realms, then ad-hoc, particularistic conceptualizations had to be rethought in terms of a specification of the *longue durée* structures of this "third arena"—including the cyclical rhythms and secular trends of their reproduction—that could be recognized over the entire life of the system. In other words, what was needed was a conceptualization analogous to those that had been conceived for the economic and political arenas.[7] The structures of knowledge approach is the outcome of this conceptual work.

From the beginning of the long sixteenth century, the practices of knowledge production took the form of a complex of processes that produced over time an intellectual and institutional hierarchy, a set of structures, within which legitimate knowledge was progressively defined as the "other" of societal and moral values. Values, the foundations on which the humanities have been built, could be based on "authorities," but in the end were open and contestable, and thus relative, whereas the universal truths produced by what eventually became the sciences were presented as singular and not open to interpretation. This evolving structure in which knowledge has been produced over the five-century *longue durée* of the modern world-system, in articulation with those sets of processes associated with the "economic" and "political" spheres, accounts for the dominant relational setting "disciplining" human cognition and intentionality, and thus forming the "cultural" parameters of possible action. The rise of visual representation and quantification that lost their association with any value components[8] and especially the emergence of what Mary Poovey has called the "modern fact" as the primary epistemological unit of valid knowledge and cultural authority[9] at the end of the European Middle Ages indicated the direction that the transformation of medieval modes of knowing were to take. The creation of the modern fact laid the groundwork for merchants to become capitalists by establishing the legitimacy of profit rooted in the virtues of "balance" inherent in the system of double-entry bookkeeping. With profit distinguished from usury, the accumulation of accumulation could take off. At the same time, however, there were effects which further redefined the structures of knowledge.

The modern fact could be affiliated with both the specifics of commerce and their generalization within a system which underwrote the individual creditworthiness of merchants and their credibility as a group. The possibility of such a double identity gave impetus to the processes of rationalization. Rationalization, the secular trend in the arena of the structures of knowledge, might be variously called "scientization" or "secularization," depending on the object of analysis or the arena of discourse involved. The pursuit of objectivity, that is, the view from nowhere that canceled agency and history, that in fact negated subjectivity however conceived, took the form of the progressive privileging of formal rationality. This formal rationality moved disinterested calculation to the fore as a generalized means of instrumental action, to the detriment of substantive rationality, the normative pursuit of specifically situated ends.

The structures of knowledge of the modern world-system are, then, like its economic and political structures, unique. No other historical system has created two antithetical, contradictory epistemological bases for the production of knowledge, one excluding human values a priori and one in which human values are an inseparable component. With the common purpose of mastering nature, two avenues in the search for truth independent of received values were charted: in the empiricist appeal to the senses and an inductive method, and in the rationalist embrace of reason and a deductive method. During the eighteenth century, the Newtonian fusion of these two produced a synthesis of experimental and empirical approaches that incorporated hypothesis construction and mathematical demonstrations. Classical science would henceforth be concerned with the discovery of universal laws governing a regular and constant nature. These would lead to the prediction of change both in the future and, retrodictively, in the past. With the displacement of the divine viewpoint to man, the humanities—which were not concerned with the ordered certitude of regularities in the world of nature but with the chaotic finitude of the unique and unpredictable in the human world of conflicting values—could call on individual creativity for a "rational" understanding of emergence and change. Along these two lines, the long-term intellectual and institutional opposition of the sciences and the humanities, what has come to be called the "Two Cultures," reached a clear definition over the course of the nineteenth century.[10]

Within this basic structure, the social sciences emerged in the nineteenth century as a medium-term solution to the tensions internal to those structures of knowledge that no longer offered practical ways of addressing the evolving geopolitics of the world-system.[11] In the aftermath of the French Revolution, it was no longer possible to imagine a static world; however, modes of interpreting social change in the human world, as marked off from the natural world, made contradictory appeals to values. The mutually exclusive alternatives were either achieving order through the authority of tradition or experiencing chaos from unfettered democracy. Neither offered a solution, on which any consensus seemed possible, to the political confrontations between conservatism and radicalism, both of which threatened capital accumulation. Eventually, from the late nineteenth century, the objective, value-neutral, problem-solving spirit of science was advanced to resolve the stand-off in the English-speaking world, and the connection between meaning or values and systematic knowledge was argued rigorously in the *Methodenstreit*, especially in the Germanys. The result was the institutionalization of a set of disciplines, the social sciences, which would function to guarantee ordered change in the name of "progress" through "scientific" control, exercised by "experts" and based on "hard facts." In political and economic terms, this amounted to liberal incrementalism, maximizing accumulation and minimizing class struggle.

The evolving hierarchical structure of the sciences, the social sciences, and the humanities, privileged, as authoritative, the universalism that was purportedly an attribute of knowledge produced in the sciences—the empirical and positivistic sphere of "truth"—over the particularism characteristic of the humanities, the impressionistic and anarchic realm of "values." In the great nineteenth-century fluctuation in the processes of reproduction of the structures of knowledge, the social sciences came to be situated in between the two super disciplines, resolving in the medium term the crisis of social knowledge production. The social sciences divided the study of the human world into isolated domains separated intellectually in disciplines and institutionally in university departments. Oriental studies and anthropology dealt with the great civilizations and the "tribes" of the non-modern world respectively; history was primarily concerned with the past of the modern world; the present of the modern world was further divided up among economics, political science, and sociology—these three treating the market, the state, and civil society as isolated fields. Although economics, political science, and sociology inclined more toward the sciences, while history, Oriental studies, and anthropology tended to have a more humanistic bent, even within the disciplines there was no consensus on the composition of their data (which could be quantitative or qualitative), or the appropriateness of their methods (they might be statistical or narrative), or the nature of their "scientific" universality (the discovery of laws or the aggregation of descriptions) on which they based the legitimacy of their claims. However, from the moment of the greatest intellectual and institutional success of this structure in the period immediately after 1945, the scholarly legitimacy of the premises underlying the separation of the disciplines and the practical usefulness of the distinctions became less and less self-evident, and after 1968 were overtly contested.

These then are the three analytically distinct but functionally, and existentially, inseparable structural arenas of the modern world-system: the axial division of labor, the interstate system, and the structures of knowledge. They define a singular "world." And that world is unique in human history in that from the time of its emergence it has expanded to incorporate the entire globe. It is this world, then, that constitutes the unit of analysis of the world-systems perspective.

A persistent question for both analysts and activists has always been why the exploited majority, although successful in agitating for improved conditions in the medium term, has never been able to entirely change the rules of the system. Historically, world-economies have been unstable and they have generally transformed into world-empires or simply disintegrated. The modern world-system, in contrast, has not (yet) met either fate. Wallerstein argues, "The secret of its strength . . . is the political side of the form of economic organization called capitalism . . . [that] as an economic mode is based on the fact that the economic factors operate within an arena larger than that which any political entity can totally control. This gives capitalists a freedom of maneuver that is structurally based."[12] What matters for the system as a whole is not where state borders are drawn (these have, in fact, changed greatly over time), but rather that there exists a mechanism per se that fragments the system into partially independent, semi-autonomous parts (the process of state formation). This in turn results in a hierarchical ordering of multiple centers of power that can unilaterally impose resolutions to struggles among competing interests, but, with maximum legitimacy and efficacy, only within their exclusive geographic confines.

Classes, on the other hand, are economic phenomena depending on a hierarchical relation to capital. They are thus formed and maintained through the mechanisms of capital accumulation at the level of the axial division of labor, that is, at the level of the world-economy. The answer to the political question, why the exploited majority simply does not rebel, is of course that it does, and does so periodically. Actual class struggle, however, always remains disjointed, leaving the overall structure intact, since political movements organize to effect change in the states because that is where the actual organs of power and decision-making are located.

This structure, or the combination of the structures of the modern world-system, has guaranteed that capital has always held the advantage over labor in the long term. Nonetheless, individual competing capitalists calculate their bottom lines in the short term, and workers have to assure their needs on a daily basis. Considering the cost of active struggle to profits and wages, any deployment of force over a significant period of time is decidedly unattractive. In the medium term, the least costly outcome of workers' struggles for a better life (a bigger share of the surplus that they produce) and capital's resistance (maintaining the level of the rate of profit) is the reestablishment of consensus, even though it entails the expense to local capitalists of granting some material gains to workers. These gains are, however, kept to a minimum, since workers have to absorb an expense as well in accepting less than they would like, by the addition of a codicil promising further progress at some unspecified time in the future. Of course, the distribution of aggregate surplus is a zero-sum game at any specific moment. Agreeing to some, even minimal, demands of labor in one locale has to be made up in another if the ceaseless accumulation of capital is to continue. Otherwise, to avoid a vicious circle that would wipe out accumulation altogether, new sources of surplus, or more exactly sources of production of surplus, labor, have to be found. Indeed, this is what has happened historically. The world-economy has expanded (a fundamental process in the reproduction of the system) to incorporate fresh pools of cheap labor at the bottom of the wage scale to make up at the system level what has been conceded in local struggles.

The contemporary "globalization" model admits implicitly that the economic processes of historical capitalism have not changed over the past five hundred years. The rhetoric of globalization ignores, however, the long-term trends of those processes and suggests that the economic decline of the past quarter century is cyclical (a downturn in comparison with the upturn of the post-1945 period) and is thus reversible. The perceived openness of the international economy and the ease with which it eludes state regulation, which globalization critics decry, acknowledges that the cycles of endless accumulation—expansion, incorporation, exploitation, and appropriation over long distances for reinvestment—take precedence over regulative policies any single state or multistate coalition might try to impose. This is exactly what "world-economy" means. A world-economy functions within and over the entirety of the "world" defined by the spatio-temporal extent of its processes; it is precisely not an aggregation of single national economies.

Although, the globalization literature has both correctly identified and perceived as important a fundamental change relating to the politics of the modern world-system, the "external" geographic boundaries of the world-economy have disappeared. The reason this is important, however, does not have to do with the cyclical downturn in the apparent capacity of the states to regulate "international" capital. The significance lies rather with the long-term trend of the process of expansion having reached its asymptotic limit, and the political consequences of the fact. There is no longer an "outside" that can be incorporated to replenish the lowest strata of the world division of labor, and thus produce the higher levels of surplus, as a consequence of lower wages, necessary to stave off class struggle while maintaining the endless accumulation of capital.

But there is a second point concerning the periodic settlements between capital and labor that must be made, and it concerns the promise of progress. As world-scale class conflict played out in localized struggles over the eighteenth and nineteenth centuries, the contradictory demands of radicals for freedom and democracy (echoing the voices of working class victims of variously coercive modes of labor exploitation), of conservatives for order over anarchy, and of capital(ists) for assured pools of cheap labor, resulted in the collapse of clear ideological alternatives on the left and the right. The result was the emergence of the "new liberalism" at the end of the nineteenth century.[13] Coming into its own with the incorporation of the last of the regions external to the capitalist world-economy, the new liberal "consensus" inscribed some groups into subordinate positions on socially constructed but politically functional status hierarchies of race and gender. These hierarchies were translated and naturalized into "nations" of cultural/historical peoples and the dominant, politically responsible social subjects, the "citizens" of which they were made up. The excluded "others" were relegated to a secondary station legitimating their exploitation. During the first half of the twentieth century, this new liberal consensus, the geoculture of the world-system, was extended worldwide in the form of Wilsonian "self-determination of nations" and Rooseveltian "economic development," the structural equivalents of universal suffrage and the welfare state at the national level within the core.[14]

This world-liberal compact relied on strengthened state structures and piecemeal reform to insure order, that is, check democratic tendencies. But the equilibrium based on the promise of progress was unstable, and although it prevailed for almost a century, it eventually lost its luster, especially for women, ethnic and racial "minorities," the young in the core, and (ex-)colonial peoples in the periphery on whose marginalization it had depended. By the 1960s there was no one left ("outside" the system) to whom the promise of progress had not been made to bring into the system to pay for its (partial) fulfillment for those to whom the promise had been made. Even the modernizers could see that the sequential development model did not describe how differential well-being was produced and reproduced in the real world, and all of the social, national, and Old Left movements that had bought into the promise by targeting state power found themselves targets, along with the powerful institutions guaranteeing the processes of endless accumulation, in the world revolution of 1968.

Over the past four decades, the crisis in the processes reproducing the organizational patterns of the modern world-system in all three structural arenas has become apparent,[15] despite neoliberal efforts bolstered by the rhetoric of globalization (the idea that there is no other choice) to extend them.

The major mechanisms through which accumulation has been guaranteed over the past five centuries (by keeping costs of production down) have been (1) the incorporation of new pools of lowest cost labor, (2) the externalization of the costs of infrastructure and ecological degradation, and (3) control over transfer payments resulting in higher taxes. These have all run up against their limits, resulting in rising costs of production at the world level that can no longer be offset locally. "The bottom line," writes Wallerstein, "is that the curve of the *overall and worldwide* costs of production has been steadily rising. This is the fundamental factor that has produced the structural crisis of the capitalist world-economy in which we find ourselves today." He goes on to say that politically, in the wake of the world revolution of 1968, the ability of states to "constrain the strength and volatility of the political action of the popular classes" has "weakened critically."[16]

Within the structures of knowledge the process of rationalization has entered into crisis as well. The manifestations of this crisis are already changing the way we view the world, from one of autonomous, but interacting, units, to one of relational systems that create their elements as actors and observables. The effect will eventually be to alter the possibilities for human action that we are able to imagine as effective and legitimate. The structuralists drew attention to the shortcomings of European humanism and positivism alike, and from the late 1960s, developments at the level of theory were paralleled on the ground of practice. Those groups who had lacked a "voice" gained admittance to the academy and began to transform it from the inside by applying their differently situated knowledges of the workings of the social world. Multiple, not always harmonious, varieties of feminism have contested the received premises of knowledge formation through a conception of values expressed in hierarchies of difference and power, and they have directly undermined the (male) universalism and objectivity by which science laid claim to a distinctive mode of knowledge production. Their work disputed essentialist categories of man and woman and situated the female body as a pivotal site, positioning women in society through scientific discourse. Similarly, scholars and activists working in the area of race and ethnicity have, in the production of their own empirical studies, built up theories of difference that challenged (Western) universalism and objectivity. Their work too highlighted the essentialism of received categories and how difference could be used to subordinate entire groups.

Over the same period, the very premises of science have been undermined from the inside.[17] It took the better part of four centuries for what we now think of as the scientific model to dominate our common sense view. That model included the discrimination between the true and the false in a world of independent, "objective" elements. It included the idea that explanations should be brief and simple and at their best could be expressed in laws that allowed for predictions to be made. These are exactly the notions that have lost their unquestioned legitimacy. They continue, however, to regulate our everyday thinking. Their great force resided in their naturalized, universal, and trans-historical character, but they were historically constructed and may be, indeed are now being, questioned particularly as regards the idea, the Newtonian ideal, that the regulative mechanisms of the natural world can be uniquely expressed in laws.

Thus, the structure of the super-disciplines of knowledge production is collapsing. Contingency, context-dependency, the collapse of essentialisms, and multiple, overlapping temporal and spatial frameworks are closing the gap between the humanities and the historical social sciences. Likewise, the indivisibility of chance and necessity that gives rise to irreversibility and creativity in natural systems is moving the sciences back toward "human studies."[18] Certainly, the subject matters we now think of as composing the humanities will not disappear. Likewise, those subject matters that we think of today as belonging to the natural sciences will not disappear either. What is changing is the overarching structure itself that categorizes and separates the humanities and the sciences. Thus, these many subject areas will not be segregated and opposed to one another according to their supposedly contradictory epistemological premises. Music and literature, biology and astrophysics, will cease to live in worlds apart; they participate equally in the production and reproduction of the human condition. Coinciding with these developments, the intellectual sanctions and practical justifications for independent disciplines in the social sciences, where epistemological ambiguities were never put to rest, are disintegrating too.

What conclusions are we to draw from the simultaneous exhaustion of the processes insuring endless accumulation and containing class struggle taking place contemporaneously with the collapse of their co-constitutive intellectual structures? The upper bound of the trajectory of historical capitalism is not a point of arrival. It is a frontier of transition implying an ethical imperative to make profoundly political choices, value-oriented choices. The real story of the post-Cold War world is not the "victory of the West" but the disintegration of the liberal compact that began in 1968 and was completed in 1989.[19] The liberal consensus, the geoculture of the world-system, was a politics of medium-term increments of reformist change adding up, it was asserted, to endless (long-term) linear progress. This vision depicted a golden "now" that could be extrapolated into the future with no allusion to the ideologies of either a future transformation (socialism) or an idyllic past (conservatism). The parallel with Newtonian dynamics is clear. Science itself offered the linear development model, based empirically and episte-mologically on independent units. But in the post–Cold War world, liber-alism has not been able to deliver on its universalist message of progress. In its neoliberal guise it has failed in its bid to reinstate the geopolitical reali-ties of the world characterized by U.S. hegemony in the post-1945 period, or, through structural adjustment, to reproduce the conditions of the Kon-dratieff A-phase economic expansion of the same period.

Science now provides us with alternative models of physical reality in the form of relationally constituted self-organizing systems and fractal ge-ometry, and of change and transition, complexity theory, and chaos theory. These all defy the law of the excluded middle that has been fundamental to the production of legitimate knowledge, and basic to common sense, for the past five centuries. The recognition of the indeterminacy of mean-ing in the humanities and the "alternative knowledges"—knowledges that found a home in the social sciences with the expansion of the faculty and the student body after 1968 to include those speaking from marginalized subject positions—have brought into sharp focus the political dimension of knowl-edge production and have undermined the idea of scholarship as a perfectly disinterested activity amenable to time-independent, objective evaluation. These developments notwithstanding, we have not reached the end of re-sponsibility; indeed, social agendas have become more important than ever.

We are hardly at the "end of history"; we are on a frontier where time and space can no longer be treated as neutral parameters, but must be viewed as socially constructed, interdependent categories. The future is decidedly one of transformation and thus full of possibilities. However, not all of the possible futures we can envision are equally desirable. This is a world at the "end of certainty," argues Ilya Prigogine.[20] The direction of fundamental change is unpredictable, but intimately dependent on our choices among the real historical alternatives that we can imagine for a more egalitarian world. "Utopistics" is the name Wallerstein gives to the mode of social analysis appropriate for these times; it is a mode of analysis that privileges the differentiation of possible from impossible alternatives for the future.[21] World-systems analysis, as Wallerstein himself has constantly and consistently maintained, has always been an interpretative approach or perspective, always taking into consideration of course that it is the modern world-system that is the unit with which the analyst is concerned, rather than a "theory" to be proven or an explanatory or causal framework grounding prediction.

In fact, some alternative conceptions of the future are already becoming clear. According to Wallerstein, these may be thought of in terms of the "spirit of Davos" (with reference to the World Economic Forum), a new historical system that like the present world would be "based on privilege, exploitation, and polarization," or the "spirit of Porto Alegre" (with reference to the World Social Forum), a new historical system "relatively democratic and relatively egalitarian."[22] Since the final outcome is unpredictable and remains to be constructed, the struggle for the future will call for committed, purposeful action in favor of what we consider the most desirable of the possible alternatives. Lasting for the next half century perhaps, the transition will be rich in fluctuations, that is, social instability—a lack of order already comprises the "new world order." Unstable systems, in fact, impose fewer constraints, entail fewer limits. The exercise of free will, for our purposes interpretative scholarly work meaningful for the times in which we live, is thus less restricted. Moreover, during this period of instability small fluctuations will be capable of massive amplification, to the point that eventually some set of irreversible and determining moral choices for a qualitatively different social world will define a new historical system with its own unique structures, processes of reproduction, and geoculture.

Notes

1. The literature is extensive. See, in particular, Wallerstein's multivolume *The Modern World-System* and his seminal articles collected in *The Essential Wallerstein*; for a schematic overview, see Wallerstein, *Historical Capitalism*; for an introduction including origins and development, see Wallerstein, *World-Systems Analysis*; and for some early thoughts on methods, see Hopkins, Wallerstein, et al., *World-Systems Analysis: Theory and Methodology*. The present exposition is made in reference to the world-systems perspective developed by Wallerstein and others who have built on his work (but excluding those devoted to comparing world-systems). These scholars generally hyphenate the concept (see Wallerstein, "The World-System," for an explanation of the significance of the hyphen; see, for instance, Denemark, Friedman, Gills, and Modelsky, *World System History* for examples of work in which the concept is not hyphenated).

2. See Anderson, *Lineages*.

3. Hopkins, Wallerstein, et al., *World-Systems Analysis*, 12.

4. Ibid., 43.

5. See Lee "Structures of Knowledge," and "The 'Third' Arena," and Lee and Wallerstein, "Structures of Knowledge," *Overcoming the Two Cultures*. Wallerstein has been sensitive to the importance of both the intellectual and material structures of knowledge production throughout his career, with his later work hinging increasingly on an explicit inclusion of the structures of knowledge in the analysis.

6. See Lee, *Life and Times of Cultural Studies*.

7. See Lee, "The 'Third' Arena."

8. See Crosby, *Measure of Reality*.

9. On the modern fact and its ambiguity, see Poovey, *A History of the Modern Fact*, chap. 1 and chap. 2 especially; this is the history of "how description came to seem separate from interpretation or theoretical analysis; the story of how one kind of representation—numbers—came to seem immune from theory or interpretation" (xii).

10. See Lee and Wallerstein, *Overcoming the Two Cultures*.

11. The place and role of the social sciences in understanding the modern world and eventually in understanding the evolution of the modern world-system since the mid-nineteenth century has long been deemed crucial by Immanuel Wallerstein. He has set out the organizational structure of the social sciences, and its significance, in numerous articles and books (e.g., Wallerstein, ed., *Open the Social Sciences*). As early as 1971, he declared, "There is no such thing as sociology if by sociology we mean a 'discipline' that is separate and distinct from anthropology, political science, economics, and history (not to speak of demography and so on). They are all one single discipline which I suppose we may call social science" ("There is No Such Thing as Sociology," 328; see also "L'organization des sciences humaines et l'objectivité").

12. Wallerstein, *Modern World-System I*, 348.

13. See Lee, *Life and Times of Cultural Studies*, chap. 2.

14. The zones of "real existing socialism" were not excluded: the Leninist program, "not world revolution but anti-imperialism plus socialist construction . . . on inspection turned out to be mere rhetorical variants on the Wilsonian/Rooseveltian concepts" (Wallerstein, *After Liberalism*, 137–38).

15. See Hopkins, Wallerstein, et al., *World-Systems Analysis*.

16. Wallerstein, "An American Dilemma," 15–17.

17. See Lee, "Complexity Studies." For a comprehensive review of this literature, see Lee, "Readings in the 'New Science.'"

18. See Prigogine, *The End of Certainty*.

19. See Wallerstein, *After Liberalism*.

20. See Prigogine, *The End of Certainty*.

21. See Wallerstein, *Utopistics*.

22. Wallerstein, "American Dilemma," 19.

Blaming the System

BRUCE ROBBINS

I take the title "Blaming the System" from Luc Boltanski's book *Distant Suf-fering*.[1] Inspired, it would seem, by the relatively successful public opinion campaigns waged by NGOs like Doctors Without Borders, Boltanski turns his attention in this book to a series of rhetorical tropes that were more and less effective in eliciting a large-scale public response. He runs these tropes through a body of thinking about compassion and philanthropy emanating mainly from the Anglo-Saxon tradition. Out of these materials he tries to build the supporting theory for a newly politicized humanitarianism. His point of departure is the situation in which suffering is observed by a non-sufferer, as in the story of the Good Samaritan. At least temporarily, the non-suffering observer is "lucky," which is to say circumstantially unequal to the sufferer. The observer is therefore not the sufferer's natural political ally. There is no affiliation between the two, neither a common interest nor a common identity that would push the observer to come to the sufferer's aid. Hence assistance to the sufferer must be won by means of some as yet non-existent sense of obligation or solidarity, brought into being by the power of speech. For Boltanski, situations of detached, disinterested inequality like this, which seem to defy the categories of politics, pose a severe but unavoid-able challenge to existing forms of rhetoric.

This challenge is at its most daunting in the case of speech across great distance, social as well as physical. An example of both would be someone addressing a First World audience on the subject of Third World poverty. In the key chapter devoted to the rhetoric of denunciation, the act by which the spectator of suffering is moved from pity to indignation and accuses those responsible, Boltanski writes: "The greater the distance between the perse-cutor and his victim," the longer the "causal chain between the unfortunate and the agent who causes his suffering," and the more rhetorical work has to be done to establish a connection (62). Consider "an unfortunate who dies of hunger in a shanty-town. His persecutor, who has never seen him, occupies an office in Paris or New York at the head office of a holding company from which he works on the financial markets. How can the connection between unfortunate and persecutor be made to stick?" (62). The ability to denounce successfully under these conditions, Boltanski says, requires the mediation of a "theory of power" (62). For only a theory of power will be able to distinguish such cases from cases of "suffering which, however distressing it may be, is inherent in the human condition" (62)—that is, from suffering that cannot properly be described as political. Let us observe in passing that such a theory of power is precisely what Immanuel Wallerstein supplies.

Boltanski notes that the borderline between what is and isn't held to be inherent in the human condition, hence between suffering for which people can and cannot be held responsible, is "constantly being drawn and redrawn" (63). But the chapter ends by facing a related and even more sobering difficulty: the denunciation of "system," or the question of how and whether accusation can be "shifted from *persons* on to larger de-individualized entities such as *systems* or *structures*" (73). Brought face to face, so to speak, with a faceless system, the rhetoric of denunciation becomes, if not paradoxical, at least "more fragile, because the extension of networks, the lengthening of connections, and the multiplication of mediations which have to be secured in order to make an accusation stick, increase the number of points on to which doubts and challenges can be hooked" (73). This confrontation might seem to replay an origin story about the discipline of sociology in which Boltanski, like Wallerstein, works. He notes that generalizing from particular unfortunates and their singular fates is what sociology has always done. Hence one would imagine sociology had long ago figured out ways of dealing with the doubts and challenges provoked by generalization. But perhaps, for Boltanski, sociology after all does not stand on firm foundations. At any rate, Boltanski does not seem to feel that the discipline's existence guarantees the feasibility of denouncing systematic abuse. Where denunciation is concerned, every baby step away from pity for a particular individual and indignation at a particular perpetrator is presented as fraught with extreme danger. Whether an individual sufferer is made representative of some larger collectivity, or a system rather than an individual is held responsible for the suffering, the emotional intensity of the listener would also seem to suffer. The same theory of power that is needed to enforce the link between sufferer and accused would also seem to threaten the latter's freedom to act otherwise, hence his or her accountability: "Accusation cannot abandon all orientation toward responsibility without falling into self-contradiction. It is the very possibility of things happening otherwise and, consequently, the existence of responsibility, which distinguishes the denunciation of suffering about which it seems reasonable to be *indignant* from the attitude of *resignation* which prevails in the case of sufferings about which nothing can be done" (75).

The moral would seem to be: the more system, the less denunciation. The chapter ends, a bit vaguely, on its own note of resignation. Regarding the possibilities for successful blaming on the collective or systematic level, perhaps nothing can be done. Boltanski quotes Ricoeur on German war guilt to the effect that accusation is only sound if it is limited to the criminal accusation of individuals (76).[2]

This argument is a provocation: it would seem to undermine any possible ground for the politicized humanitarianism Boltanski wants, or for the sort of militant cosmopolitanism (an overlapping concept) presupposed today by many projects in the humanities. This provocation makes Boltanski's argument a useful way of framing questions both about the humanities and their responsibilities in the era of so-called globalization, on the one hand, and about the strange mixture of attraction and repulsion that characterizes the intersection of the humanities and the work of Immanuel Wallerstein, on the other. The repulsion is most often seen as the result of a fundamental difference of opinion about the value and significance of "culture," a term that I will here take as standing in, however crudely, for the object of knowledge of the humanities, and will henceforth liberate from its quotation marks. The culture problem is real, but defenses of the cultural tend to be, one might say, defensive—that is, hasty, instinctive, and unedifying. Worse, they tend to ignore the rich uncertainties that we in the humanities would otherwise freely admit as to what culture is and does. Under these circumstances, perhaps it would help to reconsider the hearty but awkward relationship between Wallerstein and the humanities in something like Boltanski's terms: that is, provisionally replacing the concept of culture with the rhetorical practice of praise and blame and applying it to the challenging but highly pertinent version of "system"—world-systems theory—that Wallerstein founded. If the vocabulary of praise and blame can hardly claim to encompass all of culture's meanings, it does cover much of what actually happens when people in the humanities think about those meanings. It is reductive, of course, but it has the corresponding advantage of calling attention to the limited range of critical actions that actually tend to be performed by those invoking (that is, praising) culture's irreducible richness and variety. At the same time, as Boltanski's argument shows, terms like "denunciation" and "blame" indicate an area of common ground between actions performed on and in culture, on the one hand, and political action in and on what Edward Said has called "the world of nations." Thus the rhetoric of praise and blame would also seem to designate grounds for a fresh encounter between the humanities and Wallerstein's vision of the world capitalist system, which is to say his theory of power.

In the introduction to his career-making book *The Modern World-System* (1974), Wallerstein describes his early intellectual trajectory as a quest for the "appropriate unit of analysis." This quest resulted, he says, in a rejection of both state and society on the grounds that each of these units is limited to the scale of the nation, hence incoherent: "I decided that neither one was a social system and that one could only speak of social change in social systems. The only social system in this scheme was the world-system" (7).

The assumption that coherence, lacking at the level of the nation, is to be rediscovered at a global or transnational level is not an unfamiliar premise for humanities scholars. Thanks in part to the force of Wallerstein's arguments and his synthesis of historical scholarship, this premise has become one of the most appealed-to and productive across a wide variety of disciplines and interdisciplinary areas. Sometimes the filiation to Wallerstein himself is explicit, as in the cultural criticism of Fredric Jameson and Edward Said, and, more recently, in the intriguing theory of world literature proposed by Franco Moretti.[3] But it is no less significant when it goes unacknowledged. The index to Paul Gilroy's pathbreaking book *The Black Atlantic* (1993) has no entry for Wallerstein, but when Gilroy proposes that cultural historians "take the Atlantic as one single, complex unit of analysis" (15), the borrowing seems unmistakable.[4] If scholarly justice were to be done, many of the copious footnotes in which recent writers on transoceanic diaspora and other versions of the transnational express their methodological debt to Gilroy would simultaneously have to be credited to Wallerstein's account.

Yet if Wallerstein clearly stands among the founders of what is now very close to a scholarly consensus, the distinctness of his individual place in this distinguished company is less evident. Even many of those who cite him would probably not give full support to his identification of "system" as the single mandatory unit of scholarly analysis. And a similar lack of clarity affects the consensus itself, which like other collective enthusiasms has been loath to slow down and ask where exactly it is heading, or should be heading. I share the assumption that the transnational turn is desirable and in any case probably unavoidable. Yet it seems a good idea to ask how best to take this turn—where we are likely to end up, interpretively speaking, if we make use of any one of the intellectual vehicles available, each whipping us around the curve with various degrees of momentum and abandon. World-systems theory is one such vehicle—to its critics, not always the best-handling.[5] But the resistance to world-systems theory, of which there has been a great deal, especially in the humanities, is also a mode of conveyance. Whether or not it keeps us safe, it does not keep us in place; it takes us somewhere else. If we are going to choose between system and anti-system, it is better to know the alternative destinations.

My aim, then, is to reflect critically both on Wallerstein's commitment to "system" as privileged unit of analysis and on those habits of thinking in the humanities that appear to discourage such a commitment. One of those habits is reverence for our cultural objects, or the rhetorical practice of praise. (This is a practice that the most Wallersteinian of contemporary literary critics, Franco Moretti, has characteristically and almost uniquely chosen to forego.[6]) The practice of blaming has been less acknowledged, perhaps because the humanities have recently been accused of violating their very nature by doing too much of it. Yet blame is the inescapable counterpart of praise, and it is also, as I suggested above, a privileged link to the domain of the political. In search of greater lucidity about the conflicted nature of our commitments, as well as the promise (or perhaps the threat) of possible common ground between the humanities and Immanuel Wallerstein, it seems worthwhile to pursue the difficulties and rewards of the practice of blaming when the object in question exists, as Wallerstein proposes, on the scale of the world-system.

In his essay "The Rise and Future Demise of the World Capitalist System: Concepts for Comparative Analysis," also published in 1974, Wallerstein defined *system* as follows: "We take the defining characteristic of a social system to be the existence within it of a division of labor, such that the various sectors or areas are dependent upon economic exchange with others for the smooth and continuous provisioning of the needs of the area. Such economic exchange can clearly exist without a common political structure and even more obviously without a common culture" (74–75).[7] Politics and culture exist within the system, but neither does anything to make it systematic. What makes it systematic, hence the unit of analysis that has to be studied, is a common division of labor. From the perspective of the humanities, whose object of knowledge is culture, this privileging of the economic at the expense of the cultural has been unpopular, and understandably so.[8] The most obvious reason why the humanities have not made more of Wallerstein's work is that while culture shows up from time to time, it never plays a very significant role. Here Wallerstein differs from, say, Michel Foucault or Pierre Bourdieu. Each could be described as a systemic thinker, yet each has had a more visible individual impact on the cultural disciplines, and this despite the further fact that, unlike Wallerstein, each has had rather hostile things to say about culture. Indeed, both Bourdieu and Foucault (as theorist of discourse) could be said to attribute many of society's ills to the cultural-discursive realm. In so doing, however, each attributes great causal importance to culture, an importance that both assert is irreducible to noncultural or nondiscursive factors. This is more than enough reason for Foucault and Bourdieu to have been embraced. From the viewpoint of the cultural disciplines, *blaming* culture is a way of *flattering* culture.

Is flattery what the humanities require? I hope not. In taking culture's relative insignificance as a slap in the face, have the humanities overreacted? Perhaps. These questions offer an invitation to disciplinary self-consciousness that there is good reason to accept.

As a further motive for self-consciousness in the humanities, consider this further explanation for our resistance to Wallerstein. It's not just that Wallerstein's scheme doesn't give culture much of importance to do. From its very beginning, the concept of culture has also been deeply opposed, indeed *constitutively* opposed, to the very concept by which Wallerstein defines system, namely the division of labor. As Raymond Williams tells the story in *Culture and Society* (1958), the division of labor names the characteristic disease of social and individual fragmentation that, in the decades following the Industrial Revolution, first calls the compensatory wholeness of the culture concept into being. As an antidote to society's modern divisiveness, culture is anti-system, at least in Wallerstein's sense, from its very origins in the romantic movement.[9] Thus almost all of the "Culture-and-Society" tradition, left as well as right, identifies system as its enemy. Matthew Arnold is "eternally dissatisfied with 'the men of a system,'" that is, "with men like Comte, or the late Mr Buckle, or Mr Mill."[10] On the whole, so are thinkers and writers like Dickens and Orwell, George Eliot and T. S. Eliot. This aspect of the tradition persists bizarrely into figures who might otherwise have seemed antithetical to it. Michel Foucault was a professor of the History of Systems of Thought, but he could take over from Arnold as the pre-eminent thinker for scholars in the humanities largely because, for him as well, system seemed to name society's prime antagonist.[11] Edward Said, arguably Foucault's most important mediator in the United States, managed this mediation only by demanding a place for criticism that would be "between culture and system"—a position that despite its apparent symmetry arguably favors culture *over* system.[12] At any rate, since his death in 2003 Said has consistently been praised, in terms that he himself sometimes invited, as a fundamentally anti-systemic thinker, where "system" is a code word for the French theory-builders. Thus Abdirahman Hussein suggests in *Edward Said* that the theorist troubled other people's wisdom instead of offering any systematic wisdom of his own, rejecting methodology in order to be "open-ended" (4).[13] If these are the standard terms of praise, then Wallerstein will not often be praised by the humanities, though he is in fact praised by Said himself.

Many will judge this suspiciousness about system to be no more than common sense. And to some extent it is, even if the humanistic common sense that values the particular over the general is no less ideological than the reverse. Doubts can certainly be raised about the notion of system as pure economic necessity, unaffected in any decisive way by culture or politics. Wallerstein writes that his "concept of a grid of exchange relationships assumes a distinction between *essential* exchanges and what might be called 'luxury' exchanges. This is to be sure a distinction rooted in the perceptions of the actors and hence in both their social organization and their culture. These perceptions can change. But this distinction is crucial if we are not to fall into the trap of identifying *every* exchange as evidence of the existence of a system."[14] In an "exchange of preciosities" between two systems, he goes on, "each can export to the other what in *its* system is socially defined as worth little in return for the import of what in its system is worth much" (83). Social perception, or what we might want to call culture, is allowed to define worth for the exchange of luxuries. But the exchange of luxuries does not define a system, for it entails only "'reaping a windfall' and not obtaining a profit" (83). Or does it only entail, as Wallerstein then suggests, not obtaining a "maximum" profit? If *some* profit can indeed be reaped by an exchange of what might be called luxuries, as the word "maximum" suggests, then there can be no absolute, theoretical line between luxuries and necessities, between the purely economic logic of the division of labor and a messier logic that would have to factor in the effect of cultural perception, class struggle, and so on. In short, there would be no purely economic line between system and non-system.[15] This does not imply that there cannot be any such thing as system, but only that if there is—and in any given case it seems advisable not to assume in advance that system does in fact exist—then culture cannot ipso facto be excluded from what makes it systematic. In other words, all significant causal necessity cannot be denied to non-economic factors like politics and culture.[16] Indeed, Wallerstein himself cannot flesh out the recent history of the world-system without making continual reference to these factors.[17]

To say this, however, is not necessarily to embrace the classic critique of world-systems theory (to many humanists, a conclusive critique) articulated by the anthropologist Marshall Sahlins. Indignant at the idea of culture as merely a passive reflection of economic relations, Sahlins insisted that in indigenizing Western economic and cultural exports, so-called peripheral peoples were shaping their own history, not allowing it to be shaped by a world system. World-systems theory made "colonized and 'peripheral' peoples the passive objects of their own history and not its authors," thus leaving nothing for anthropology to do—you could as easily substitute comparative literature here—"but the global ethnography of capitalism. Anthropology would be manifest destiny. For other societies were regarded as no longer possessing their own 'laws of motion'; nor was there any 'structure' or 'system' to them, except as given by Western-capitalist domination."[18] The logic here takes for granted the absolute claims of the particular—not universally, as it were, but at the level of the discipline. If you are right, Sahlins complains, what will become of my discipline? Anthropology's disciplinary object would become insignificant. Therefore you can't be right.

This is what might be called disciplinary special pleading. It cannot be allowed to settle the question. For the humanities, the fact that Wallerstein doesn't accept the premise that culture is causally decisive or relatively autonomous or otherwise especially significant ought on the contrary to be taken as a valuable aid to reflection. We can hardly ask anyone outside the humanities to accept the value of our work if we take our self-serving premises for granted and never expose them to a hostile or merely skeptical scrutiny. Your true friends are not the ones who politely withhold that scrutiny. They are the one who force you to make the case.

A response that would look better in public would have to engage more directly with the motives and results of Wallerstein's work—not necessarily in its own terms, but at least as translated into a cross-disciplinary ethical lingua franca. Such translation would not be difficult. As seen with nonspecialist eyes, Wallerstein's research seems to have had a relatively simple and compelling motivation: a desire to understand the sad state of the post-colonial world in the 1970s, the failure of seemingly victorious movements of national liberation to change the basic political and economic inequality between developed and underdeveloped countries. What was needed, it seemed, was a deeper level of causality. In search of it, Wallerstein went back to the acquisition of European political and economic superiority in the Early Modern period, when a division was established, he argued, between core and periphery. The modern world-system that he saw taking shape in that period worked to ensure the systematic transfer of surplus from the periphery to the core without military conquest but merely by means of market exchange. The result, in other words, was a theory of power at the global scale, a theory that was all the more persuasive because it accounted not only for how the present inequality of power and resources at the level of the planet came to exist, but also, crucially, for how it managed to perpetuate itself despite seemingly dramatic clashes and reversals, like the movements of national independence.

This theory does not interpellate social scientists alone. Anyone recognizing and wishing to change the present continuing state of global inequality, whatever her or his discipline, would seem to have an unavoidable interest in such a theory. This would include most humanists I know. To the extent that planetary injustice matters to us, humanists cannot in good conscience stand up for our particular zone of expertise without trying to show what effect phenomena within that zone (and/or our expert way of interpreting such phenomena) are capable of having on the fate of planetary injustice. This is a task that Sahlins, for example, does not undertake. In *Genealogies of Religion: Discipline and Reasons of Power in Christianity and Islam*, Talal Asad comments on Sahlins's "protest against the idea that the global expansion of capitalism, or the World System so-called, has made the colonized and 'peripheral' peoples the passive objects of their own history and not its authors" (3). Asad objects, reasonably enough, that "no one is ever entirely the author of her own life" (4). "To the extent that what Sahlins calls the larger system determines the conditions within which things take on meaningful places," Asad continues, "all peoples can be said to be the passive objects of their own history and not its authors" (5). Furthermore, he writes, "to take the extreme example: even the inmates of a concentration camp are able, in [Sahlins's] sense, to live by their own cultural logic. But one may be forgiven for doubting that they are *therefore* making their own history" (4). The system cannot be treated (here Asad's object is Sherry Ortner) as if it were an abstraction or "a mere fiction" (5). In fact, Asad asserts, "some theoretical idea of world capitalism is necessary if its historical consequences are to be recognized" (5). Asad concludes, with powerful understatement: "If anthropology's distinctive contribution requires it to take a *ground level* view of things, it is difficult to see how confining oneself to that level is sufficient to determine in what degree and in what way other levels become relevant" (6).

That people make their own history should not be pious dogma, cut loose from all pragmatic concern about global injustice and how to work against it. It should be an open question: how far have people actually been able to make their own history in this case or that, under these circumstances or those? Phrased as a genuine uncertainty, this proposition can guide research that will be genuinely valuable precisely because it will help us understand what can and can't be done about global injustice and thus how our interpretive puzzles do or don't contribute to that goal.

The lack of clarity that results when scholars in the humanities, reacting against systematicity, refuse to ask Asad's question, or Wallerstein's—the question of whether or how far culture really does make a difference to inequality at the world scale—can be illustrated by an article in *PMLA* called "Beyond Discipline? Globalization and the Future of English." The author, Paul Jay, declares that although the nation-state persists, "the rapid circulation of cultural commodities . . . has come at the expense of the nation-state's ability to control the formation of national subjectivities and ideologies. . . . Culture is now being defined in terms less of national interests than of a shared set of global ones" (32).[19] As a result, Jay declares, the prime task of "English" today is to wean itself away from its national and nationalist paradigm and adapt instead to the new global givens. But what does this mean? What version of the transnational turn is he describing? Initially, the answer is: Wallerstein's. But having laid out Wallerstein's theory of the world capitalist system, Jay immediately steps back from it, complaining that this notion of system is primarily economic. On this point he takes the side of what he calls "globalization theorists." Globalization theorists, from whom literary and cultural studies will properly take their cue, hold that "culture is not subordinated to the economy. Rather the two are interdependent" (35). Here the crucial figure is Arjun Appadurai (38ff), whose object is "'the social work of the imagination.'"[20] For Appadurai, "Globalization cannot be reduced to Westernization or Americanization" (39).

This sounds innocuous enough; indeed it sounds like a point that in many situations still very much needs to be made. But to say that culture and economics are "interdependent" (neither of them causally privileged at the expense of the other) is not quite accurate, at least where Appadurai is concerned. The title of Appadurai's position-defining essay was "Disjuncture and Difference in the Global Cultural Economy," and the word "disjuncture" marked a crucial and very explicit insistence, not on the interdependence of the cultural and the economic, but on the disjoining of culture from economics. In cutting the legs out from under the Americanization thesis by asserting (rightly) that indigenization often trumps homogenization and that flows of capital do not dictate the one true meaning of flows of culture, Appadurai went further: he asserted in effect that there is no system that links the two sorts of flows. There is no system, period.[21] That's why the global cultural economy is divided into a series of so-called "scapes," each distinct and disconnected from the others. When Appadurai says that Wallerstein's theory has "failed to come to terms with what Lash and Urry calls disorganized capitalism" (275), disorganization is a synonym for disjuncture, which is the antithesis of system. The result, considered as a way of taking the transnational turn, is to conflate that turn with an emancipatory flowering of the cultural, but one that is disjoined from other dimensions of the project of emancipation.

Like the humanities generally, Jay does not seem to take the full measure of his own hesitation in the face of system and what it entails. He is critical of Appadurai for not considering the "class differences" that "mark these cultural flows and transformations" (40). The criticism may not be unfair, but Jay has forfeited his right to make it. For in opting for the piety of "interdependence" and allowing that piety to replace any actual theory (necessarily less pious) of what is in fact more or less dependent on what— in other words, in rejecting "system" as such—Jay has ruled out just the sort of explanation that he criticizes Appadurai for not proposing. Appadurai, having floated the slogan of disjuncture, is perfectly consistent in evading the weighty yoking of culture to class. For theories of class are theories of inequality, theories of systematic injustice—theories of the conjoining of culture to economics. To add class is to give up on disjuncture. Trying to add class as if it were a random constituency, as if the researcher had an obligation to ask how globality looks to the inhabitants of Sioux Falls or Fall River, Jay is asking for something he doesn't want: a systematic account of inequality. If we want class, then we want system, or want to be able see real (if always provisional and imperfect) systematicity wherever it may exist.

And we cannot be critical of Wallerstein for being committed to system in this sense.

In defense of Appadurai and Sahlins, it would be possible to object that their arguments do not in fact ignore the question of global injustice, as they seem to, but rather imply an alternative view of it. For Appadurai, disjuncture is not only the rule, but it is "growing" (280). If disjuncture is growing, then Appadurai seems committed, as I hinted above, to an undeclared metanarrative in which culture is gradually escaping from beneath the heavy heel of economics. This emancipatory narrative immediately gets him into epistemological hot water. For if the increasing independence of culture and imagination from economic determination is simply real, then culture and imagination cannot have jurisdiction over the history of their own liberation. If they did have such jurisdiction, then that history could not be presented as empirical fact. Yet that is precisely how the narrative is presented. Whether the linear narrative is convincing or not, its *telos* hides, in a familiar diachronic camouflage, the author's interpretive priorities, his positive values.[22] Appadurai seems to be telling us, in other words, that history is moving toward greater global justice, and this precisely because more voices can now make themselves heard, because there is increasing emancipation at the level of cultural self-expression.[23] This is the bandwagon we should be climbing aboard.

Do Wallerstein's critics really mean to imply this alternative view of injustice? It would seem that they must. But if they do, one notes that it is rarely declared and defended explicitly. Perhaps this is because it has so little chance of satisfying anyone but those who, for disciplinary reasons or others, are already convinced. Who else would choose cultural silencing as our world's characteristic version of injustice, while ignoring, say, political subjection or economic deprivation? This choice gets a well-deserved scolding in the account that fellow cultural anthropologist James Ferguson offers of the phrase "alternative modernities," a slogan that has had all the success in the transnational zone of the humanities that world-systems theory itself has not.[24] What is the effect of that success? Ferguson writes: "The deployment of the idea of alternative modernities in Africa has a rather different significance than it has in Asia. East and Southeast Asian versions of alternative modernity have mostly argued for the possibility of a parallel track, economically analogous to the West but culturally distinctive. Broadly, the idea has meant the possibility of achieving a First World standard of living, while retaining so-called Asian values, or maintaining a more restricted version of individual rights, or avoiding the West's perceived moral vices. But in Africa, where the idea of economic convergence has lately lost so much of its plausibility, pluralizing the concept of modernity has proven attractive for very different reasons" (173). All cultures are now modern, in the sense of being (1) historical rather than traditional and (2) not incompatible with the successful manipulation of today's high-tech habitat. As such, all cultures have won the right to equal respect. But this is not the modernity, Ferguson notes, that Africans want. The modernity they want, knowing perfectly well that they don't already have it, is "economic convergence." And that is something that all the cultural pride in the world cannot supply.

Perhaps out of fidelity to the bitterness of his African subjects, Ferguson writes with a certain bitterness of his own about this academic effort to pass off a prescriptive, universal equality of cultural respect as a substitute for what Africans themselves might recognize as equality: equality of living standards, equal access to the goods of the earth. There is no excuse, he implies, for focusing on the "happy story about plurality and nonranked cultural difference" to the neglect of a second, much less happy story which results in "relatively fixed global statuses" in a "world socioeconomic hierarchy" (179). What Ferguson calls "hierarchy" is more or less what Wallerstein calls "system." The slogan "alternative modernities" allows anthropologists to tell their happy story about culture without bringing that story into any confrontation with system in the zero-sum sense of global economic hierarchy. It is another way of suggesting that there *is* no system. But it is little short of obscene to talk about cultural liberation if diverse and imaginative cultures, once liberated, have so little effect on the hierarchical order of power and wealth in which those cultures are obliged to scratch out a living. This is not to say that they *cannot* have an effect, but only that in any given case strong evidence is needed that they are indeed having one.

When Ferguson speaks of "relatively fixed global statuses," he seems to be both invoking and avoiding a global concept of class, a concept something like "class-among-nations."[25] The neologism is not a bad way of describing Wallerstein's core-periphery vision of world-system. The absence Jay bemoans in Appadurai, and could well have bemoaned in the discourse of alternative modernity as well, can be filled in at the global level only by something like what Wallerstein offers.

I do not claim that what Wallerstein offers supplies anything and everything the humanities might need in order to turn their scholarship more effectually against global injustice. There is also a sense in which Wallerstein fits into and flatters a paradigm by which the already-existing humanities both lay claim to politics at a global scale, on the one hand, and evade the shifting contingencies of direct political commitment, on the other.

The world Ferguson presents is one in which Africa has not risen, but China has. China's rise, though it is not Ferguson's subject, would seem to make an immense difference to how and in whose interest the world-system is thought to be operating. Yet in Wallerstein's view, China's rise doesn't seem to make any difference at all. For Wallerstein, transfer of surplus from the periphery to the core would not be affected by sudden Chinese prosperity, since even if China were to become part of the core, the theory posits that there would be equal need for a periphery: in this case, to return to Ferguson's example, Africa. As Jan Pieterse puts it: "According to the theory, these shifts [earlier ones] are of no consequence as long as the system itself does not change; it does not matter whether Brazil or Britain occupies a particular world market niche, whether particular countries rise or decline in the system: 'since the system as a whole creates pressures to maintain a certain mix of core, semiperipheral, and peripheral activities.'"[26] Thus Wallerstein writes: "We have had very large shifts of production from North America, western Europe, and even Japan to other parts of the world-system, which have consequently claimed that they were 'industrializing' and therefore developing. Another way of characterizing what happened is to say that these semiperipheral countries were the recipients of what were now less profitable industries" (51). Both the "claimed" and the scare quotes around "industrializing" express a barely concealed reluctance to see any genuine shift here. The reason is clear. If his theory holds that there is something like class-among-nations, then the rise of a peripheral nation to become an economic superpower, especially a peripheral nation that holds as high a proportion of the earth's people as China, raises the possibility of a drastic change in the system, and thus a possible need for more or less drastic adjustments to the theory.[27] The prospect of a country from the periphery becoming hegemonic is a very different thing from the usual musical chairs since the 1500s among various core nations.[28] Thus Wallerstein doesn't register the new and tricky political challenges that such a shift might entail—for example, how to deal with the temptations of left-wing economic nationalism over the vexed question of "lost jobs."

Long-time readers of Wallerstein will notice in his refusal to be impressed by the economic rise of East Asia a characteristic intellectual gesture. Events, actions, and movements tend not to register on Wallerstein's screen as more than blips. According to "The Rise and Future Demise," the end of slavery (95), decolonization (98), and the rise of socialism (101) were all something less eventful than they seemed; indeed, each was more or less what the system wanted.[29] That's counting out quite a bit of what would otherwise appear to be significant history. Wallerstein often finds that wars end in "truce more or less at the starting point" (*Decline*, 37). This is said here about the Korean War, and it is said elsewhere of the Gulf War. Are there no wars about which this would not be true? Another characteristic move is to claim that "the very success of the antisystemic movements has been the major cause of their undoing" (*Decline*, 39).[30] But the same thing is also asserted about *hegemonic* movements. For Wallerstein, it seems to be true of *any* movements, or any successful ones. But if there is so little difference in the end between the results of systemic movements and of anti-systemic movements, then the real dividing line would seem to fall not between system and non-system. Everything is (or threatens to become) system. The real division is between movement itself and stasis, with stasis seemingly predestined to win out. Thus stasis would become the deep or functional truth of system as such. In a signature effect of his rhetoric, Wallerstein announces that the attacks of September 11, 2001, seemed "dramatic and shocking" (*Decline*, 1) but were actually much less significant than they at first appeared. Wallerstein notes somewhere that his notion of system was inspired by the solar system, which of course can be observed in its coherence but not interfered with and which exists on a time-scale utterly divorced from our own—a system that is functionally if not absolutely immortal.[31]

The sort of change that Wallerstein has no trouble acknowledging is change for the worse. Military aggression may tend to leave a country's borders where they started, and will not, Wallerstein assures us, improve its economic fortunes, but it can certainly hasten a power's decline. This was the case for Germany in the twentieth century, he suggests, and is again the case for the United States now. In both cases this may well be true, but it leaves a question mark hanging over imperialism and more generally over coercion—the very element of Wallerstein's most daring and successful revision of Marx—as a possible agent of historical change.[32] Does coercion matter, or not?

Only a programmatic commitment to change for the worse can explain Wallerstein's emphatic proposal of the unfashionable (and to me, untenable) thesis that capitalism has produced absolute immiseration. In *Historical Capitalism*, Wallerstein writes: "I wish to defend the one Marxist proposition which even orthodox Marxists tend to bury in shame, the thesis of the absolute (not relative) immiseration of the proletariat. I hear the friendly whispers. Surely you can't be serious; surely you mean relative immiseration?" (100–101). Adding the (historically implausible) idea that "sexism and racism" form "a new framework of oppressive humiliation which had never previously existed" (102), he arrives at the conclusion that "in both material and psychic terms (sexism and racism), there was absolute immiseration" (104). Both the content and the tone—a tone suggesting a position that is not the result of empirical assessment, but an a priori, unavailable to further review—ought to be familiar to humanists.[33] Breaking with Marx— "It is simply not true that capitalism as a historical system has represented progress over the various previous historical systems that it destroyed or transformed" (98)—Wallerstein carries the anti-progressive impulse that he shares with the humanities even further than most humanists would be tempted to. Here he sounds very like those anti-progressive thinkers the humanities have most eagerly embraced, Matthew Arnold and Michel Foucault.

The thesis of absolute immiseration ought to provoke humanists to consider whether we too may not have come to a collective decision in advance, independent of actual evidence: a decision that our culture *must* be responsible, at least in part, for the suffering of the world, one that takes for granted, both that there must be an absolute sufferer, and that we must be linked up to that suffering. Are we sure that what looks like system is not in fact the self-flattery that can hide in self-blame—a response to the disciplinary imperative to achieve self-importance, an unearned guarantee of a significance for culture that might otherwise be doubted? The humanities are making a case for culture; Wallerstein is making a case for the periphery. The overlap of course comes at the point where culture and periphery coincide: the cultures of the Third World. It does the Third World no favors to force its cultures to serve as the invisible evidence by which the study of culture in general is legitimated, the foundation on which a First World program of intellectual examination is based.

The same doubts that could be raised about culture have already been raised about Wallerstein's implicit case for the significance of the periphery. Robert DuPlessis writes, for example: "By inflating the small-scale, loosely articulated international trading networks of the mercantilist age into an integrated world-economy, and then investing that system with causal primacy, Wallerstein not only substantially overestimates the contribution of the periphery for growth in the core but overlooks forces for change and divergence internal to each of the three zones."[34] If Sahlins accused Wallerstein of giving too little importance to the periphery (at the level of culture and agency), DuPlessis says the problem is that he gives too much importance to it. The absoluteness of the absolute immiseration thesis suggests that, beyond the actual suffering on the periphery, which is not in short supply, peripheral suffering also plays a systemic role, so to speak, at the level of the argument. Built into the logic, it must be protected from any shifting in the historical facts. It would be inconvenient if the facts were suddenly to reconfigure themselves. In this sense, Wallerstein might be said to veer toward a fundamentally ethical, rather than an empirical or indeed a political, position.

In the humanities, this constellation of features ought to be recognizable. Taking for granted that our vocation is to foster remembrance of what society wants to forget and not (as politics would demand) some contingent mixture of remembering and forgetting, we tend to jump to the conclusion that the more inclusive the temporal viewpoint, the better. The long, almost inhuman temporal perspectives that result are inimical to the urgencies of topical intervention. The aesthetic, as I have suggested elsewhere, is sometimes nothing more or less than a version of retrospect, that structural remove from political commitment that is presumed by making judgments about the past rather than the present. About the past, no commitment in the strongest sense is possible.[35] These hidden commonalities between Wallerstein and the humanities, commonalities in the chosen time-scale (the long term) and the deferral or dilution of political agency (an anti-interventionist ethos that might also be called aesthetic), will I hope be somewhat disquieting to both pro- and anti-system readers.

Wallerstein's belief in system (as definitive and exclusive object to be blamed) seems the very antithesis of the humanist's disbelief in system. For the humanist, what must be blamed is, precisely, thinking systematically. Yet as I've suggested, these apparent opposites have similar and disquieting (that is, quietist) political effects. And the counterintuitive symmetry goes further. If I have shown that Wallerstein has more in common with the humanities than he appears to, I hope I have also managed to suggest that the humanities need more of Wallerstein's sense of system than they admit. For if system makes blaming difficult, as Boltanski says in the argument with which I began, it is no less true that without system, blaming in Boltanski's sense is not really possible. In order to blame well, one has to know that this is not just any random suffering, the result of nature or accident or perhaps even the fault of the sufferer. The recent fashion in the humanities has been to avoid such knowledge — to view the suffering body in close-ups that leave the potentially explanatory background out of focus or out of the frame. It's as if humanists could not bear the threat that, once allowed into the picture, the background would throw epistemological or ethical doubt on the fact of suffering, which is properly left autonomous and indisputable. Lacking or deliberately evading any theory of power, we find ourselves imitating the news media and the news-dependent humanitarian NGOs, which do not want the flow of sympathy and dollars checked by worry about wasted or badly bestowed efforts. (A notorious example of the latter is international support for hungry, homeless Hutu refugees after the Rwandan genocide of 1994, which turned out in effect to be support for those who had committed genocide.) Without system, you get celebrity humanitarians like Bernard-Henri Lévy, pointing to themselves pointing to a victim and programmatically refusing any theoretical explanation that might link the lives of their entranced tele-spectators to those of their telegenic victims, thereby breaking out of the theory-free mode of moral appeal.

But this linkage may help extricate us from the paradox in which Boltanski's argument had placed us. The paradox is this: you can't blame without system, which teaches you what must and what can be changed, what is and isn't merely the work of nature, human or otherwise. But you also can't blame with it, for system fatally weakens the link between individual sufferer and individual perpetrator, hence between the suffering and the listener. The only solution I can see to this paradox is another one: we can only come to act as Good Samaritans if we realize that we are not Good Samaritans, at least according to Boltanski's paradigm of the disinterested observer.

The Samaritan, it turns out, may not have been as disinterested as he seemed. According to my Israel guidebook, which locates the biblical scene on the road between Jerusalem and Jericho, on what is now the West Bank, in fact near one of the larger fortified settlements, the Good Samaritan was, like me, a sort of Jew.[36] The story is that when most of the Jews were sent into exile after the Assyrian conquest around 720 BC, some were left behind. "Returning from exile in 538 BC, the Jews shunned the Samaritans for their intermarriage with the conquerors, although the Samaritans claimed strict adherence to the Mosaic Law" (283). There is thus some question as to whether the Samaritans were simply enemies of the Jews or something more intimate and more confused, and thus whether the Good Samaritan can stand for something as simple as a disinterested spectator. Perhaps this charitable action was closer to solidarity, or to the specific overcoming of a specific hostility.

Like the Good Samaritan, we Americans are not quite disinterested spectators of the world's suffering. If every ethics presupposes a sociology, as Alasdair MacIntyre teaches, then the sociology behind Boltanski's dilemma—what do you say to get people in France or the United States to show compassion about things that happen far away?—would seem evident enough. I quote George Orwell, who had notable opinions on "why words matter" in a political context. In *The Road to Wigan Pier* Orwell writes as follows: "Under the capitalist system, in order that England may live in comparative comfort, a hundred million Indians must live on the verge of starvation—an evil state of affairs, but you acquiesce in it every time you step into a taxi or eat a plate of strawberries and cream" (140). These may not be the right words—in fact I think they're rather problematic words—but we need words like them in order for Americans to see how far from disinterested they are. To put it crudely: every American except the very poorest has an objective and appreciable interest in the continuing exploitation of the rest of the world, the siphoning off of resources there so as to support a disproportionate level of comfort here. In spite of the dramatically unequal distribution inside America of the benefits brought to America by our government's hypocritical mixture of dogmatic free trade and actual protectionism, backed up by military as well as economic power, American hegemony has paid real across-the-board dividends. Even the poor in this country are on the whole much better off than the majority of the population of many other countries, and the majority of Americans are obscenely better off. Thus the American left is asking Americans not to throw off their chains, but to surrender their privileges. It is because of our interest that disinterestedness is a political project we cannot refuse.

Notes

1. Boltanski, *Distant Suffering*.

2. It is worth noting here that Boltanski's major institutional inspiration, Médecins sans frontières, came into existence because of a perceived need for humanitarianism that would be less neutral, in other words more ready to blame, than the Red Cross.

3. Said praises Wallerstein as critic of Eurocentrism and exemplary champion of "a genuinely cosmopolitan or internationalist perspective" (53). Said praises his con-

tribution to our understanding of "our global system" in the same book (138). Said, *Humanism and Democratic Criticism*.

4. Gilroy, *The Black Atlantic*.

5. Pieterse writes, for example: "In the indexes to Wallerstein's books . . . one looks in vain for any reference to 'system' and from the outset it is clear that we are dealing with an untheorized use of 'system'" (30). "No reasons are given as to why the existence of a division of labor over an area should be considered to give rise to a social system. Why a *system*? And why a *social* system? It would be more obvious to speak of an economic system" (31). Pieterse, *Empire and Emancipation: Power*. Pieterse goes on: "The unit of analysis (classes, strata, nations) remains unclear, and is switched ambiguously from one to another" (40).

6. Moretti cites Wallerstein in *Modern Epic*. For literary criticism without the assumption of reverence, see Moretti's *Atlas of the European Novel 1800–1900* and *Graphs Maps Trees: Abstract Models for a Literary Theory*.

7. Wallerstein, "The Rise and Future Demise of the World Capitalist System," in *The Essential Wallerstein*.

8. When Wallerstein describes the world capitalist system as "a unit with a single division of labor and multiple cultural systems" (75), one notes that cultures are themselves recognized as systems, hence presumably endowed with their own coherence. This becomes an issue for other commentators, who claim either that Wallerstein denies such coherence to sub-world units, whether cultural or social, or that he is inconsistent on this point. Yet even if this coherence exists, it is irrelevant to that larger coherence in which the multiple cultures reside, the singleness that overrides cultural multiplicity and determines the proper unit of analysis: a single, shared division of labor.

9. Williams, *Culture and Society 1780–1950*.

10. Arnold quoted in Eagleton, *The Eagleton Reader*, 174.

11. This is a bit unfair, as readers are sometimes too quick to add to Foucault's diagnosis of system the assumption that Foucault was *hostile* to system, or hostile to it as such.

12. Said, "Criticism between Culture and System," 178–225. The essay was originally published in 1978.

13. I will not insist here on the pro-systemic side of Edward Said's work, which is obvious enough. In dialogue with Tariq Ali in 1994, Said described the genesis of his book *Orientalism* as a discovery that "distortions and misrepresentations [of the Arabs in Western discourse] were systematic, part of a much larger system of thought that was endemic to the West's whole enterprise of dealing with the Arab world" (62). Said's sense of what sort of enemy we are up against—a category from which, as he had learned from his French interlocutors, we can never exclude ourselves—does not permit any simple distinction between system and anti-system, humanism and antihumanism. Tariq Ali, *Conversations with Edward Said*.

14. Wallerstein, "The Rise and Future Demise of the World Capitalist System," 82–83.

15. Appadurai, ed., *The Social Life of Things*. In his introduction to the volume, Appadurai explains that many of the commodities dealt with "have a strong luxury dimension and thus appear to constitute a sample that is bound to favor a cultural approach in a way that humbler, more mass-produced commodities might not" (40). He proceeds to ignore this qualification, so that the cultural approach is made to work for all. It may be relevant that culture is itself often imagined as a luxury.

16. Steve J. Stern notes how much support the Caribbean experience of slavery lends to "Wallerstein's theoretical stance on units of analysis and capitalist combinations of free and coercive labor" (35). Yet after long examination he concludes that local factors were more decisive than systemic ones in explaining, say, recourse to coerced labor in the Caribbean and Brazil (46). Stern, "Feudalism, Capitalism, and the World-System in the Perspective of Latin America and Africa," 23–83.

17. In *The Decline of American Power*, Wallerstein refers to many different causal factors and attributes varying degrees of power to them. His account of 1968, for example, carries a suggestion that culture matters quite a bit after all. The decline of American power can be dated from events whose significance was mainly symbolic: "The direct political consequences of the world revolutions of 1968 were minimal, but the geopolitical and intellectual repercussions were enormous and irrevocable" (19). The same could be said of September 11, 2001, which "posed a major challenge to U.S. power" (22). Admittedly this book is a popularization, hence looser and more narrative than the work that produced Wallerstein's account of the world-system. Still, there remains some question about how far the original work is itself narrative in its essence, an account of a single unrepeatable sequence of events rather than a theory properly speaking, which would have to extend to other times and places.

18. Sahlins, "Cosmologies of Capitalism: The Trans-Pacific Sector of 'the World System,'" 412–13.

19. Jay, "Beyond Discipline?"

20. Appadurai, ed., *The Social Life of Things*.

21. This assumption is concealed by the fact that the word "system" continues to appear with regularity in Appadurai's work, as in *Fear of Small Numbers*, 26, 129–30, and passim.

22. Appadurai, "Disjuncture and Difference in the Global Cultural Economy."

23. Wolf's version of what Wallerstein does is similarly a choice, as if it were nothing but a choice: "To understand how the core subjugated the periphery, and not to study the reactions of the micro-populations habitually investigated by anthropologists" (23). Wolf, *Europe and the People without History*.

24. Ferguson, "Decomposing Modernity: History and Hierarchy after Development."

25. Ferguson reveals the power of the culture concept, even in an anthropologist

as clear-eyed as himself, when he talks of "relatively fixed global statuses." It might have seemed that the category he was looking for was not status but class, which puts the emphasis where he wants it: on forms of structural inequality that are unyielding and systematic. Status, on the other hand, which is more subjective, allows for a more disordered, less hierarchical diversity; it makes the global hierarchy seem *merely* cultural—exactly the position that Ferguson is trying to get away from.

26. Pieterse, *Empire and Emancipation*, 38.

27. Anderson, "Confronting Defeat."

28. For a recent reiteration of the same vision—the decline of the U.S. and the rise of East Asia, without any questioning that this might constitute a significant shift in the system itself—see Wallerstein, "The Curve of US Power."

29. On decolonization, compare, for example, Stephen Howe, for whom decolonization was "one of the most profound transformations that the world political system ever experienced" (*Empire*, 104).

30. If they became part of the system, which seems the implication when he says "the antisystemic movements were in power" (40), then why continue to call them anti-systemic?

31. The recent relegation of Pluto to sub-planetary status does not seem to me to interfere with this conclusion.

32. It would be interesting to speculate at length about the role of force in Wallerstein's work. If he rescues coercion from its neglected place in Marx, where it is upstaged by free wage labor, does he also bring it back as a cause (in the form of strong nation policy) of the core–periphery system? And if so, does coercion make a sort of deconstructive return, unsettling the coherence of a world-system defined by the supposed long-term capacity to function at a deeper level, relatively untroubled by the surface tumult of wars and rebellions?

33. Wallerstein is scornful of "the 'progressive' politics of the past several hundred years" (104) as resulting merely in a "diminution of the unequal distribution of world surplus-value among the small group who have shared it" (104).

34. DuPlessis, "The Partial Transition to World-Systems Analysis in Early Modern European History," 20.

35. Note how Wallerstein's lack of epistemological anxiety here rejoins Appadurai's insistence on the trouble that "uncertainty" brings into the modern (non)system (Appadurai, *Fear of Small Numbers*, 88ff.). And Wallerstein's certainty about the causal power and knowability of the system converges with a common version of anti-system in the humanities, which makes unknowability similarly programmatic and irremediable. "Auschwitz, Gulags, and ethnic purification all occurred within the framework of a historical social system, the capitalist world-economy," Wallerstein writes. "We have to ask what it is about this system that produced such phenomena and allowed them to flourish in the twentieth century, in ways and to a degree that hadn't occurred before" (41). He insists "that the explanation must be found in the

functioning of the system" (42). One can raise an eyebrow at the outlandish confidence of the claim that the system can explain Auschwitz without committing oneself in advance to the impossibility of explanation. Surely it would be better to remain agnostic on the point of when, where, and how much of the unknown must remain unknown.

36. Stedman, *Palestine with Jerusalem*.

PART TWO

Literature: Restructured,

Rehistoricized,

Rescaled

World-Systems Analysis,
Evolutionary Theory,
Weltliteratur

FRANCO MORETTI

A friend brought me the first volume of *The Modern World-System* from the United States in the late seventies. The book made an enormous impression on me, and I remember wondering how it could affect, and change, the study of literature. But I found an answer only several years later, when I realized that world-systems analysis offered a very good way to account for the mix of "all-inclusiveness" and chaos that had often been noticed in Modernist texts (*Ulysses, The Waste Land, Cantos* . . .), but never truly explained. In the light of world-systems analysis, this strange combination could be recognized as an attempt to represent a world that had simultaneously become *one* (whence the all-inclusiveness), but full of disparities and contradictions (whence the chaos). "World texts," I called these works, and in a book called *Modern Epic* (the epic is the literary genre of totality), I traced their lineage forward in time from the 1920s to Magic Realism, and backward, through Wagner and Melville and others, to Goethe's *Faust*, which was composed between 1770 and 1830, during one of the great expansions of the capitalist world-system.

The first contribution of world-systems analysis to literary history, then, was this: it allowed us to "see" a new literary genre—and not just any genre, but the one trying to represent *the world as a totality*: a possibility that our discipline had never even envisioned, because it lacked the concepts to do so. (When I presented my thesis at Harvard, around 1990, the title of the talk was turned by the organizers into "Word texts," without the "l," so odd must have seemed the conjunction of world and text. . . .) And then, second contribution, world-systems analysis threw light on a geographical peculiarity of this genre that was, at first sight, extremely disconcerting: the nearly complete absence of French and English works. Disconcerting, because between 1650 and 1950 these two literatures are unquestionably the core of the world literary system—and yet, in the most ambitious genre of all, they are replaced by German, American, Irish, Latin American writers. . . . Why? And what do all these writers have in common, that they write in such a similar vein? For traditional literary history, nothing. But within world-systems analysis, a common ground emerges: they are all writers from the semiperiphery, who were probably encouraged by their intermediate and dynamic position to grapple with the world as a whole.

With these last remarks, we have already moved beyond the initial thematic approach—the world-system as a theme; the world-system "inside" literature, so to speak—to a second perspective, which reverses the relationship, by focusing instead on *literature inside the world-system*. Here, we encounter one of the most celebrated terms of literary history, coined by Goethe almost two centuries ago: *Weltliteratur*. World literature. A neologism that was, at the time, more prophecy than description, and that in its long life (which includes an appearance in the *Communist Manifesto*) has never fully shed its initial tentativeness—thereby also leaving its object in a sort of conceptual limbo. Needless to say, this essay will not solve the problem. But it will take a first step, by sketching a comparison of two theories that have often struck me as excellent candidates for the task: evolutionary theory, and, indeed, world-systems analysis. I will begin by outlining how the two models may help us define world literature; then, I will discuss their intellectual compatibility; and finally, after a brief detour on the making of cultural hybrids, I will try to delineate the consequences of all this for our idea of *Weltliteratur*.[1]

It is easy to see why evolution is a good model for literary history: it is a theory that explains the extraordinary variety and complexity of existing forms on the basis of a historical process. In a refreshing contrast to literary study—where theories of form are usually blind to history, and historical work blind to form—for evolution form and history are really the two sides of the same coin; or perhaps, better, the two dimensions of the same tree.

A tree is famously the only image included in the *The Origin of Species*; it appears in the fourth chapter, "Natural Selection," in the section on "Divergence of Character."

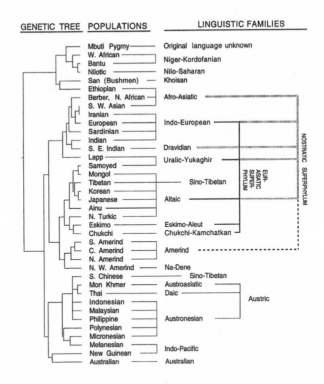

Figure 1. Genetic tree comparing linguistic families and superfamilies.

A tree, or a "diagram," writes Darwin, whose point lies in visualizing the interplay of the theory's two variables: history along the vertical axis, where every interval corresponds, hypothetically, to "one thousand generations"— and form along the horizontal one, which follows the morphological diversification that eventually leads to "well-marked varieties," or to entirely new species.

The horizontal axis follows formal diversification. . . . But Darwin's words are stronger: he speaks of "this rather perplexing subject," whereby forms don't just change, but do so by always and only *diverging* from each other (remember, the tree appears in the section on "Divergence of Character"). Whether as a result of geohistorical accidents, or under the action of a specific "principle"—as far as I can tell, the question is still open—divergence pervades for Darwin the history of life, and shapes its morphospace accordingly. "A tree can be viewed *as a simplified description of a matrix of distances*," write Cavalli-Sforza, Menozzi, and Piazza in the methodological prelude to their *History and Geography of Human Genes*; and figure 1, where genetic groups and linguistic families branch away from each other in geography and morphology at once, makes clear what they mean: a tree is a way of sketching *how far* a given form has moved from another one, or from their common point of origin.

A theory that takes as its central problem the *multiplicity of forms* existing in the world; that explains them as the result of *historical divergence*; and that bases their divergence on a process of *spatial separation*: here is what evolutionary theory has to offer to literary history. Many different forms, in a discontinuous space: not bad, as an idea of world literature.

In world-systems analysis the coordinates change, as the onset of capitalism brusquely reduces the many independent spaces needed for the origin of species (or of languages) to just three positions: core, periphery, semiperiphery. The world becomes *one*, and *unequal*: one, because capitalism constrains production everywhere on the planet; and unequal, because its network of exchanges requires, and reinforces, a marked power unevenness between the three areas.

Here, too, it's easy to understand the theory's appeal for literary study. On its basis, we can grasp the *unity* of world literature—one, as in Goethe's (and Marx's) *Weltliteratur*—as well as its *internal differentiation*: just like capitalism, *Weltliteratur* is unified but unequal, as the development of all national and local literatures is profoundly constrained by their position within the system. Itamar Evan-Zohar (whose "polisystem theory" has a strong resemblance to world-systems analysis) speaks in this respect of the "asymmetry" of the literary system: where powerful literatures from the core "interfere" all the time with the trajectory of peripheral ones, whereas the reverse almost never happens, making the inequality of the system grow over time.

While studying the market for novels in the eighteenth and nineteenth century, I reached very similar conclusions to Evan-Zohar's. Here, the crucial mechanism was that of *diffusion*: books from the core were incessantly exported into the semi-periphery and the periphery, where they were read, admired, imitated, turned into models—thus drawing those literatures into the orbit of core ones, and indeed "interfering" with their autonomous development. And then, diffusion imposed a stunning *sameness* to the literary system: wave after wave of epistolary fiction, or historical novels, or *mystères*, took off from London and Paris and dominated the scene everywhere—often, like American action films today, even more thoroughly in the smaller peripheral markets than in the French or British core.

The *international constraints* under which literature is produced, and the *streamlining of formal solutions* imposed by the world market on the literary imagination: these were the central findings of a world-systems approach to literary history. But did they agree with those of the evolutionary approach?

———————————

Not really. Evolution foregrounds the *formal diversification* produced by speciation; world-systems analysis, the *formal sameness* (or at any rate, reduction) enforced by diffusion. I am simplifying of course, evolution includes mutation *and* selection (i.e., both the production and the elimination of diversity), just as world-systems analysis specifies *different* positions within the international division of labor. But still, think of those titles: *The Origin of Species*, plural, and *The Modern World-System*, singular: grammar is a good index of the opposite research paths. And the geographical substratum of the two theories reinforces the antithesis: Darwin's breakthrough famously occurred in an *archipelago*, because the origin of species needs a world made of discrete spaces, separated by vast expanses of water; but world-systems analysis shows how long-distance trade *bridges* even the widest of oceans, creating a single, continuous geography all over the planet.

A theory of diversification in a discontinuous space; a theory of sameness in a unified geography. Clearly, the two were incompatible. Just as clearly, they both explained important aspects of world literature. They were both true: but they *could not* be both true.[2] Or perhaps, better, they couldn't—*unless literature itself functioned in two completely incompatible ways.*

This assertion may sound absurd, but there is a historical and morphological rationale behind it. The historical argument is simple: the drive toward diversification and the—opposite—drive toward sameness are both present in literary history, because they arise from different social mechanisms, and in different epochs. Diversification is the result of the (relative) isolation of human cultures from their origins until a few centuries ago; sameness appears much later, around the eighteenth century, when the international literary market becomes strong enough to unify and subjugate those separate cultures (with an interesting delay on the markets for material goods and for money). Here I am simplifying again, there had been episodes of widespread diffusion well before the eighteenth century (like the Petrarchist epidemics of late medieval Europe), just as there have been episodes of diversification after it; but the point is that each of the two principles has an elective affinity with a different socio-historical configuration, and that, by and large, we have moved from the supremacy of diversification to that of sameness.

This, in broad strokes, is the historical argument. The morphological one is different. So far, I have implicitly accepted the evolutionary assumption that in literature, just as in nature, *diversity equals divergence*: that new forms can only arise by branching out from pre-existing ones via some kind of mutation. Now, if this were always the case, diffusion (and with it the world-systems approach that, in literature, so heavily relies on it) would have nothing to say on literary morphology: great at explaining how forms *move*, a theory of diffusion cannot account for how they *change*, for the simple reason that diffusion does not try to multiply forms, but rather to *reduce* their number by maximizing the space occupied by just one of them.

But . . . is it true that in literature, just as in nature, diversity equals divergence?

This question will strike many readers as a mere rhetorical flourish. "Darwinian evolution," writes Stephen Jay Gould, "is a process of constant separation and distinction. Cultural change, on the other hand, receives a powerful boost from amalgamation and anastomosis of different traditions. A clever traveler may take one look at a foreign wheel, import the invention back home, and change his local culture fundamentally and forever."[3] The clever traveler is a poorly chosen example (it's a case of diffusion, not of amalgamation), but the general point is clear, and well expressed by the historian of technology George Basalla: "Different biological species usually do not interbreed," he writes. "Artifactual types, on the other hand, are routinely combined to produce new and fruitful entities."[4]

Routinely combined. . . . That's it: for most scholars, convergence—interbreeding, grafting, recombination, hybridization—is the basic, if not the *only* mode of cultural change. Elsewhere, I have criticized this idea, countering it with a sort of division of labor between divergence and convergence;[5] here, I will only add that, once more, the decisive turning point coincides with the establishment of the international literary market: divergence being the main path of change before its advent, and convergence afterward. Thomas Pavel's morphological reflections in his great book, *La Pensée du Roman*—based on a very different conceptual framework from the present paper—offers excellent (because independent) corroboration for this thesis: for him, the *separation* of narrative forms from each other is the driving force in the first fifteen centuries of the novel's existence, and their *recombination* in the last three, from the eighteenth century onward.

From the eighteenth century. . . . Or in other words: convergence makes its appearance in literary life *at exactly the same time as diffusion*. And one wonders: is this merely a temporal coincidence, or is there a functional relationship between the two?

Let me begin with a concrete example. Years ago, one of the greatest critics of our time, Antonio Candido, wrote a tryptich of essays (on Zola's *Assommoir* [1877], Verga's *Malavoglia* [1881], and Azevedo's *Cortiço* [1890]) in which he followed the diffusion of the naturalist novel from the core (France), through the semi-periphery (Italy), and into the periphery (Brazil) of the world literary system. And he discovered, among many other things, an odd disjunction in the process of diffusion: whereas Zola's plot model was largely retained by Verga and Azevedo, his style was deeply transformed—in Verga, by his Sicilian-Tuscan orchestration of collective speech, and a thick texture of old popular proverbs; in Azevedo, by the explicit recourse to a form of racial-political allegory, and by the narrator's frequent ethical intrusions (especially in sexual matters).[6]

Now, Verga's and Azevedo's behavior is far from being unique. In the late nineteenth century, as European narrative models reach with increasing regularity peripheral cultures, their greatest writers frequently subject them to a similar process of stylistic rewriting, replacing the analytico-impersonal style which had been the great invention of nineteenth-century France with judgmental, loud, sarcastic, emotional voices. Aside from *Malavoglia* and *Cortiço*, we find variations of this basic arrangement in Multatuli's anti-imperialist classic, *Max Havelaar, or The Coffee Sales of the Netherlands Trading Company* (1860), and in Rizal's Filipino masterpiece, *Noli me tangere* (1886–87); in Futabatei's *Drifting clouds* (1887), the "first modern Japanese novel," and in Tagore's Rashomon-like political parable, *Home and the world* (1916).

Italy, Brazil, Indonesia, Philippines, Japan, Bengal. . . . The specifics obviously differ from case to case, but the formal logic is always the same: all these novels are indeed, in Gould's formula, "amalgamations of different traditions"—and all of the same kind: they mix *a plot from the core*, and *a style from the periphery*.[7] Which means that, in the journey of novelistic models from the center to the periphery of the world literary system, plots survive more or less intact, whereas styles become somehow "unglued" from them—and are replaced by different ones.

But how can plot and style become unglued from each other?

They can, because the novel is a composite form, made of the two distinct layers of "story" and "discourse"—or, in my slight simplification, of plot and style: plot presiding over the internal concatenation of the events, and style over their verbal presentation. Conceptually, the distinction is clear; practically, a lot less so, because the two are usually so tightly interwoven that their separation is hard to imagine. And yet, as diffusion "moves" novels across the literary system, they seem to pass through a giant literary sieve, where their basic ingredients are filtered and separated: plots are allowed to pass, and remain fairly stable throughout the process of diffusion—whereas styles find all sorts of obstacles, and are profoundly transformed.

Why these different destinies? Two reasons. First, the plot is usually the main point of a novel, and hence it must be extremely resilient to external pressures. What makes it so resistant is the presence of those episodes that Boris Tomashevsky baptized "bound motifs": crucial turning points in the narrative, that "cannot be omitted . . . without disturbing the whole causal-chronological course of events."[8] And since bound motifs cannot be "omitted" (nor changed, of course), "they are usually distinguished," concludes Tomashevsky, "by their 'vitality': that is, they appear unchanged in the works of the most various schools"—and just as unchanged, we may add, in the works of the most various countries.[9]

The second reason is not structural, but linguistic. Diffusion usually entails translation: a movement, not only from one space to another, but also from one *language* into another. Now, plot is fundamentally *independent* from language, and it remains more or less the same even from one sign system to another (from novel, say, to illustration, film, ballet . . .). Style however is nothing *but* language, and hence its translation—*traduttore tra-*

ditore—is always a potential betrayal: in fact, the more complex a style is, the "better" it is, the greater the chance that its most significant traits will be lost in translation.

Diffusion makes literature pass through a sieve . . . *two* sieves, actually: a narrative, and a linguistic one. In both cases, the nature of the filter is such that plots are (largely) preserved, while styles are (largely) lost, and replaced by Brazilian, Italian, Filipino, or Japanese solutions. The result is indeed Gould's "amalgamation of different traditions." But the amalgamation is in its turn rife with contradiction, because in "replacing" the old style, the new one also acts as a powerful *counterpoint* to the original story.

The fact is totally clear in Multatuli and Rizal, where melodramatic invective and bitter sarcasm accompany throughout the "European" plot of lost illusions and political defeat; it operates more obliquely in Futabatei, whose verbal reticence casts an aura of incomprehensibility around the sentimental education of his hero, and in Verga, where the *longue durée* of village mentality is only slowly undermined by the new reality of capitalism. But in one way or another, a dissonance between plot and style is typical of all these books, making them aesthetically rather unsteady (if not quite "the greatest mess imaginable," as Lawrence said of *Max Havelaar*). Beyond aesthetics, though, the dissonance highlights a *political* tension between the story that came from the core, and style that had arisen in the periphery. In this respect, these hybrid texts are not—as is routinely assumed in contemporary criticism—a sign that power differences *have been overcome*, but rather a *specific embodiment* of those differences: they are a microcosm of the world literary system, and of its endless spiral of hegemony and resistance.

———

Weltliteratur. . . . But the singular is misleading. There are *two* distinct world literatures—one that precedes the eighteenth century, and one that follows it. The "first" *Weltliteratur* is a mosaic of separate "local" cultures;[10] it is characterized by strong internal diversity; it produces new forms mostly by divergence; and is best explained by (some version of) evolutionary theory. The "second" *Weltliteratur* (which I would prefer to call the world literary system) is the product of a unified market; it shows a growing, and at times shocking degree of sameness; it produces new forms mostly by convergence; and is best explained by (some version of) world-systems analysis.

What are we to make of these two world literatures? They offer us a great chance to rethink the place of history in literary studies. A generation ago, only the literature of the past was considered "worth" studying; today, the only "relevant" literature is that of the present. In a sense, everything has changed; in another, nothing has, because both positions are profoundly *normative* ones, much more concerned with value judgments than with actual knowledge. And instead, the past and the present of literature (a "long" present, beginning in the eighteenth century) should be seen, not as "superior" or "inferior" to each other, but as two epochs that are structurally so different that they require two independent theoretical approaches. Learning to study *the past as past*, then, with the help of evolutionary theory, and *the present as present*, with the help of world-systems analysis: here is a possible research program for *Weltliteratur* in the twenty-first century.

Notes

1. Embarrassingly enough, I have used evolution and world-systems analysis for many years—even in the same book!—without ever considering their compatibility. Evolution was crucial for the morphological argument of *Modern Epic*, whose thematic aspect was in turn strongly shaped by world-systems analysis. A few years later, world-systems analysis played a major role in *Atlas of the European Novel*, and in the articles "Conjectures on World Literature" and "More Conjectures," while evolution was the basis for "The Slaughterhouse of Literature" and "Graphs, Maps, Trees" (a few passages from this article are more or less repeated in the present text).

2. Obviously enough, I am here speaking of their truth *when applied to literature*; in their original fields (biology and economic history) the two theories are simply incomparable.

3. Gould, *Full House*, 220–21.

4. Basalla, *The Evolution of Technology*, 137–38.

5. See "Graphs, Maps, Trees."

6. Candido, *O discurso e a cidade*.

7. It can hardly be a coincidence that the greatest problematizer of narrative voice in western European literature—Joseph Conrad—had himself worked in the colonies, and owed his formal breakthrough (Marlow's laborious, defensive irony) to his wish to re-present the periphery to a metropolitan audience. In his case, of course, the ingredients of the amalgamation are reversed: a plot from the periphery—and a style from the core.

8. Tomashevsky, "Thematics," 68.

9. Here, the analogy with biological mutation is arresting. "In DNA and protein regions of vital importance for function, one finds perfect—or almost perfect—conservation," write Cavalli-Sforza, Menozzi, and Piazza in *The History and Geography*

of Human Genes: "This indicates strong selective control against changes that would be deleterious; it also shows that evolutionary improvement in this region is rare or absent. However, variation is quite frequent in chromosome regions that are not of vital importance" (15). Within narrative structure, bound motifs are the equivalent of the "protein regions of vital importance for function," where one finds "near perfect conservation"; whereas the "chromosome regions that are not of vital importance," and where variation is therefore quite frequent, have their parallel in the "free motifs" of Tomashevsky's model, which "may be omitted without destroying the coherence of the narrative," and which are as a consequence quite variable ("each literary school has its characteristic stock [of free motifs]").

10. Speaking of "local" cultures does not exclude the existence of large regional systems (Indo-European, East Asian, Mediterranean, Meso-American, Scandinavian . . .), which may well overlap with each other, like the eight thirteenth-century "circuits" of Janet Abu-Lughod's *Before European Hegemony*. But these geographical units are not yet stably subordinated to a single center like that which emerged in eighteenth century France and Britain.

The Scale of World Literature

NIRVANA TANOUKHI

This is his home; he can't be far away.
Sophocles, *Philoctetes*

Distance has long been a thorny issue for Comparative Literature. Whether one tries to explicate a foreign text, map a course of influence, or describe an elusive aesthetic, there's the problem of crossing considerable divides without yielding to the fallacy of decisive leaps. And yet, a condition conducive to methodological malaise found consolation in a fixed literary geography that justified comparison, ingeniously, with the very fact of incommensurability. Impossible distances beg to be crossed *precisely* because they cannot be. And for crossings to be attempted, each book, each author, each device— each canon, nation, or interpretive community—would assume its rightful place. While comparative literature, it was said, would "occupy" the-space-in-between conventional places. And so, by a euphoric celebration of displacement, the comparative method became unquestionably subversive: in practice it exacted "shock value,"[1] institutionally it was a "thorn in the side,"[2] in ideological wars it proffered a "symbolic weapon."[3] But really, may that not be overstating the case? I want to consider why the comparative method, in the first instance, made a *cartographic* claim to scale. Why dedicate a discipline to the task of charting zones, paths, and crossroads obscured by strict adherence to "national traditions"—when logically, comparison depends for its existence on the entrenchment of nation-based geography?

Comparison's cartographic commitment (and its poetics of distance) is worth examining not only as a logical paradox, but also as a possible key to the recent disciplinary revival of the concept "World Literature"—which I take to be the latest, most pronounced attempt to diffuse the teleological thrust of literary history with a radically synchronic outlook. With this slide from literary history to world literature the literary discipline makes a belated entry into the globalization debates,[4] a time-honored social-scientific inquiry into the time and place of uneven development. But what kind of possibilities does this move open up for comparative literary analysis,[5] and what are the risks involved? Here's my answer: On the one hand, the discussion about literary globalization has already launched us, however slowly or implicitly, on a disciplinary critique of the very concept *scale*, which by necessity moves us away from metaphorical deployments of "space" toward concrete discussions about the materiality of literary *landscapes*. I suggest that the concept scale, properly theorized, would enable a more precise formulation of the role of literature, and literary analysis, in the history of the production of space. But, in the meantime, though such a critique seems imminent, "world literature" threatens to become a hardened (albeit enlarged) image of the old literary history, where *geography* evokes a figurative solidity that assumes the guise of materiality. My aim is to hasten the literary critique of scale by making cracks in the geography of "world literature." The "post-colonial novel"—perhaps one of the most geographically constituted objects of literary history—offers an ideal weak spot to get us started.

Man with a Novel

A most interesting insight about the comparative view of the novel comes in an essay by the cultural philosopher Anthony Appiah, where he describes a particular geographic outlook that makes futile both the writing of the post-colonial novel, and by extension, its cultural critique. Appiah argues that so long as the novel is taken as a representative sample of African culture, Western intellectuals are bound to drown in misconceptions about the popular mentality of the continent. By "popular" he means non-literate, which is why he proposes African sculpture as an alternate sample-object of African cultural history.[6] *Man with a Bicycle*, a Nigerian sculpture (see figure 1), is presented as the epistemological antithesis of the African novel, an object whose cultural ethos eludes Western critics (suggests Appiah) precisely because they insist on approaching it *as a novel*. Appiah reprimands the sculpture's critics and curators as follows:

> I am grateful to James Baldwin for his introduction to the [Nigerian sculpture] *Man with a Bicycle*, a figure who is, as Baldwin so rightly saw, polyglot—speaking Yoruba and English . . . someone whose "clothes do not fit him too well." He and other men and women among whom he

mostly lives suggest to me that the place to look for hope is not just to the postcolonial novel, which has struggled to achieve the insights of Ouologuem and Mudimbe, but to the all-consuming vision of this less-anxious creativity. It matters little whom the work was made *for*; what we should learn from is the imagination that produced it. *Man with a Bicycle* is produced by someone who does not care that the bicycle is the white man's invention: it is not there to be Other to the Yoruba self; it is there because someone cared for its solidity; it is there because it will take us further than our feet will take us; it is there because machines are now as African as novelists . . . and as fabricated as the kingdom of Nakem. (357)

One cannot be surprised by Appiah's admiration for *Man with a Bicycle*, a contemporary Nigerian wooden sculpture whose nonchalant protagonist stands firm, it seems, because impervious to the anxieties of influence. We understand why he would draw force from such a *man* lacking in hesitation, who grabs a machine simply because it works. In fact, the *man* seems to be at such ease that we almost wonder whether he takes the bicycle, not simply, but unthinkingly. His apparent comfort in the solidity of things resonates for us uncomfortably with the primitivism of Lévi-Strauss's *bricoleur* who can make do precisely because he does not reflect. We are a little surprised by Appiah's effortless conflation (or confusion) of the maker of the statue with the figure he carves out: the producer, "someone who does not care that the bicycle is the white man's invention," and the wooden personage, "someone whose 'clothes do not fit him too well'" (357). For sculpture to be an improvement on the novel—a "less-anxious" alternative, as Appiah says—the author and his hero must become one, such that the "hope" of the creator passes into the happiness of his creature, showing the "dark vision" of the novel to be gruesome in comparison. We're meant to see how, as a sculpture, *Man with a Bicycle* conveys in itself the solidity of its conception, a man's matter-of-fact contentment in his clothing, regardless of whether they fit or not. As if to say that writing a *novel*—imagine a hypothetical novel called *Man with a Bicycle*—about this man would have been akin to using his clothes to tell his story, which would lead inevitably to a novel *about* his clothes, because their "fit," being imperfect after all, would have become a problem (or the story) itself. At best, such a novel could be about the man's contentment *despite* his clothes, which is already not the same thing. Because surely, in this case the man would "care" not only about his clothes, but the status of the bicycle as "the white man's invention," so on and so forth. . . .

Figure 1. *Man with a Bicycle*, Yoruba, Nigeria, 20th century. Wood, 353/4″.
Collection of The Newark Museum, Purchase 1977 Wallace M. Scudder
Bequest Fund and The Members' Fund. Photo: Jerry Thompson, 1986.

Is this true, then? That in a sculpture, bicycles (and borrowed clothes) can be mere conveniences, while in a novel a mere bicycle (or ill-fitting clothes) must be a problem? Does the postcolonial writer's "struggle" with the novelist's mantle truly brand the hero with an anxious temperament, and by extension, the postcolonial novel with its "dark vision"? For now, instead of asking *whether* this is true, let's look at Appiah's own inadvertent explanation for *how* it's true. What is fundamentally historical about the postcolonial novel, he says, is its foreignness to African soil (a premise that, as we shall see later, echoes comparative wisdom on the subject). For this reason—unlike in the case of sculpture—the novel's geographic displacement becomes the context by which it can be properly historicized. This is, for him, the generic difference that escapes the interpreters of *Man with a Bicycle*, who mistake a piece of wooden handiwork for a modernist work of "high culture", burdening it with residues of the kinds of expectations we bring to a novel. And where do we see the critics making the mistake? Well, observes Appiah, when they "contextualized [the sculpture] only by the knowledge that bicycles are new in Africa" (339).

To contextualize an African novel, then, is *not* exactly to historicize. What Appiah captures is the peculiar "contextual" work done by a so-called "historical" detail, where the bicycle's novelty serves as the seed from which springs a whole psychic landscape with which the postcolonial novel is identified. One exhibit caption stresses the same detail to "explain" the sculpture as follows: "The influence of the Western world is revealed in the clothes and bicycle of this neo-traditional Yoruba sculpture which probably represents a merchant en route to market" (341). As for Baldwin, he observes that "his errand might prove to be impossible. . . . He is challenging something—or something has challenged him." The critics' "knowledge" of the bicycle's novelty is of course far from random, it is a "fact" chosen to mark a particular location: "new in Africa," not elsewhere. Since Appiah is far from interested in making a case for the African novel, the extent of his claim is that each genre is decipherable by a hermeneutic—a logic of contextualization—to which it's individually suited. The claim *betrayed* by his line of reasoning is far more interesting: that a wooden bicycle is turned into a sign of novelty by *a way of reading*, which not only pulls together identity and landscape in *Man with a Bicycle* such that they become inextricable—but more impressively, they mystify the man's journey, turning garb and transport into hurdles along his way. It's a way of reading that elicits a novel's dark vision:

"His errand might prove impossible"—a way of reading that prevents the *Man* from reaching his destination.

Even as Appiah seems to be corroborating a common view of the post-colonial novel as "anxious creativity," he illuminates the obscure makings of its "landscape." By doing so, he has taken us where we wanted: the symbolically historical place that is Africa-of-the-novel, where each object is potentially a hurdle and distance is the threshold of motion.[7]

Distance, Scale, Location

We must linger on the nature of distance, in light of places like Africa-of-the-Novel. "The making of place," says Neil Smith, always "implies the production of scale in so far as places are made different from each other; scale is the criterion of difference not between places so much as between different kinds of places."[8] Smith is inviting us, here, to enlarge our schoolish association of scale to maps. From the perspective of a human geographer,[9] the fact that the distance between two adjacent neighborhoods of unequal wealth cannot be measured numerically necessitates an understanding of geographic scale as a process—a process that establishes distances dually: by differentiating places *qualitatively* and demarcating boundaries *quantitatively*.

The cartographic sense of scale—of representation through mapping—is only one of three senses of the term that Smith lists in the revised entry for "Scale" in the *Dictionary of Human Geography*:

> *Cartographic scale* refers to the level of abstraction at which a map is constructed . . . therefore crucial in determining what is included and excluded in a map and the overall image a map conveys. . . . [*Methodological scale*] is largely determined by some compromise between the research problem (what kind of answer is anticipated), the availability of data, and the cost of data-acquisition and processing. . . . If these first two definitions refer to the conceptualizations of scale—cartographic and methodological—*geographic scale* is of a different order. "Geographic scale" refers to the dimensions of specific landscapes: geographers might talk of the regional scale, the scale of the watershed, or the global scale, for example. These scales are also of course conceptualized, but the conceptualization of geographical scale here follows specific processes in the physical and human LANDSCAPE rather than conceptual abstractions lain over it. . . . Geographical scale is in no sense natural or given. There is nothing inevi-

table about global, national, or urban scales. . . . These are specific to certain historical and geographical locations, they change over time, sometimes rapidly sometimes slowly, and in some cases a scale that operates in one society fails to appear in another. (724–26)

So, three senses of scale: cartographic, methodological, geographic—each accentuating a particular kind of limitation the geographer will encounter in practice. The first is epistemological and recognizes the limits of looking through a particular frame. The second, empirical, acknowledges the necessity of compromise with pre-existing conditions of research. In both cases, scale is a more or less a matter of choice. But the third, more materialist definition of scale—what Smith properly calls *geographic* scale—sounds more complex and elusive. Though geographic scales are arbitrary, says Smith, they *emerge* (for the geographer) as objectifiable elements in the course of *following* the material process that shapes a landscape. It is this very notion, implied here, of a scale-sensitive procedure—a procedure that "conceptualizes" by "following"—which, I think, carries significant consequences for the idea, method, and perhaps the ethics of comparison.

Smith takes "space" to be the kind of seemingly simple, abstract category (not unlike "labor") whose conceptualization, articulation, and manifestation in social life must be examined and understood within a history of intercourse between humans and the physical universe of which they are part. "In the advanced capitalist world today, we all conceive of space as emptiness, as a universal receptacle in which objects exist and events occur, as a frame of reference, a co-ordinate system (along with time) within which all reality exists." This, Smith explains, is a particular conception of space that resulted from a distinction made by Newton between *absolute space* and *relative space*: "Absolute space in its own nature, without relation to anything external, remains always similar and unmovable. Relative space is some movable dimension or measure of the absolute spaces; which our senses determine by its position to bodies."[10] Thus, we may speak metaphorically of spaces that "connect," "house," or "anchor"—but only as a way of gauging the navigability of a situation: "Absolute location is simply a special case of relative location, one in which we abstract from *the social determinants* of distance (83, my italics)." Smith gives the medieval city as an example: "In Euclidean terms, the distance from the ground floor to the fourth floor of a city tenement may be equivalent to the height of a tree in the primal forest beyond the city walls. But the same distance between floors of the tenement can also be measured in terms of social rank and class whereas the height of the tree cannot" (78). Though we could of course imagine a situation in which the height of the tree itself would matter as the center of a social dispute or transaction.

As comparatists, therefore, we must approach spaces wherever we find them, as the articulation of distance within a particularly spatialized system of social relations. In a landscape like Africa-of-the-Novel, we must reconstruct the process by which the space of the postcolonial novel becomes differentiated, gaining the contours of a place and the fixity of a cultural location. Only by "following" the dynamics of a landscape will we be able to unearth "the social determinants of distance."[11] If we can indeed imagine a literary history that is entangled in the history of the production of space, it is time for comparative literature to develop both a critique of scale, which would examine the spatial premises of comparison—and eventually, a phenomenology of scale, which would help us grasp the actually existing landscapes of literature. Let us begin with the first problem, by turning once again to the postcolonial novel, and the "conceptual abstractions lain over it."

A Sensitive Genre

The postcolonial novel, it would seem, lacks the serenity that comes with provincialism. It is a place-sensitive genre that supposedly intuits its geographic displacement as the condition of its impossibility. "An anxious creativity," Appiah says; nor are most critics of the postcolonial novel as generous. "Compromise," not "creativity," is the central trope in criticism of the postcolonial (or "peripheral") novel, according to Franco Moretti.[12] This idea of compromise appears so prevalent in the secondary literature, Moretti goes further, that one would think it "a law" of literary evolution: "Four continents, two hundred years, over twenty independent critical studies, and they all agreed: when a culture starts moving towards the modern novel, it's always as a compromise between foreign form and local materials."[13] And nowhere is the compromise more evident, say his sources, than in the narrator's anxiety. "Which makes sense," for Moretti, since "the narrator is the pole of comment, of explanation, of evaluation . . . when foreign 'formal patterns' . . . make characters behave in strange ways . . . then of course comment becomes uneasy—garrulous, erratic, rudderless." If indeed a law could be extracted, for him it would look like this: "Foreign form, local material—*and local form*. Simplifying somewhat: Foreign *plot*; local *characters*; and then, local *narrative voice*: and it's precisely in this third dimension that these novels seem to be most unstable—most uneasy." Moretti takes "compromise" to mean something like "refunctionalization," the concept conceived by Shklovsky to describe formal adaptation to historical change. However, when he applies it to describe a process of adaptation to geographic change (when refunctionalization becomes a process of domestication), an interesting tautology arises. "Local form" is initially proclaimed the synthesis of "foreign form and local materials." But when "form" is simplified quickly into "narrative voice," it emerges as a symptom of incomplete refunctionalization (of impossible domestication). For Moretti and his informants, as with Appiah, the postcolonial compromise with the novel's foreignness forecloses the condition in the symptom; the landscape in the detail; the "law" (60) in the "unit of analysis" (61).

But no matter how intriguing this idea of the postcolonial novel's impossibility, or how poignant this malaise of compromise, it takes an "anxious" genre to illustrate methodologically the possibility of the project "world literature." And to even have a debate, it helps (as I hope to emphasize) that the novel's comparative potential is a matter of disciplinary consensus. Moretti defends his "law" as a scientific abstraction of a ubiquitous critical repetition, but more importantly he authorizes it explicitly as an empathetic reformulation of the testimonies compiled. Even the fiercest critiques of Moretti's law do not question the substance of the secondary literature, nor do they contest his description of the object itself (the postcolonial novel). I take the thesis of "formal compromise," which has remained remarkably invisible in the otherwise intense debate triggered by Moretti's essay, to point to a theoretical status quo.

Objections to the law itself have been generally procedural, targeting either Moretti's disengagement from textual hermeneutics, or the law's limited cartographic potential. On the one hand, we have the critics of "distant reading" who are most concerned with the displacement of hermeneutic authority, and perhaps the implication that they may be mere specialists to whom close-reading would be conveniently outsourced. For this reason, they raise the problem of second-hand information as one of reliability (not objectivity for instance). Their quarrel with Moretti is: "How do you know they're right without *seeing* for yourself?" as opposed to "What can one make of this *kind* of repetition?" Then there's the second group, who wants to beat Moretti at his own game, claiming that his seemingly ambitious

model actually circumscribes the full cartographic potential of the comparative enterprise. Appropriately enough, this group offers recommendations
on how to hone and refine the proposed model, while implicitly agreeing
that the schematization of literary space is the greatest and most significant
challenge of a world literature.[14] Important questions are raised about how
to balance the representation of centripetal and centrifugal tendencies, or
differentiate the portability of certain genres over others. But there is little
self-reflexivity about the cartographic impulse, and the logic that accepts
"portability" as a category of comparison. Overall, the principle of world
literature as a cartographic program that would adjudicate the scope of foreign interference resonates both with structuralist theories of influence (literary interference, dependence, debt, etc.)[15] and also with poststructuralist
theories of reappropriation (literary resistance, subversion, cannibalization,
etc.).[16] Even Moretti's swift concession to his critics is a victory of sorts, for
instituting that question which must remain the center of comparative controversy: "Yes, 'measuring' the extent of foreign pressure on a text, or its
structural instability, or a narrator's uneasiness, will be complicated, at times
even unfeasible. But a diagram of symbolic power is an ambitious goal, and
it makes sense that it would be hard to achieve."[17] (Here, we must mention a
third ascetic group who reject this imperative of diagramming on principle,
choosing to abstain altogether from comparative schematizations lest they
should fall into the temptations of universalism. But even there, the category
"mobility" resurfaces as a theoretical axis in the metaphors of translatability
and translation.)[18]

The problem, to my mind, lies not in the nature of "measuring." Nor, as
Pascale Casanova has famously suggested, in the impossibility of measuring distances established "in the mind": "The structure [of literary relations
is] so hard to visualize [because] it's impossible to place it at a distance, as a
discrete and objectifiable phenomenon."[19] But rather, in the fact that as literary critics, we often begin with strong ideas about what needs to be measured—for me, this is the most compelling justification offered by Moretti
for pursuing a new comparative science: that "we are used to asking only
those questions for which we already have an answer."[20] But are we posing
a new question when we set out to investigate the *extent* of "foreign pressure
on a text"; "its structural instability"? It's not that such measuring endeavors
are "unfeasible"; what is worse, they appear superfluous, because the mystery is already solved: "a narrator's uneasiness." Between Moretti's tragic
conception of formal compromise (the postcolonial novel's yearning for in-

dependence) and Casanova's more conciliatory version (of literature as the willful realization of a compromise: "The majority of compromise solutions achieved within this structure are based on an 'art of distance'"),[21] we have transformed the comparative concern with xenocentrism into something like Xeno's paradox, where the riddle of distance produces either the *need* or the *will* to shape compromises with literary laws of motion.

This kind of paradox of course increases the novel's fortune in "comparative" controversy.[22] Let me explain by turning back briefly to *Man with a Bicycle*. I began with Appiah's insight that the novel's anxiety derives, at least in part, from a mode of contextualization, which "grounds" an African hero by circumscribing his mobility. As to what makes the African novel itself conducive to this kind of reading, says Appiah, the problem lies with the author. Or more precisely, the African novelist's obligation to what he calls the "space clearing gesture": an explicit departure from intellectual predecessors without which an author in the modern Western sense cannot make a claim to distinction.[23] Because literary producers must assert an authorial status, says Appiah, the African novelist vacillates discontentedly between the national and Western traditions, hoping to claim a sensible parameter of influence. Baldwin, on the other hand, offers a clue that suggests that the novelist's problem lies elsewhere: "He's grounded in immediate reality by the bicycle . . ." and then, "He's apparently a very proud and silent man" (339). Not only must the hero of our hypothetical novel, *Man with a Bicycle*, worry about his clothes and his bicycle. Unlike his wooden counterpart, he is not afforded the stoic stance of a sculpture. The novel seems to demand that the African hero speak, and it's the force of this imperative that unleashes (in the mind of the novel's critics) the question of what, if anything, distinguishes the utterance of a postcolonial hero—what makes the postcolonial novel amenable to comparison—or better, what opens it to geographic explanation. Moretti correctly identifies voice as a possible point of political convergence between the comparatist's moral and empirical ambition, on the one hand, and his informants' anxieties, on the other. But is the convergence real? What is the sociology of this term "compromise" so often repeated in the second-hand testimonies, and what is its theoretical hold on the comparative imagination?

New Anxieties

The thesis of cultural "compromise" is much more than a law of literary history; it is the most powerful and lasting cultural program to originate from the development era, and was devised by emergent postcolonial intelligentsia to resolve the contradictions of "transition" in what was then candidly called the Third World. Partha Chatterjee has provocatively described this agenda as "alternative modernity" to insist on the cognitive and political work expended by Asian and African societies to formulate an independent path of progress from colonial patronage to indigenous state-formation.[24] But, in a remarkable development, the synchronic connotation of an "alternative modernity" appealed to analysts of contemporary cultural forms who sought a way of describing an increasingly integrated cultural world without recourse to teleological narratives of modernization. Adopted as an analytical framework, "alternative modernity" has proved immensely fertile, producing a rich descriptive literature that demonstrates the versatility and creativity of local forms despite compromises with larger forces of homogenization. But the anachronism that belies this critical gesture is unmistakable. Is it really possible to borrow the cultural slogan of an era of economic optimism to describe the uneven world that emerged in its painful aftermath? This spirited body of work must neglect, as Jim Ferguson has observed, that the early postcolonial investment in cultural alterity lost currency when the prospect of economic progress became dim. That in fact, when economic convergence was no longer believed a historical inevitability, cultural alterity appeared more like the symptom (or even the cause) of permanent economic troubles. The language of alternative modernity thus disguises a real dissonance between an academic thesis that celebrates the periphery's specificity, and a local outlook that experiences "specificity" as a mark of inferiority. Speaking of his colleagues, Ferguson says: "Anthropologists today, working to combat old stereotypes, are eager to say how modern Africa is. Many ordinary Africans might scratch their heads at such a claim."[25]

What is "accomplished," he asks, by saying that Africa is "differently" or "alternatively" modern? We could indeed ask this question of Moretti whose eagerness to proclaim the postcolonial novel the rule, not the exception, recalls Ferguson's description of anthropologists. We must consider the possibility that alternative modernity is currently a powerful horizon of world-scale literary analysis, and that Moretti's conjecture on "formal compromise" is neither a coincidence nor an isolated move. The thesis of "formal compromise," says Moretti,

> completely reverse[s] the received historical explanation of [influence]: because if the compromise between the foreign and the local is so ubiquitous, then those independent paths that are usually taken to be the rule of the rise of the novel (the Spanish, the French, and especially the British case)—*well, they're not the rule at all, they're the exception*. They come first, yes, but they're not at all typical. The "typical" rise of the novel is Krasicki, Kemal, Rizal, Maran—not Defoe.[26]

Moretti's goal of provincializing the European novel appears worthwhile, even to his harshest critics. First of all, he avoids placing novelistic traditions in a chain of "influence" that defines literary modernity as literary westernization. Second, he reveals that the "path" to literary modernity is *normally* alternative; and by extension, that the European novel is in fact a deviation from the norm. None of this could have been done without fulfilling comparative literature's unflinching commitment to scale, "You become a comparatist for a very simple reason: *because you are convinced that your viewpoint is better*. It has greater explanatory power; it's conceptually more elegant; it avoids that ugly 'one-sidedness and narrow-mindedness.'" (68). In short, by looking at the production of the novel "on a world scale" (66),[27] you are able to reframe (if not redirect) the traffic of influence. But what if Ferguson is right? If, as he suggests, the ethos of development is the historical condition that allowed the two terms "alternative" and "modernity" to be sensibly conjoined, what seems most troubling about the anachronistic redeployment of "alternative modernity" is that it *should* bear some *trace* of the actual decomposition that befell the paradigm of development, and that broke the once reassuring tie between cultural ascendance and economic progress. An immediate question for a program of "world literature" becomes: *How* indeed does the theoretical framework of alternative modernity manage to do its work without bearing such a trace? When Moretti moves from "description" to "explanation" without raising questions about the very sociology of "compromise," what exactly did he borrow from a bygone narrative of postcolonial transition that proved surgically extractible?

Here, we must go back to Chatterjee who, in his account of alternative modernity as paradigm of postcolonial transition, described more than an agenda that called for adapting foreign forms to local reality. Chatterjee's description is most vivid and convincing when he reconstructs a complex mode of cognitive mapping that split social life into an external economic domain, and an internal spiritual domain. This zoning of the national consciousness offered a society, for better or worse, a way "to choose its site of autonomy" amidst a project of cultural normalization.[28] And after staking out the spiritual domain as a zone of autonomy, culture was again conceived as a *place* where foreign and native elements are allowed to mix by way of careful but creative compromises and negotiations.[29] This intricate mapping of the social terrain allowed the intelligentsia to evoke two contradictory views of culture: looking outward from the spiritual domain, culture looked like a defensive space that needed to be protected and differentiated from the sphere of commerce; whereas looking inward, culture looked like a space of experimentation and innovation.[30]

In recent deployments of alternative modernity, the cartographic impulse is emulated but economics and culture are taken as antagonistic *agents*, not mutually differentiated *spaces*. Ferguson finds that in anthropology "the application of a language of alternative modernities to the most impoverished regions of the globe has become a way of *not* talking about the noneserialized, detemporalized political economic statuses of our time—indeed a way of turning away from a radically worsening global inequality and its consequences" (23). In the case of comparative literature, I believe the picture looks different. It's not that the "detemporalized economic statuses of our time" are ignored. Instead they are routinely evoked as the "real" material condition to which postcolonial societies respond with defensive acts of cultural creativity. We no longer have the tension produced by the forced separation of economics and culture within a national sphere, instead economic pressure is experienced as an external force of "foreign interference."[31] As we saw with *Man with a Bicycle*, political statuses have so hardened as an *African* "reality" that they've become the "objective" limit of a work's interpretation. And the more these statuses' detemporalization is asserted, the more literary production at the periphery is imagined, in this context, as a mode of creativity under duress. In a place like Africa-of-the-Novel, where problems are chronic and solutions short-term, there is no time for literary projects, only literary acts of survival: generic reappropriation, reversal, refunctionalization, subversion, the list goes on. This helps us better understand Pascale Casanova's *World Republic of Letters* as a particular kind of *place*:

> To speak of the center's literary forms and genres simply as a colonial inheritance imposed on writers within subordinated regions is to over-

look the fact that literature itself, as a common value of the entire space, is also an instrument which, if re-appropriated, can enable writers—and especially those with the fewest resources—to attain a type of freedom, recognition and existence within it.

More concretely and directly, these reflections on the immense range of what is possible in literature, even within this overwhelming and inescapable structure of domination, also aim to serve as a symbolic weapon in the struggles of those most deprived of literary resources, confronting obstacles which writers and critics at the centre cannot even imagine.[32]

"An inescapable structure of domination," continues Casanova, that "enables [the most unprivileged] writers . . . to attain a type of freedom." An ingenuous logic, which leaves us with a literary universe whose internal differentiation into zones may be theoretically attributed (according to Casanova) to the uneven distribution of literary capital—but which is differentiated *from a methodological point of view* by a fundamentally unequal capacity among zones for *sustainable* modes of literary production: large-scale projects like forms, genres, or literature itself expand out of Central Europe, while small-scale endeavors like techniques, styles, or texts transpire locally.[33] In such a universe, where "writers within subordinated regions" are oppressed-and-freed by the task of "writing back," a misplaced genre like the postcolonial novel is the quintessential object of comparison. In theory, the postcolonial novel points us in two directions: either to celebrate the reappropriation of a Western genre on the periphery, or lament the perpetual struggle borne of cultural colonialism. The framework of alternative modernity allows us to indulge both sentiments in a single interpretive procedure: first, we *describe* the periphery as a region of economic struggle; then we *explain* individual novels as local acts of resistance or appropriation.

The brilliance of this formulation is that it reconciles two contradictory horizons of comparison: on the one hand, economic accounts of a single world made of unequal and connected regions; and on the other, cultural accounts of multiple universes that are intelligible in their own right. While the first precludes in principle the notion of comparison (as Wallerstein would put it, "You do not *compare* 'parts of a whole'"),[34] it often defines "unequal" peripheral regions comparatively in terms of their relative location to the center. And the second, while it considers location *de facto* a guarantor of specificity (an incomparability inviting comparison), it ignores the dependence implied by this state of separateness: "If separate, then *from* what?" But there's no need to dwell too much on such contradictions. These two approaches have co-existed peacefully by a tacit division of labor: ecumenical models fulfill the function of describing a lamentably homogenous economic world, while localized models illuminate, through case-by-case analytical care, a multifarious cultural universe. One could say that the economistic view has served the congenial role of springboard for culturalist arguments. After all, "alternative," "critical," and "other" cultural modernities need to be championed against the existing menace of a "singular" economic modernity.[35] In the shadow of a consolidating neoliberal order, the comparative imagination shouldered the responsibility of illuminating local spaces of hope. Thinking back to the cognitive map drawn by Chatterjee, we could say that the comparatist has not only mastered the cartographic impulse, but also assumed the position of a transcendental witness who can look both inward *and* outward from culture. In this way, comparison can become a spatialized escape route from the teleological claims of a singular modernity. The comparative method can double-up, as it were, as antidote and supplement to periodization. But as a condition, "scale" would have to remain a flat, untheoretical concept—the geographic foil of a cartographic enterprise heralding spaces of its own creation.

Indeed, for a human geographer and theorist of scale like Neil Smith, the conceptual framework of alternative modernity is a particular instance of what he describes as "the metaphorical uses of space that have become so fashionable in literary and cultural discourse."[36] In terms that recall Ferguson's remarks about anthropologists of contemporary Africa, Smith describes a subtle form of ideological complicity that belies the liberal dispensation of spatial metaphors, even (and increasingly, it seems) in the most ethically disposed cultural criticism.

> Much social and cultural theory in the last two decades has depended heavily on spatial metaphors. The myriad "decenterings" of modernism and of reputedly modern agents (e.g., the working class), the "displacement" of political economy by cultural discourse, and a host of other "moves" have been facilitated by a very fertile lexicon of spatial metaphors: subject positionality, locality, mapping, grounding, travel, (de/re) centering, theoretical space, ideological space, symbolic space, conceptual space, spaces of signification, territorialization, and so forth. If such metaphors functioned initially in a very positive way to challenge, aerate, and even discard a lot of stodgy thinking, they may now have taken on

> much more independent existence that discourages as much as it allows
> fresh political insight. . . . Metaphor works in many different ways but it
> always involves an assertion of otherness. . . . Difference is expressed in
> similarity. Some truth or insight is revealed by asserting that an incom-
> pletely understood object, event, or situation is another, where the other
> is assumed known. . . . To the extent that metaphor continually appeals
> to some other assumed reality as known, *it* systematically disguises the
> need to investigate the known [at hand]. . . . (63–64)

Smith's insistence that we "investigate the known" at hand, implies an
important shift in the ethical horizon of comparison. A metaphorical space
like postcolonial culture, when conceived as an operative counter-force to
the world-economy, indeed "disguises the need to investigate" the particular spatial relations which shape the landscapes of the postcolonial novel.
It makes it impossible to recognize Africa-of-the-Novel as a differentiated
place that embodies, in part, the ethical anxieties of the culturally "permitting" Western critic, national commentators, and the producers of novels.
A literary critique of scale would regard Africa-of-the-Novel as a dialectically "motivated" *landscape* (to use a key term of formal analysis) where the
so-called laws of motion, progress, and probability unfold according to a
logic of spatial differentiation—or better, as would say an anthropologist,
in a process of scale-making. What better program for a geographically enlarged literary history than to conceptualize the dialectic of lived time and
lived space in and around literature—in order to understand the entanglement of literature in the history of the production of space. There can, of
course, be no productive conceptualization of literary scale that can be limited to a single genre.[37] And yet, the novel seems to offer a ready oppor-
tunity to begin tackling directly the stakes of "literary globalization" as a
historical, theoretical, and ethical conundrum: by returning us to one of
the most time-honored problems of comparative literary history—the problem of historical contextualization—this time, for the purpose of considering the geographic thinking that grounds comparative claims to context-
dependency.

Instead, in the world-literature debate we witness distanciation, a notion
that may well qualify as the common sense of the discipline, undergo yet
another radical revival. And the repetition suggests that the comparative
imagination is hitting a chronotopic limit. Again we are told what every
comparatist already knows: that by enlarging the frame of inquiry beyond

the nation-scale, by stepping back, as it were, to revision the literary terrain from afar, one becomes privy to broader connections: clusters, homologies, specificities, exchange, trails of influence. This is a cultural geography that will continue to harden, as I have suggested, to make crossings possible. But also, in the midst of familiar provocations, globalization is presented as an impetus to rethink the "evidence" of literary phenomena, and the relationship of the literary object to its milieu. And this is where, to my mind, the simple logic of distance begins to disintegrate.[38] We are at a juncture where we must pursue directly a literary phenomenology of the production of scale, which can begin to elucidate the diverse forms of entanglement between literary history and the history of the production of space—and the function of literary criticism as an intermediary poetics. By doing so, we leave behind what Neil Smith describes as "the metaphorical uses of space." Unlike schoolchildren for whom scale is the relation between distance on a map and distance in reality, literary comparatists conceptualize scale as the social condition of a landscape's utility.

Notes

1. Apter, *The Translation Zone*. Apter's critique of comparative literature begins by examining the cultural and racial biases of the discipline's founders, most notably Erich Auerbach and Leo Spitzer.

2. Moretti, "Conjectures on World Literature." Moretti's short essay, and the wide response it has solicited from "comparatists" and "specialists" alike is significant, primarily because it allows us to gauge a critical status quo. Responses include, but are not restricted to: Prendergast, "Negotiating World Literature," Orsini, "Maps of Indian Writing," Kristal, "'Considering Coldly,'" Arac, "Anglo-Globalism?," Apter, "Global *Translatio*," Parla, "The Object of Comparison," Ferguson, "Comparing the Literatures: Textualism and Globalism," Dimock, "Genre and World System: Epic and Novel on Four Continents," Spivak, "World Systems and the Creole," and her discussion of Moretti's distant reading in *Death of A Discipline*, 108. The list goes on.

3. Casanova, "Literature as a World." Casanova's application of Pierre Bourdieu's sociological construct of the "field," to describe a tightly knit international sphere of literary production that emerges in the seventeenth century and which gradually guarantees for literature relative autonomy from politics, has received general approval in U.S. and British academic circles, upon publication of an English translation *The World Republic of Letters* (2005) of her French book *La republique mondiale des lettres* (Paris: Le Seuil, 1999). Terry Eagleton calls the book "a milestone in the history of modern thought" in *Newstatesman* (11 April 2005) and in "Union Sucrée"

29. "Language . . . became a *zone* over which the nation first had to declare its sovereignty and then had to transform in order to make it adequate for the modern world" (my italics) (Chatterjee, *Nation*, 7).

30. These two views of culture proved contradictory, shows Chatterjee, when "modern women" became anxiously perceived as the barometers of compromise. *Nation*, 135–57.

31. Gibson-Graham has offered a critique of a political economy which increasingly endows "the economy" with the quality of an abstract and unchanging "Real," in *The End of Capitalism (As We Knew It): A Feminist Critique of Political Economy*.

32. Casanova, "Literature," 90. See note 3.

33. In this logic, it matters little that some products are more far-reaching than others, because all modes of production are aesthetically equal.

34. This has long been Wallerstein's position, and is expressed explicitly in relation to the comparative method in "Call for a Debate about the Paradigm" in *Unthinking Social Science*.

35. Anna Tsing explores the relationship between modernization and globalization as historiographical tools in her influential essay, "The Global Situation," where she proposes "scale-making" projects as an object of ethnography.

36. Smith, "Contours," 62.

37. It has been argued, with validity, that the novel's centrality in discussions of world literature and literary globalization must itself be scrutinized and explained. See note 4.

38. The term "scale" has recently attracted some specialists of American literature, such as Wai Chee Dimock and Laurence Buell who argue that what appears to be a national American literature can in fact be shown to be transnational; this is finally done by asserting the multiculturalism of a presumably homogenous American canon, *Shades of the Planet: American Literature as World Literature*. Hsuan Hsu ("Literature and Regional Production") also introduces the language of scale to the debate among Americanists about regionalism, most recently reactivated by Sara Blair's article, "Cultural Geography and the Place of the Literary." Hsu associates scale with the ability of literary texts to negotiate the experience of belonging to geographic spheres of experience that vary in scope, and consequently chooses to examine instances where conventional geographic scales (such as the world, the nation, the home) are named and questioned, or when the word "scale" emerges in the discourse of American writers. Also see Brigham's "Productions of Geographic Scale and Capitalist-Colonialist Enterprise in Leslie Marmon Silko's *Almanac of the Dead*," which draws widely from Neil Smith's work.

PART THREE

Respatializing, Remapping,

Recognizing

The Space of the World

Beyond State-Centrism?

NEIL BRENNER

According to Immanuel Wallerstein, significant strands of twentieth-century social science have been locked into an indefensibly state-centric epistemological framework in which national states are viewed as self-enclosed territorial containers of social, economic, political, and cultural relations.[1] Through his rejection of internalist, society-centered modes of explanation, his sustained emphasis on the world scale of capitalist development, and his subsequent development of world-systems analysis, Wallerstein had already launched a powerful "protest" against these and many other inherited social-scientific assumptions as of the early 1970s.[2] However, it was not until at least a decade later, with the intensification of scholarly interest in the various restructuring processes associated with globalization, that the limits of state-centric ontologies and nationally focused modes of analysis came to be appreciated more widely. Since this time, a wide range of globalization researchers have followed Wallerstein's pioneering example by attempting to construct methodologies that are attuned to the worldwide scale of political-economic relations and, on this basis, challenge the "iron grip of the nation-state on the social imagination."[3] This increasingly interdisciplinary and even postdisciplinary effort to transcend state-centric epistemologies arguably represents one of the unifying theoretical agendas underlying contemporary research on globalization.

However, as the editors of this volume indicate, the kind of scale shift advocated by Wallerstein presents a variety of methodological dilemmas, not only for those who embrace his own version of world-systems analysis, but for any researcher who is concerned to examine world-scale processes, whether from a political-economic, cultural studies, or literary point of view. This chapter confronts one such challenge—the need to develop an alternative mapping of world capitalism that avoids the state-centric geographical assumptions Wallerstein and others have been concerned to criticize. I view this challenge as essential to any confrontation with what the editors of this volume have aptly termed "the problem of the world." As Henri Lefebvre recognized in the 1970s, around roughly the same time that Wallerstein was launching his own research program, the notion of the world contains many layers of philosophical meaning—but it necessarily requires reflection on the historically changing, always contested *spatialities* of social relations.[4] Accordingly, this chapter asks: to what degree does the work of Wallerstein and other globalization researchers succeed in transcending the geographical assumptions associated with state-centric approaches? To what degree do these researchers offer a viable mapping of "the space of the world" under contemporary capitalism?[5]

These goals are, in practice, considerably more difficult to accomplish than is usually recognized, for they entail much more than an acknowledgment that transnational or global processes are gaining significance or than an emphasis on the worldwide scale. As I suggest below, the overcoming of state-centrism requires a comprehensive re-conceptualization of entrenched understandings of space as a fixed, pre-given container or platform for social relations. Despite the persistent efforts of spatially attuned scholars in recent decades to unsettle such assumptions, the conception of space as a realm of stasis, fixity, and stability—which contains but is not substantively modified by social action—is still surprisingly pervasive. Even within contemporary globalization studies, in which debates on the problematic of social spatiality have been proliferating with particular intensity, many analyses are still grounded on relatively static, atemporal geographical assumptions and/or various forms of methodological territorialism. Indeed, I argue below that Wallerstein's own approach to world-systems analysis can be subjected to this line of critique: he successfully expands his unit of analysis to the world scale, but he paradoxically continues to conceive the space of the world in methodologically territorialist terms, as a globally stretched but morphologically static territorial matrix. Such considerations suggest that one of the central intellectual barriers to a more adequate understanding of contemporary global transformations is that we currently lack appropriately *historical* and *dynamic* conceptualizations of social space that are attuned to the possibility of systemic transformations within established political-economic and sociocultural geographies.

But the challenges of transcending state-centric modes of analysis do not end here. Even when static, territorialist models of social spatiality are effectively overcome, the question of how more adequately to conceptualize the space of the world—and, specifically, of globalization processes—remains thoroughly contentious. Those globalization researchers who have successfully transcended such state-centric, methodologically territorialist geographical assumptions have frequently done so by asserting that national state territoriality and even geography itself are currently shrinking, contracting or dissolving due to alleged processes of "deterritorialization."[6] A break with state-centrism is thus secured through the conceptual negation of the national state and, more generally, of the territorial dimensions of social life. However, this methodological strategy sidesteps the crucially important task of analyzing the ongoing reterritorialization and re-scaling of political-economic relations under contemporary globalizing capitalism. Consequently, within most standard accounts of deterritorialization, the goal of overcoming state-centrism is accomplished on the basis of a seriously one-sided depiction of currently emergent sociospatial forms, and a resultant inability to grasp the emerging spatialities of what Lefebvre termed *mondialité*, a concept that can be loosely translated into English as "world-ness."[7]

In contrast to these positions, the present chapter advances the contention that world capitalism is currently experiencing (*a*) the transcendence of the nationalized sociospatial arrangements that prevailed throughout much of the twentieth-century; and, concomitantly, (*b*) the production of new, rescaled sociospatial configurations that cannot be effectively described on the basis of purely territorialist, nationally scaled models. An essential, if apparently paradoxical, corollary of this thesis is the claim that state-centric mappings of social spatiality limit our understanding of the national state's own major role as a site, medium, and agent of contemporary global restructuring. Therefore, the effort to transcend state-centric modes of analysis does not entail a denial of the national state's continued relevance as a major locus of political-economic regulation. What such a project requires, rather, is a re-conceptualization of how the geographies of state space *and* worldwide space are being transformed under contemporary geo-economic conditions.[8]

In the next section, I summarize the conceptualization of sociospatial restructuring under capitalism that grounds my analysis of the globalization debates. On this basis, I develop an interpretation of the epistemology of state-centrism, and I indicate various ways in which the contemporary round of global restructuring has undermined state-centric modes of analysis. Then, through a critical analysis of two major strands of globalization research—labeled, respectively, "global territorialist" approaches and "de-territorialization" approaches—I criticize the methodologically territorialist foundations of Wallerstein's world-systems analysis as well as the equally problematic methodological consequences of recent attempts to dissolve or transcend the category of territory, perhaps most influentially elaborated in Hardt and Negri's account of "Empire." Through these critical engagements, the chapter sketches an alternative interpretation of contemporary global restructuring as a contradictory process of reterritorialization and re-scaling. A concluding section outlines various key methodological challenges for studies of global restructuring.

Capitalist Development and the Creative Destruction of Sociospatial Configurations

At core, the notion of globalization is a descriptive category denoting the spatial extension of social interdependencies on a worldwide scale.[9] To the extent that worldwide social interdependencies are being enhanced, this development must be interpreted as the aggregate consequence of a variety of interrelated (economic, political, and cultural) tendencies rather than being viewed as the expression of a single, internally coherent causal mechanism.[10] From this perspective, an adequate analysis of globalization must differentiate the multifaceted causal *processes* that have underpinned this worldwide extension of social relations, while simultaneously attempting to trace the variegated, uneven *effects* of such processes in different political-economic contexts. In other words, "Globalisation as an outcome cannot be explained simply by invoking globalisation as a process tending towards that outcome."[11] Considerable methodological reflexivity is therefore required in order to circumvent some of the many "chaotic" presuppositions and explanations that underpin mainstream accounts of contemporary globalization.[12]

Before examining more closely the geographical contours of the contemporary globalization debate, it is necessary first to explicate some of the key theoretical assumptions upon which my own understanding of sociospatiality and sociospatial restructuring is grounded. The starting point for this analysis is a processual conceptualization of sociospatial forms under modern capitalism.[13] In this view, space is not opposed to time and historicity, but must be viewed as a co-constitutive, dialectically inseparable moment of the latter. Thus, while concepts such as space, territory, geography, place, and scale are generally used to connote fixed objects, pre-given platforms or static things, I deploy them here as shorthand labels for more precise, if also more stylistically cumbersome, terminological formulations—such as spatialization processes, territorialization processes, geography-making, place-making, and scaling. In other words, all aspects of social space under modern capitalism must be understood as presuppositions, arenas, and outcomes of dynamic processes of continual social contestation and transformation. Such a conceptualization entails the replacement of traditional Cartesian notions of "space-as-thing" or "space-as-platform" with a dialectical, social-constructionist notion of "space-as-process."

For the sake of stylistic convenience, I shall continue to use standard terms such as space, territory, place, and scale—but it must be emphasized that these labels connote ongoing *processes* of spatialization, territorialization, place-making, and scaling rather than fixed, pre-given, or static entities. A foundational question for any study of the production of space under capitalism is how such processes of spatialization, territorialization, place-making, scaling, and so forth mold and continually reshape the geographical landscape.[14] In the present context, I build upon Harvey's conceptualization of the production of spatial configuration under capitalism as a basis for examining the distinctively geographical parameters of contemporary forms of global restructuring.

According to Harvey, capitalism is under the impulsion to eliminate all geographical barriers to the accumulation process by seeking out cheaper raw materials, fresh sources of labor-power, new markets for its products, and new investment opportunities.[15] This deterritorializing, expansionary tendency within capitalism was clearly recognized by Marx, who famously described capital's globalizing dynamic as a drive to "annihilate space by time" and analyzed the world market as its historical product and its geographical expression.[16] Thus, for Harvey, as for Marx, capital is oriented simultaneously toward temporal acceleration (the continual acceleration of turnover times) and spatial expansion (the overcoming of geographical barriers to the process of accumulation). Insofar as they eliminate historically specific territorial barriers to accumulation, these tendencies may be said to embody capital's moment of *deterritorialization*.

At the same time, Harvey insists that the impulsion to reduce the socially necessary turnover time of capital and to expand its spatial orbit necessarily hinges upon the production of relatively fixed and immobile sociospatial configurations. Indeed, according to Harvey, it is only through the production of historically specific socio-geographical infrastructures — composed, for instance, of urban built environments, industrial agglomerations, regional production complexes, systems of collective consumption, large-scale transportation networks, long-distance communications grids, and state regulatory institutions — that processes of time-space compression can unfold. In this sense, each moment of deterritorialization hinges upon an equally essential moment of *reterritorialization* in which relatively fixed and immobile spatial arrangements are established or modified as a basis for extending and accelerating capital's orbit. From this perspective, the historical evolution of capitalism has entailed the increasing replacement of inherited, pre-capitalist landscapes with specifically capitalist sociospatial configurations. Each framework of capitalist sociospatial organization is closely intertwined with historically specific patterns of uneven development insofar as it entails the systemic privileging of some locations, places, territories, and scales, and the marginalization or exclusion of others.

Harvey refers to these historically specific sociospatial configurations as capital's "spatial fix" — a "tendency towards . . . a structured coherence to production and consumption within a given space."[17] By providing a relatively fixed and immobile basis upon which capital's circulation process can be organized, each spatial fix entails "the conversion of temporal into spatial restraints to accumulation."[18] However, Harvey also insists that no spatial fix can ever permanently resolve the endemic crisis-tendencies that pervade capitalism; consequently, each sociospatial configuration is merely temporary. On this basis, Harvey interprets the historical geography of capitalism as a process of continual restructuring in which sociospatial configurations are incessantly created, destroyed, and reconstituted anew.[19] For Harvey, then, the endemic tension "between the rising power to overcome space and the immobile spatial structures required for such a purpose" provides the analytical key to the investigation of processes of sociospatial restructuring under capitalism.[20] Capitalist sociospatial configurations are produced as historically specific geographical preconditions for capital's globalizing dynamism, only to be eventually torn down and recreated during successive waves of systemic crisis-induced restructuring. Through this tumultuous process of creative destruction, inherited geographical landscapes are reshaped, as major factions of capital strive to amortize the full value of existing spatial configurations, to "wash away the dead weight of past investments" and thus to wrest open new possibilities for accumulation.[21]

Harvey's conceptualization has significant implications for interpreting the diverse restructuring processes that are today generally subsumed under the rubric of "globalization." As indicated, globalization is a multifaceted concept that refers, at core, to the extension of spatial interdependencies on a worldwide scale.[22] While it would clearly be problematic to reduce this tendency to any single causal mechanism, Harvey's conceptualization of capitalist sociospatial configurations provides a useful analytical basis on which to interpret some of its core spatio-temporal dynamics. From this perspective, the contemporary round of global restructuring can be interpreted as the most recent historical expression of the *longue durée* dynamic of creative destruction that has underpinned the production of capitalist spatiality throughout the modern era.[23] As in previous rounds of crisis-induced sociospatial restructuring, contemporary global shifts have entailed a multifaceted, dialectical process through which: (*a*) the movement of commodities, capital, and people through geographical space has been expanded and accelerated; (*b*) relatively fixed and immobile socio-territorial infrastructures have been produced in order to enable such movement; and (*c*) inherited patterns of uneven spatial development have been systematically reworked. Therefore, much like earlier periods of creative destruction under capitalism, the contemporary round of global restructuring has been grounded upon a multiscalar, dialectical interplay between deterritorializing and reterritorializing tendencies.

This conceptualization of contemporary global restructuring will be developed in more detail below, through a critical analysis of major strands of the globalization literature. At this juncture, it is essential to emphasize that national states must be viewed as essential geographical arenas and agents of contemporary forms of global restructuring rather than as the passive or helpless victims of these processes.[24] While numerous authors have usefully underscored the activist role of national states in facilitating the contemporary round of geo-economic integration,[25] I am concerned here to underscore the *territorializing* operations of state institutions in relation to capital at both national and subnational spatial scales. For, much like urban-regional agglomerations, national states have long operated as relatively fixed and immobile forms of (re)territorialization for successive rounds of time-space compression, particularly since the second industrial revolution of the late nineteenth-century.[26] With the consolidation of national-developmentalist political regimes during that period, national states became ever more central to the promotion, regulation, and financing of capitalist expansion—

above all through their role in the construction of large-scale geographical infrastructures for industrial production, collective consumption and long-distance market exchange, transportation and communication. From this perspective, late nineteenth- and early twentieth-century forms of geo-economic integration entailed the consolidation of the national state's role as a territorialized scaffolding for accelerated capital circulation and as an institutional interface between subnational and supranational scales. Throughout this period, processes of globalization and (national) territorialization proceeded in tandem, mutually reinforcing one another in powerful ways.[27]

One of the core claims of this chapter is that, under contemporary geo-economic conditions, national states continue to operate as key forms of territorialization for the social relations of capitalism, but that the *scalar* geographies of these state-organized territorialization processes have been fundamentally reconfigured. This development has systematically undermined inherited, state-centric conceptions of political-economic space. But what sorts of geographical assumptions do such state-centric visions entail?

Hidden Geographies and the Epistemology of State-Centrism

The epistemology of state-centrism can be defined most precisely in terms of its three most essential, if usually implicit, geographical assumptions: (*a*) the conception of space as a static platform of social action that is not itself constituted or modified socially; (*b*) the assumption that social relations are organized within territorially self-enclosed spatial containers; and (*c*) the assumption that social relations are organized at a national scale or are undergoing a process of nationalization. The first assumption results in a *spatial fetishism* in which space is seen as being timeless, and therefore immune to historical change. The second assumption results in a *methodological territorialism* in which territoriality—the principle of spatial enclosure—is treated as the necessary spatial form for social relations. The third assumption generates a *methodological nationalism* in which the national scale is treated as the ontologically primary locus of social relations. Taken together, these assumptions generate an internalist model of societal development in which national territoriality is presumed to operate as a static, fixed, and timeless container of historicity. While all three of these assumptions have pervaded the mainstream social and human sciences, a mode of analysis may be said to be state-centric, in the terms proposed here, when the assumption of spatial

fetishism is linked either to methodological territorialism or methodological nationalism.

Defined in this manner, a state-centric epistemology has pervaded the
modern social sciences since their inception during the late nineteenth century. Not surprisingly, political science has been the most explicitly state-
centric among the social sciences. States have been viewed as politically
sovereign and economically self-propelled entities, with national state territoriality understood as the basic reference point in terms of which all subnational and supranational political-economic and sociocultural processes
are to be classified. On this basis, the (national) state has been viewed as the
container of (national) society, while the interstate system has been mapped
in terms of a distinction between "domestic" politics and "foreign" relations
in which national state boundaries are said to separate "inside" from "outside."[28] Crucially, however, the above definition extends the problematic of
state-centrism well beyond those fields of inquiry that are focused directly
upon state operations and political life to various modes of anthropological,
sociological, economic, and humanistic analysis in which the concept of the
state may not even be explicitly deployed. For instance, as defined above, a
state-centric epistemology has arguably underpinned significant strands of
sociology (due to its focus on nationally configured societies and communities), anthropology (due to its focus on bounded, territorialized cultures),
macroeconomics (due its focus on purportedly self-contained, self-propelled
national economies), and even comparative literature (to the extent that it
focuses on "national" literary traditions).[29]

This unhistorical conception of spatiality can be usefully characterized as
a *state*-centric epistemology because its widespread intellectual plausibility
has been premised upon a naturalization of the modern state's specifically
national/territorial form. Among the most rudimentary features of territoriality in social life is its role as a strategy grounded upon the parcelization
and enclosure of space.[30] However, in the modern interstate system, territoriality has assumed an historically specific geographical significance. With
the dissolution of feudal hierarchies in late medieval Europe, political space
came to be organized in terms of exclusive state control over self-enclosed
territorial domains.[31] This development is generally said to have been institutionalized in the Treaty of Westphalia of 1648, which recognized the existence of an interstate system composed of contiguous, bounded territories
ruled by sovereign national states committed to the principle of noninterfer-

ence in each other's internal affairs. The consequence of this transformation has been the long-term enclosure of political, economic, and military power within a global grid of mutually exclusive yet geographically contiguous national state territories.

Clearly, the notion of territoriality is a polysemic category and not all of its meanings refer to this statist global and national geography. However, since the late nineteenth century, the social sciences have come to presuppose a territorialist, nationalized image of social space derived from the form of territory-sovereignty nexus that has been produced and continually re-inscribed at a national scale within the modern interstate system. By the mid-twentieth century, each of the conceptual building blocks of the modern social sciences—in particular, the notions of state, society, economy, culture, and community—had come to presuppose this simultaneous territorialization and nationalization of social relations within a parcelized, fixed, and essentially timeless geographical space. The resultant state-centric epistemology entailed the transposition of the historically unique territorial and scalar configuration of the modern interstate system into a generalized model of sociospatial organization, whether with reference to political, societal, economic, or cultural processes. Within this framework, sociohistorical change is said to occur within the fixed territorial boundaries of a national state, society, culture, or economy, rather than through the transformation of those boundaries, their scalar contours, and the political-economic practices they putatively enclose. State-centric modes of analysis acquired a doxic, taken-for-granted character during the course of the twentieth century, as their "spatial premises enter[ed] into the realm of 'common sense' where interrogation is deemed both unnecessary and quite uncalled for."[32]

Particularly from an early twenty-first century vantage point, it is crucial to recognize that the epistemology of state-centrism was not merely a fantasy or an ideological projection. Indeed, its widespread intellectual plausibility was derived from the late nineteenth- and early twentieth-century historical-geographical context in which the social sciences first emerged, during which the territorial state's role in "encaging" socioeconomic and politico-cultural relations within its boundaries dramatically intensified.[33] This intensified territorialization of social relations at a national scale suggests that "the state-centric nature of social science faithfully reflected the power containers that dominated the social world it was studying."[34] However, the theorization outlined previously points toward a somewhat different interpretation. From this perspective, the epistemology of state-centrism is to be viewed less as a faithful "reflection" of its historical-geographical context than as a politically mediated *misrecognition* of that context.

The epistemology of state-centrism was tightly enmeshed within the national-developmentalist round of deterritorialization and reterritorialization that unfolded during the late nineteenth and early twentieth centuries. On the one hand, processes of deterritorialization intensified dramatically in conjunction with the second industrial revolution, the globalizing expansion of the world economy and the imperialist forays of the major capitalist national states. On the other hand, this dramatic spatial extension and temporal acceleration of capitalism was premised upon the construction of qualitatively new forms of territorialization—including, most crucially, the production, distribution, and consumption infrastructures of major industrial city-regions; newly consolidated, nationalized networks of market exchange, transportation, and communication; and the highly bureaucratized institutional-regulatory systems of national states. The essence of state-centric modes of analysis is to focus one-sidedly upon a single term within this dialectic of deterritorialization and reterritorialization, that of territorial fixity, as embodied in the national state's bounded, territorialized form. In this manner, state-centric modes of analysis conflate the historical *tendency* toward the territorialization of social relations on a national scale—which has undoubtedly intensified during much of the twentieth century—with its full historical *realization*. Processes of territorialization and nationalization are thus represented as pre-given, natural conditions of social life rather than being seen as the products of historically specific strategies of parcelization, centralization, enclosure, and encaging at a national scale.

The crucial point here, then, is that territorialization, on any spatial scale, must be viewed as an historically specific, incomplete, and conflictual *process* rather than as a pre-given, natural, or permanent condition. To the extent that the national scale, or any other geographical scale, acquires tendential primacy as an organizational arena for social, political and economic relations, this must be viewed as an historically contingent outcome of scale-specific projects and strategies, rather than being conceived as an expression of ontological necessity. By contrast, state-centric epistemologies freeze the image of national state territoriality into a generalized feature of social life, and thereby neglect to consider the ways in which the latter has been produced and continually transformed during the geohistory of capitalist development.

Rescaling Territoriality: From Globalization
to the Relativization of Scales

The geographies of capitalism thus have been profoundly transformed since the 1970s, leading many commentators to acknowledge the socially produced, and therefore malleable, character of inherited formations of political-economic space. To date, however, most globalization researchers have grappled with the challenges of analyzing sociospatiality in one of two deeply problematic ways—either (*a*) through an analysis of the global scale in implicitly state-centric terms, as a globally stretched territorial grid; or (*b*) through an emphasis on processes of deterritorialization that purportedly trigger the erosion of national state territoriality as such. The former approach, which is manifested most prominently in Wallerstein's writings, transposes state-centric mappings of space onto the global scale, and thus remains trapped within a basically territorialist understanding of contemporary capitalism. The latter approach, which is particularly prevalent in the influential work of Hardt and Negri and within the emergent field of global cultural studies, transcends the territorialist epistemology of state-centrism on the basis of two equally problematic assumptions: (*a*) the notion that globalization is an essentially nonterritorial, borderless, supraterritorial or territorially disembedded process; and (*b*) the notion that globalization entails the contraction or erosion of national state power. In the remainder of this chapter, I argue that neither of these methodological strategies can provide an adequate mapping of contemporary sociospatial transformations. In the course of this discussion, I also begin to sketch a more general interpretation of contemporary re-scaling processes (elaborated at greater length in Brenner, *New State Spaces*).

The crux of my argument is the proposition that the contemporary round of global restructuring has radically reconfigured the *scalar organization* of territorialization processes under capitalism, relativizing the primacy of the national scale while simultaneously enhancing the role of subnational and supranational scales in such processes. The contemporary round of global restructuring arguably represents a major new wave of deterritorialization and reterritorialization in which global socioeconomic interdependencies are being significantly extended in close conjunction with the establishment, or restructuring, of relatively fixed forms of capitalist sociospatial organization at diverse, subglobal geographical scales. Crucially, however, the political-economic and sociocultural geographies of this process are today being fundamentally rescaled relative to the nationally configured patterns in which it has unfolded since the late nineteenth century. Whereas previous rounds of deterritorialization and reterritorialization occurred largely within the geographical framework of national state territoriality, the current round of worldwide sociospatial restructuring has significantly decentered the role of the national scale as the primary institutional arena for the territorialization of capital.

Collinge has aptly characterized these multifaceted shifts as a "relativization of scales" in which, in marked contrast to earlier configurations of capitalist sociospatial organization, no single level of political-economic interaction currently predominates over any others.[35] As this process of scale relativization has proceeded apace, a range of subnational and supranational sociospatial configurations—from global city-regions, industrial districts, regional state institutions, and cross-border zones, to multinational economic blocks, supranational regulatory institutions, and regimes of global governance—have acquired major roles as geographical infrastructures for the reproduction of global capitalism. These re-scaling processes represent a conflictual dynamic of "glocalization" in which global sociospatial integration is proceeding in tandem with a pervasive triadization, regionalization, and localization of social relations.[36] In this sense, "globalization is not just about one scale becoming more important than the rest; it is also about changes in the very nature of the relationships between scales."[37]

The central consequence of these re-scaling processes has been to thrust the apparently ossified, entrenched fixity of national state territoriality abruptly and dramatically into historical motion, radically redefining its geographical significance, its organizational configuration, and its linkages to both subnational and supranational scales. Processes of territorialization remain endemic to capitalism, but today they are jumping at once above, below, and around the national scale upon which they tendentially converged during much of the last century. Consequently, state territoriality currently operates less as an isomorphic, self-enclosed block of absolute space than as a polymorphic, multiscalar institutional mosaic composed of multiple, partially overlapping institutional forms and regulatory configurations that are neither congruent, contiguous nor coextensive with one another.[38] I view this re-scaling of national territoriality as the *differentia specifica* of the currently unfolding round of global sociospatial restructuring. Even though contemporary forms of deterritorialization have partially eroded the container-like qualities of national borders, national states con-

tinue to operate as essential political and institutional sites for, and media-
tors of, the territorialization of social, political, and economic relations.[39]
The key point is that the political-economic geographies of this territorialization process are no longer focused predominantly on any single, self-
enclosed geographical scale.

In the next two sections, the notion of a re-scaling of national territoriality is further developed through a critical analysis of the two major strands
of globalization research mentioned above, with particular attention to
Wallerstein's world-systems analysis and Hardt and Negri's influential account of a deterritorialized "Empire" of capital. Because so much of globalization research remains grounded upon state-centric or otherwise problematic geographical assumptions, I view this type of epistemological critique
as a crucial prerequisite for the project of developing more geographically
reflexive and scale-sensitive approaches to the investigation of contemporary sociospatial transformations.

Global Territorialism: State-Centrism on a World Scale

A significant strand of globalization studies conceives global space in essentially state-centric terms, as a pre-given territorial container or as a form of
territoriality stretched onto the global scale. The deployment of this "global
territorialist" methodology is frequently quite explicit, as in Albrow's definition of globalization as "those processes by which the peoples of the world
are incorporated into a single world society, a global society."[40] The concept of "world society" has played a defining role within a major strand of
mainstream research on globalization, according to which globalization entails not only the growing interconnectedness of distinct parts of the globe,
but—in Waters's characteristic formulation—the construction of "a single
society and culture occupying the planet."[41] Other globalization researchers have elaborated closely analogous accounts of "global culture," "transnational civil society," and "global unicity."[42]

In each case, the modifier "global" or "world" is positioned before a tra-
ditionally state-centric, territorialist concept—society, civil society, or culture—in order to demarcate a realm of social interaction that transcends
the borders of any single state territory. Whether this sphere of interaction
is understood in normative terms (for instance, as a site of universalistic
values such as human rights, equality, peace, and democracy), institutionally (for instance, as a framework of globally standardized economic, politi-

cal, educational, and scientific practices) or experientially (for instance, as a worldwide diffusion of American, European, or Western cultural influences), world-society approaches share an underlying conception of global space as a structural analog to state territoriality. Insofar as the interpretation of global space is derived directly from an understanding of the territorially configured spaces of national societies and national cultures, the question of the qualitative sociospatial organization of world-scale processes is essentially foreclosed through a choice of conceptual grammar. The difference between global and national configurations of social space is thereby reduced to a matter of geographical size. Meanwhile, because globalization is understood primarily as a world-scale process, the role of national and subnational territorial transformations in contemporary processes of global restructuring cannot be explicitly analyzed. In this sense, even as their unit of analysis is extended beyond national territorial boundaries, world-society approaches remain embedded within a state-centric epistemology that conceives space—on both global and national scales—as a timeless, territorial container of social relations. The pre-constituted geographical space of the globe is presumed simply to be filled by the social practices associated with the process of globalization rather than being produced, reconfigured, or transformed through the latter.

A more theoretically nuanced and more influential form of global territorialism can be found within Wallerstein's approach to world-systems analysis, which is otherwise among the most sustained, powerful critiques of explicitly state-centric frameworks yet to be developed in the social sciences. By demonstrating the *longue durée* and macro-geographical parameters of capitalism, Wallerstein's pioneering studies have also served as a useful corrective to excessively presentist interpretations of the post-1970s wave of globalization that exaggerate its discontinuity with earlier historical configurations of capitalist development. Despite these substantial achievements, however, Wallerstein's theoretical framework arguably replicates on a global scale the methodological territorialism of the very state-centric epistemologies he has otherwise criticized so effectively. To elaborate this claim, the intersection of global space and national state territoriality in Wallerstein's approach to world-systems analysis must be examined more closely.

Wallerstein conceptualizes capitalism as a geographically integrated historical system grounded on a single division of labor. Worldwide space is conceived neither as a society, a culture, or a place, but rather in terms of the more geographically and historically specific notion of the "modern world-system." Although Wallerstein defines the capitalist world-system on multiple levels—for instance, in terms of the drive toward ceaseless accumulation; the commodification of production, distribution, and investment processes; and the antagonistic class relation between capitalists and wage-laborers—he argues repeatedly that its unique *scalar* form is one of its constitutive features.[43] In contradistinction to previous historical systems ("world-empires"), in which the division of labor, state power, and cultural forms overlapped more or less congruently within the same territorial domains, capitalism is composed of "a *single* division of labor but *multiple* polities and cultures."[44] It is through this abstract contrast between two geometrical images—world-empires in which the division of labor is spatially congruent with structures of politico-cultural organization; and world-economies in which a single division of labor encompasses multiple states and multiple cultural formations—that Wallerstein delineates the geographical foundations of modern capitalism. In essence, Wallerstein grasps the specificity of capitalist spatiality in terms of the territorial non-congruence of economic structures ("singular") with politico-institutional and cultural forms ("multiple"). According to Wallerstein, the long-run reproduction of capitalism has hinged crucially upon the durability of this scalar arrangement, which has provided capital with "a freedom of maneuver that is structurally based [and has thereby] made possible the constant economic expansion of the world-system."[45] On this basis, Wallerstein outlines the long-run history of world capitalism with reference to three intersecting spatio-temporal processes—first, the Kondratieff cycles, secular trends, and systemic crises of the world-scale accumulation process; second, the cycles of hegemonic ascension and decline among the core states; and third, the geographical incorporation of external areas until, by the late nineteenth century, the international division of labor had become coextensive with most of the planet's physical-geographical surface.

However, considering Wallerstein's avowed concern to transcend state-centric models of capitalist modernity, national state territories occupy a surprisingly pivotal theoretical position within his conceptual framework. Although the division of labor in the capitalist world-economy is said to be stratified into three supra-state zones (core, semi-periphery, and periphery), Wallerstein argues that its most elemental geographical units are nevertheless national states, or more precisely, the bounded territories over which national states attempt to exercise sovereignty. To be sure, Wallerstein maintains that the division of labor within the world-system transcends the territorial boundaries of each national state; yet he consistently describes the historical dynamics of the world-economy in terms of the differential positions of national states within its stratified core-periphery structure, rather than, for instance, with reference to firms, industries, circuits of capital, urban-regional systems, or spatial divisions of labor. For Wallerstein, then, the economic division of labor is intrinsically composed of states; capitalist enterprises are in turn said to be "domiciled" within their associated national state territories.[46] Wallerstein's conception of world space is thus most precisely described as an *interstate* division of labor: national state territoriality serves as the basic geographical unit of the world-economy; meanwhile global space is parcelized among three zonal patterns (core, semi-periphery, periphery) that are in turn said to be composed of nationally scaled territorial economies. National state territoriality and world space are thereby fused together into a seamless national-global scalar topography in which the interstate system and the world-economy operate as a single, integrated system.

In this sense, Wallerstein's concern to analyze the world scale as a distinctive unit of analysis does not lead to any qualitative modification in the way in which this space is conceptualized. In Wallerstein's framework, the primary geographical units of global space are defined by the territorial boundaries of national states, which in turn constitute a single, encompassing macro-territoriality, the world interstate system. The national scale is thereby blended into the global scale while the global scale is essentially flattened into its national components. As in the tale of the traveler Gulliver who encounters identical micro- and macro-scopic replications of human society, a society of midgets and a society of giants, the global and the national scales are viewed as structural analogs of a single spatial form—territoriality.[47] Thus conceived, the global scale simply multiplies national territoriality throughout a global patchwork without modifying its essential geographical attributes. Wallerstein's approach to world-systems analysis therefore entails the replication of a territorialist model of space, not only on the national scale of the territorial state, but on the global scale of the entire world-system.

Wallerstein's methodological fusion of the global and the national scales also leads to an interpretation of contemporary globalization primarily as a physical-geographical expansion of the capitalist system, rather than as a rearticulation or transformation of the political-economic or sociocultural spaces on which it is based. To be sure, Wallerstein conceives global space as a complex historical product of capitalist expansion, but he acknowledges its historicity only in a limited sense, in contrast to previous historical systems such as world-empires. For, within the capitalist historical system, space appears to be frozen into a single geometric crystallization—"one economy, multiple states"—that cannot change qualitatively without dissolving capitalism's identity as a distinctive type of historical system. In Wallerstein's framework, each long wave of capitalist expansion is said to reproduce the structurally invariant geographical pattern upon which capitalism is grounded, a grid of nationally organized state territories linked through a core-periphery structure to a global division of labor. Paradoxically, then, Wallerstein's definition of the modern world-system as a global amalgamation of national spaces generates a fundamentally state-centric methodological consequence—namely, the assumption that a specifically capitalist form of globalization can unfold only among nationally scaled forms of political-economic organization. The possibility that the process of capitalist development might unhinge itself from this entrenched national-global scalar couplet to privilege other subnational or supranational sociospatial configurations is thereby excluded by definitional fiat.

Two general methodological conclusions may be derived from this critical analysis of global territorialist approaches.

1. An emphasis on the global spatial scale does not necessarily lead to an overcoming of state-centric epistemologies. Global territorialist approaches represent global space in a state-centric manner, as a pre-given territorial container within which the process of globalization unfolds, rather than analyzing its historical production, reconfiguration, and transformation. As noted, one of the major deficiencies of state-centric modes of analysis is to conceive territorialization as a static condition rather than as an ongoing, dialectical process. Global territorialist approaches are premised on the transposition of this state-centric misrecognition from the national to the global scale. The current round of global restructuring does indeed appear to be intensifying globally scaled forms of interaction and interdependence. However, global territorialist approaches reify this emergent, contradictory tendency into an actualized, globally scaled territorial system and thus circumvent the key methodological task of analyzing global space as an historically constituted, polymorphic arena composed of multiple, superimposed spatial forms.

2. State-centric conceptions of global space mask the national state's own crucial role as a site and agent of global restructuring processes. The global territorialist approaches discussed above treat national state territoriality as a static institutional framework over and above which globalization occurs, and thereby bracket the profound transformations of state territorial and scalar organization that have played a crucial enabling role in the contemporary round of global restructuring. The persistence of state-centric epistemologies in globalization studies thus represents a major barrier to a more adequate understanding of currently emergent forms of national state territoriality and state scalar organization.

These arguments are summarized schematically in table 1.

Table 1: The Epistemology of Global Territorialism: Schematic Overview

---

Main features: Two of the three key components of state-centric modes of analysis—spatial fetishism and methodological territorialism—are transposed from the national to the global scale.

Consequently: the global scale is analyzed (*a*) as a pre-given, unchanging arena for social relations; and/or (*b*) as a grid of national territorialities stretched onto the global scale.

Prominent examples: "World society" approaches (Meyer, "The Changing Cultural Content of the Nation-State"; Spybey, *Globalization and World Society*; Wapner, "Politics Beyond the State"; Waters, *Globalization*,); Robertson's (*Globalization*) cultural sociology of globalization; Wallerstein's approach to world-system analysis (Wallerstein *The Modern World-System I*, *The Modern World-System II*, *The Politics of the World-Economy*, *The Modern World-System III*).

Problems and limitations:

(1) Neglects to examine systematically (*a*) the historical constitution and continual transformation of the global scale as an outcome of diverse social, economic and political processes or (*b*) the complex, continually changing interdependencies between global and subglobal relations.

(2) Territoriality is conceived as the natural form in which sociospatial processes are organized; consequently, the polymorphic geographies of the global scale are described in a narrowly territorialist conceptual grammar.

(3) Neglects to examine (*a*) the key role of national states in contemporary processes of global restructuring; and (*b*) the ways in which national states are in turn being reshaped through their role in animating and mediating these processes.

As suggested above, the contemporary round of global restructuring can be fruitfully conceived as a conflictual rearticulation of political-economic space on multiple, superimposed geographical scales. These sociospatial transformations can now be examined more closely through a critical discussion of deterritorialization approaches to globalization studies.

Jumping Scales: The Dialectics of Deterritorialization and Reterritorialization

In contrast to global territorialist approaches, analyses of deterritorialization confront explicitly the task of analyzing social spatiality in an historically specific manner. From this perspective, territoriality is viewed as an historically specific form of sociospatial organization that is currently being systematically decentered. New supraterritorial geographies of networks and flows are said to be supplanting the inherited geography of state territories that has long preoccupied the social-scientific imagination. Deterritorialization researchers have analyzed these emergent, purportedly post-territorial geographies as the outcomes of diverse causal processes, including the deployment of new informational, military, and transportation technologies; the internationalization of capital, monetary, and financial markets; the virtualization of economic activity through electronically mediated monetary transactions; the global crisis of territorialized definitions of state regulation and citizenship; the expanded activities of transnational organizations, including multinational corporations and NGOs; the intensified role of electronic media in organizing sociocultural identities; the proliferation of worldwide ecological problems; and the increasing density and velocity of transnational diasporic population movements.[48]

In most research on deterritorialization, the spaces of globalization (based upon circulation, flows, and geographical mobility) and the spaces of territorialization (based upon enclosure, borders, and geographical fixity) are represented as mutually opposed systems of social interaction. Thus, for O'Brien global financial integration has generated a situation in which "geographical location no longer matters, or matters less than hitherto . . . . Money . . . will largely succeed in escaping the confines of the existing geography."[49] Likewise, in their widely discussed book, *Empire*, Hardt and Negri speak of a "general equalization or smoothing of social space" in which capital supersedes entrenched territorial borders and the power of national states is effectively dissolved.[50] More generally, for Scholte "Global space is placeless, distanceless and borderless—and in this sense 'supraterritorial.' In global relations, people are connected with one another pretty much irrespective of their territorial position. To that extent they effectively do not have a territorial location, apart from the broad sense of being situated on the planet earth. Global relations thus form a non-, extra-, post-, supra-territorial aspect of the world system. In the global domain, territorial boundaries present no particular impediment and distance is covered in effectively no time."[51]

This image of world space as a "placeless, distanceless and borderless" realm is the geographical essence of deterritorialization approaches. From Castells's account of the "space of flows," Jameson's theorization of "postmodern hyperspace" and Appadurai's concept of "ethnoscapes," to Hardt and Negri's notion of "Empire," analyses of deterritorialization have generally been premised upon this basic conceptual opposition between the purportedly supraterritorial or deterritorialized spaces in which globalization occurs in diverse subglobal territories, localities and places.[52] Indeed, Hardt and Negri explicitly criticize Wallerstein's differentiation of the world-system among core, semi-peripheral, and peripheral zones, which they view as an excessively rigid territorial mapping of a geography that is, in their view, based on "fluid infra- and supranational borders."[53]

The logical corollary of this conceptualization is the contention that globalization entails the decline, erosion, or disempowerment of the national state. Whereas Wallerstein's global territorialist approach maps global space essentially as a territorial state writ-large, deterritorialization theorists such as Hardt and Negri invert this territorialist epistemology to emphasize the increasing permeability or even total negation of national state territoriality. The decline of national state power is viewed at once as the medium and as the result of contemporary processes of deterritorialization. On the one hand, the erosion of nationally scaled forms of territorial enclosure is said to open up a space for increasingly nonterritorial forms of interaction and interdependence on a global scale. On the other hand, these globally scaled processes of deterritorialization are in turn said to accelerate the state's loss of control over its national borders and thus further to undermine its territorial self-enclosure. In this sense, the state-decline thesis and the notion of deterritorialization entail cumulative, mutually reinforcing rather than merely additive, externally related conceptions of global sociospatial transformation. Global space can be viewed as nonterritorial in form precisely because it is defined through the trope of an eroding or disappearing national scale.

Meanwhile, the thesis of state decline is elaborated not through an account of the national scale per se, but rather with reference to the role of various globally scaled, purportedly supraterritorial and deterritorializing socioeconomic processes.

By emphasizing the historicity and potential malleability of territoriality, deterritorialization approaches have begun to articulate an important challenge to the epistemology of state-centrism. This methodological denaturalization of territoriality has also enabled deterritorialization researchers to construct alternative geographical categories for describing currently emergent sociospatial forms without presupposing their enclosure within territorially bounded spaces. This important accomplishment may partially explain the immense interdisciplinary influence of works such as Hardt and Negri's *Empire* and Appadurai's *Modernity at Large*, which have obviously resonated with scholars' concern to develop new frameworks for the understanding of contemporary worldwide sociospatiality. Nevertheless, when examined through the lens of the conception of capitalist sociospatial configuration outlined above, deterritorialization approaches contain three serious deficiencies.

1. The historicity of territoriality is reduced to an either/or choice between two options, its presence or its absence. Consequently, the possibility that territoriality is being reconfigured and rescaled rather than eroded cannot be adequately explored.

2. The relation between world space and national territoriality is viewed as a zero-sum game in which the growing importance of the former is presumed necessarily to entail the decline of the latter. By conceiving geographical scales as mutually exclusive rather than as co-constitutive, relationally intertwined levels of social interaction, this dualistic conceptualization cannot adequately theorize the essential role of subglobal transformations—whether of supranational political-economic blocs, national state territories, regions, cities, localities, or places—in contemporary processes of global restructuring.

3. Most crucially for the argument here, deterritorialization approaches bracket the various forms of spatial fixity, spatial embedding, re-scaling, and reterritorialization on which global flows are premised. From this perspective, processes of deterritorialization are not delinked from territoriality; indeed, their very existence presupposes the production and continual reproduction of fixed socio-territorial infrastructures—including, in particular, urban-regional agglomerations and state regulatory institutions—within,

upon, and through which global flows can circulate. Thus the apparent de-territorialization of social relations on a global scale hinges intrinsically on their reterritorialization within relatively fixed and immobile sociospatial configurations at a variety of interlocking, subglobal scales.

This chapter began by suggesting an interpretation of contemporary global restructuring as a rescaling of the nationally organized sociospatial configurations that have long served as the underlying geographical scaffolding for capitalist development. In the context of this ongoing scalar shift, processes of deterritorialization can be reinterpreted as concerted yet un-coordinated strategies to decenter the national scale of political-economic organization. If territoriality operates as a strategy grounded on the enclosure of social relations within a bounded geographical space,[54] deterritorialization may be understood most coherently as a countervailing strategy to "jump scales," that is, to circumvent or dismantle historically entrenched scalar hierarchies.[55] From this point of view, one of the most significant geographical consequences of contemporary processes of deterritorialization has been to unsettle and rearticulate the entrenched, nationally scaled configurations of political-economic organization on which capitalist industrial growth has been grounded since at least the late nineteenth century. This de-nationalizing, scale-jumping strategy has also been closely intertwined with various conflictual forms of reterritorialization through which new subnational and supranational sociospatial configurations are being constructed. Crucially, however, the national territorial state—albeit now significantly rescaled and reterritorialized—has continued to serve as a crucial geographical infrastructure for this multiscalar dialectic of deterritorialization and reterritorialization. These arguments may be specified further through a critical reinterpretation of two commonly invoked forms of deterritorialization—the deterritorialization of capital; and the deterritorialization of the national state.

The Rescaling of Capital

The concept of deterritorialization was first developed in the early 1970s to describe the apparently footloose activities of transnational corporations in coordinating globally dispersed production networks.[56] Since this period, the notion of deterritorialization has acquired a broader meaning to encompass as well the role of new information and communications technologies in linking geographically dispersed parts of the globe to create a temporally

integrated world economy. The massive expansion in the role of transnational finance capital since the demise of the Bretton Woods currency controls in the early 1970s presents a further indication of capital's increasing
velocity and geographical mobility in the world economy. Under these circumstances, the worldwide circulation of capital can no longer be analyzed
adequately with reference to self-enclosed, discrete national economies or,
more generally, on the basis of strictly territorial representations of space.

Nonetheless, no matter how rapidly turnover times are accelerated, the
moment of territorialization still remains endemic to capital, a basic structural feature of its circulation process. Capital remains as dependent as ever
upon relatively fixed, localized, and territorially embedded technological-
institutional ensembles in which technology, the means of production,
forms of industrial organization and labor-power are productively combined to extract surplus value. For, as Yeung succinctly remarks, capital is
"'place-sticky.'"[57] The processes of deterritorialization associated with the
current round of geo-economic integration are best conceived as one moment within a broader dynamic of sociospatial transformation in which
the reindustrialization of strategic subnational economic spaces—such as
global cities, industrial districts, technopoles, offshore financial centers, and
other flexible production complexes—has played a constitutive role. These
shifts have been closely intertwined with a marked rescaling of corporate
accumulation strategies as key factions of industrial, financial, and service
capital attempt to secure competitive advantages within global production
chains through the exploitation of locally and regionally specific conditions
of production.[58] Although the growth of these urban and regional territorial
production complexes has been crucially conditioned by national political-
economic frameworks, a number of scholars have suggested that, due to
these new forms of global localization, urbanized regions are today increasingly superseding national economies as the most rudimentary geographical
units of world capitalism.[59] This pervasive rescaling of capital is illustrated
schematically in figure 1.

The essential point here is that capital's drive to diminish its place-
dependency does not, in practice, entail the construction of a quasi-
autonomous, placeless, or distanceless space of flows, as writers such as
Hardt and Negri, among others, have implied. We are witnessing, rather,
a profoundly uneven re-scaling and reterritorialization of the historically
entrenched, state-centric geographical infrastructures that underpinned the
last century of capitalist industrialization. From this point of view, scholarly

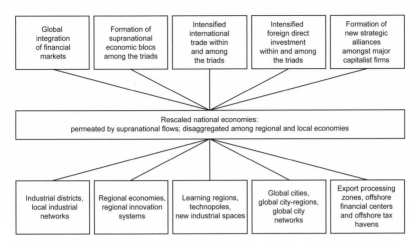

Figure 1. Rescaling of capital.

representations of contemporary global capitalism as a "smooth world"[60] or as a borderless "space of flows"[61] are grounded upon an uncritical appropriation of a neoliberal myth. Such arguments, as Radice remarks, amount to "ideological cover for the policy preferences of big business."[62] In a forceful critique of Castells, Smith elaborates this point:

> Capital . . . may entertain the fantasy of spacelessness and act accordingly, but in practice, every strategy to avoid and supersede 'historically established mechanisms' [i.e. places] and territories of social control involves not the extinction of place per se but *the reinvention of place at a different scale*—a capital-centered jumping of scale. Indeed, the perpetuation of control by these organizations (and classes) depends precisely on this reinvention of discrete places where power over and through the space of flows is rooted.[63]

Deterritorialization must therefore be viewed as a distinctively geographical accumulation strategy, as a mechanism of global localization through which major capitalist firms are attempting to circumvent or restructure the nationally organized systems of social, monetary, and labor regulation that prevailed under the Fordist-Keynesian regime of accumulation.[64]

To be sure, capitalist strategies of deterritorialization may well succeed in partially circumventing the constraints imposed by national territorial boundaries. But, even when successful, such strategies do not translate into a situation of pure capital hypermobility or placelessness. As capital strives to jump scale, it is forced to reconstitute, or create anew, viable sociospatial infrastructures for its circulation process at other scales—whether through the reorganization of existent scales or through the construction of qualitatively new scales. In this sense, capital's apparent transcendence of nationally scaled regulatory systems in recent decades has been inextricably bound up with the production of new subnational and supranational spaces of accumulation and state regulation that provide the place- and territory-specific conditions for accumulation. Thus, rather than releasing capital from its endemic dependence upon places, cities, regions and territories, the current round of geo-economic integration has hinged upon a rearticulation of inherited spatial divisions of labor.[65] The drive towards deterritorialization incessantly re-inscribes the role of capitalist sociospatial configurations while, at the same time, reconfiguring their scalar architecture in pursuit of locationally specific productive capacities and competitive advantages.

Rescaling the State

As noted, accounts of deterritorialization conceptualize the emergence of global space through the trope of a declining or eroding state territoriality. The current round of geo-economic integration has indeed rendered states more permeable to transnational flows of capital, money, commodities, labor, and information. However, this development has not entailed the demise, erosion, or weakening of the state as such. Instead, there has been a significant functional, institutional, and geographical reorganization of statehood at a range of spatial scales. While these trends have unsettled the nationalized formations of statehood that have long preoccupied social scientists, they have not undermined the centrality of state institutions—albeit now significantly reterritorialized and rescaled—to processes of political-economic regulation.

As I have argued at length elsewhere, the consolidation of post–Keynesian competition states in contemporary Western Europe has indeed been closely intertwined with fundamental, if often rather haphazard, transformations of state spatial and scalar organization.[66] These ongoing reterritorializations and re-scalings of state space cannot be understood merely as defensive responses to intensified global economic competition, but represent expressions of concerted political strategies through which state institutions are attempting, at various spatial scales, to facilitate, manage, mediate, and redirect processes of geo-economic restructuring. On a continental scale, states have promoted geo-economic integration by forming supranational economic blocs such as the EU, NAFTA, ASEAN, and the like, which are intended at once to enhance structural competitiveness, to facilitate capital mobility within new continental zones of accumulation, and to provide protective barriers against the pressures of global economic competition. Supranational agencies such as the IMF, the WTO, and the World Bank have likewise acquired key roles in enforcing neoliberal, market-led strategies of political-economic restructuring throughout the world-system.[67] At the same time, even as national states attempt to fracture or dismantle the institutional compromises of postwar Fordist-Keynesian capitalism in order to reduce domestic production costs, they have also devolved substantial regulatory responsibilities to regional and local institutions, which are seen to be better positioned to promote industrial (re)development within major urban and regional economies. This downscaling of regulatory tasks should not be viewed as a contraction or abdication of national state power, however, for it has frequently served as a centrally orchestrated strategy to promote transnational capital investment within major urban regions, whether through the public funding of large-scale infrastructural projects, the mobilization of localized economic development policies, the establishment of new forms of public-private partnership or other public initiatives intended to enhance urban territorial competitiveness. Figure 2 provides an initial, schematic representation of the rescaled landscape of statehood that has been forged through these transformations.

These ongoing transformations of state institutional and spatial organization do not herald the end of territoriality as such, as deterritorialization theorists contend. Rather, polymorphic, reterritorialized political geographies are being consolidated in which territoriality is redifferentiated among multiple institutional levels that are not clustered around a single predominant center of gravity. Whereas the traditional Westphalian image of political space as a self-enclosed geographical container does today appear to have become increasingly obsolete, territoriality nevertheless remains a fundamental characteristic of statehood and an essential institutional scaffolding for the process of political-economic regulation at all spatial scales.[68] Territoriality is no longer organized predominantly or exclusively on the national scale, for subnational and supranational levels of sociospatial organization have today come to play essential roles in processes of political-economic regulation.

By indicating the ways in which an historically entrenched form of na-

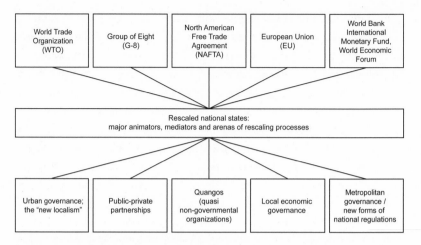

Figure 2. Rescaled landscape of statehood.

tional state territoriality is being superseded, deterritorialization researchers have made an important contribution to the project of theorizing social space in an explicitly historical manner, and they have productively opened up the problem of developing mappings of worldwide social space that transcend methodological territorialism. However, because they recognize the historicity of territoriality primarily in terms of its disappearance, obsolescence, or demise, deterritorialization approaches cannot analyze the types of qualitative reconfigurations and rescalings of territoriality that have been outlined above. Even if the role of the national scale as an autocentric territorial container has been unsettled, national states continue to play a key role in producing the geographical infrastructures upon which the process of capital circulation depends and in regulating political-economic life at all spatial scales. The reterritorialization and re-scaling of inherited, nationally organized institutional forms and policy-relays represent an important political strategy through which national states are attempting to adjust to, and to (re)assert control over, a rapidly changing geoeconomic context. Table 2 provides a schematic summary of the preceding critique of deterritorialization approaches to globalization studies.

Table 2: The Epistemology of Deterritorialization Approaches:
Schematic Overview

Main features: Territoriality is said to be declining, eroding, or disappearing as
    placeless, distanceless, and supraterritorial geographies of networks and flows
    proliferate throughout the world system.
Consequently: The capacity of national states to regulate their territorial
    jurisdictions is said to be weakening or eroding.
Prominent examples: Appadurai's ("Disjuncture and Difference") theory of "global
    cultural flows"; Castells's (*The Rise of the Network Society*) theory of the "space of
    flows"; Hardt and Negri's (*Empire*) concept of "Empire."
Major accomplishments: In contrast to methodologically territorialist approaches,
    the historicity and potential malleability of territoriality are emphasized.
    Introduces alternative geographical categories for describing currently emergent
    spatial forms that do not presuppose their enclosure within territorially
    bounded geographical spaces.

Problems and limitations:
(*a*) The historicity of territoriality is reduced to an either/or choice between two
    options, its presence or its absence; thus the possibility that territoriality is
    being reconfigured, reterritorialized, and rescaled rather than being eroded
    cannot be adequately explored.
(*b*) The relation between global space and national territoriality is viewed as a zero-
    sum game in which the growing importance of the former necessarily entails
    the decline of the latter; consequently, the role of subglobal transformations
    (for instance, of national states, regions, and cities) in processes of global
    restructuring cannot be examined.
(*c*) Brackets the various forms of spatial fixity, embedding, and (re)territorialization
    —particularly at national, regional, and local scales—upon which global flows
    are necessarily premised.

Conclusion: Rethinking the Geographies of Globalization

Like the forms of state-centrism that have dominated the social sciences for
much of the last century, the methodological opposition between global
territorialist and deterritorialization approaches to globalization studies can
be viewed as a real abstraction of contemporary social practices. Throughout this discussion, I have argued that each of these approaches grasps
real dimensions of contemporary social reality, albeit in a truncated, one-
sided manner. Capital has long presupposed a moment of territorial fixity

or place-boundedness as a basic prerequisite for its ever-expanding circulation process. Whereas state-centric epistemologies fetishize this territorialist moment of capitalism, deterritorialization approaches embrace an inverse position, in which territoriality is said to erode or disappear as globalization intensifies. The bifurcation of contemporary globalization studies into these opposed methodological approaches reflects these contradictory aspects of contemporary sociospatial transformations without critically explaining them.

The alternative theorization of global restructuring introduced here suggests that deterritorialization and reterritorialization are mutually constitutive, if highly conflictual, moments of an ongoing dialectic through which political-economic space is continually produced, reconfigured, and transformed under capitalism, at all geographical scales. Thus conceived, the contemporary round of global restructuring has entailed neither the absolute territorialization of societies, economies, or cultures onto a global scale, nor their complete deterritorialization into a supraterritorial, distanceless, placeless, or borderless space of flows. What is occurring, rather, is a multiscalar restructuring of worldwide sociospatial configurations, coupled with a reshuffling of entrenched hierarchies of scalar organization, leading in turn to qualitatively new geographies of capital accumulation, state regulation, and uneven development. A crucial challenge for future research on the geographies of capitalism is to develop an epistemology of worldwide social space that can critically grasp these processes of deterritorialization and reterritorialization as intrinsically related moments of contemporary sociospatial transformations, as well as their variegated, path-dependent consequences in specific political-economic contexts. This discussion has attempted to outline some methodological foundations for confronting this task.

At the most general level, this analysis is intended to reinforce Wallerstein's claim that state-centric geographical assumptions have underpinned the social sciences throughout most of the twentieth century, and that such assumptions significantly constrain our ability to understand the logics and illogics of modern capitalism.[69] However, while Wallerstein implies that such assumptions were always purely ideological, this discussion has suggested that they were embedded within a configuration of global capitalism in which national state territories did indeed figure crucially—albeit within a worldwide division of labor—as an organizational basis for political-economic and sociocultural life. Concomitantly, I have suggested that such assumptions have been seriously undermined during the post-1970s wave of worldwide sociospatial restructuring, which has reterritorialized and rescaled inherited formations of national territoriality and produced new constellations of political-economic organization across the world economy. These developments have led many scholars of globalization to develop more reflexive, dynamic, and historically specific understandings of social spatiality as they struggle to decipher the radically transformed political-economic and sociocultural geographies that are emerging in our midst.

Five methodological challenges for contemporary studies of global sociospatial restructuring flow from the preceding discussion.

1. *The historicity of social space.* The contemporary round of global restructuring has put into relief the distinctive, historically specific character of national state territoriality as a form of sociospatial organization. As the primacy of national state territoriality has been decentered and relativized, the historical, and therefore malleable, character of inherited formations of political-economic space has become dramatically evident both in sociological analysis and in everyday life. The overarching methodological challenge that flows from this circumstance is to analyze social spatiality, at all scales, as an ongoing historical *process* in which the geographies of social relations are continually molded, reconfigured and transformed.[70]

2. *Polymorphic geographies.* National state territoriality is today being intertwined with, and superimposed upon, an immense variety of emergent sociospatial forms—from the supranational institutional structures of the EU to global financial flows, new forms of transnational corporate organization, post-Fordist patterns of industrial agglomeration, global interurban networks, and transnational diasporic communities—that cannot be described adequately as contiguous, mutually exclusive, and self-enclosed blocks of territorial space. Under these circumstances, the image of political-economic space as a complex, tangled mosaic of superimposed and interpenetrating nodes, levels, scales, and morphologies has become more appropriate than the traditional Cartesian model of homogenous, self-enclosed and contiguous blocks of territory that has long been used to describe the modern interstate system (Lefebvre). New representations of sociospatial form are urgently needed in order to analyze these newly emergent polymorphic, polycentric, and multiscalar geographies of global social change (Sheppard). A crucial methodological challenge for contemporary sociospatial research is therefore to analyze currently emergent geographies in ways that transcend the conventional imperative to choose between purely territorialist and deterritorialized mappings of political-economic space.

3. *The new political economy of scale*. The current round of global restructuring has significantly decentered the national scale of political-economic life and intensified the importance of both subnational and supranational scales of sociospatial organization. These transformations undermine inherited conceptions of geographical scale as a static, fixed, and nested hierarchy, and reveal its socially produced, historically variegated and politically contested character. From this perspective, geographical scales must be viewed not only as the products of political-economic processes but also as their presupposition and their medium (Smith). Scalar arrangements are thus never fixed in stone but evolve continuously in conjunction with the dynamics of capital accumulation, state regulation, social reproduction, and sociopolitical struggle. Under these conditions, a key methodological challenge is to conceptualize geographical scales at once as an institutional scaffolding within which the dialectic of deterritorialization and reterritorialization unfolds and as an incessantly changing medium and outcome of that dialectic.

4. *The remaking of state space*. This discussion has emphasized the key role of national states in promoting and mediating contemporary sociospatial transformations, and concomitantly, the ways in which national states have in turn been reorganized—functionally, institutionally, and geographically—in conjunction with this role. Contemporary state institutions are being significantly rescaled at once upward, downward, and outward to create qualitatively new, polymorphic, plurilateral, institutional geographies that no longer overlap evenly with one another, converge upon a single, dominant geographical scale, or constitute a single, nested organizational hierarchy. These developments undermine traditional, Westphalian models of statehood as an unchanging, self-enclosed national-territorial container and suggest that more complex, polymorphic, and multiscalar regulatory geographies are emerging than previously existed. Under these conditions, an important methodological challenge is to develop a spatially attuned and scale-sensitive approach to state theory that can grasp not only the variegated regulatory geographies associated with inherited, nationalized formations of political space, but also the profoundly uneven reterritorializations and rescalings of statehood that are currently unfolding throughout the world system.

5. *The space of the world*. Finally, it is worth returning to the theme of this volume—the "problem of the world." This problem has many dimensions—philosophical, political-economic, cultural, representational, literary. I have explored it here from a reflexively *spatial* point of view. As Lefebvre notes,

the worldwide is a spatial arena, medium and outcome of the activities of capitalist firms, state institutions, and diverse politico-cultural movements, both revolutionary and reactionary.[71] Equally, Lefebvre emphasizes, the world has become an emergent space of possibility, a horizon for projections into a variety of imaginable futures, from the humane to the catastrophic. In this sense, the task of theorizing the space of the world encompasses, but also points beyond, the approach to territorialization and deterritorialization on which the preceding arguments have been grounded. It involves not only an analysis of how extant sociospatial configurations are being creatively destroyed, but a diagnosis of any transformative political possibilities that may be latent within contemporary rescalings and reterritorializations. Whatever my criticisms of Wallerstein's sociospatial categories, it is appropriate to view his ongoing confrontation with the world scale as an effort to grapple with this problematic. For him, as for Lefebvre, the space of world capitalism is not only a realm of structural constraint, domination, exploitation, crisis, and catastrophe, but, at least potentially, an arena of collective social choice: it is thus also a horizon for social transformation, the basis on which a radically different type of world-system may be both imagined and pursued, through creativity and struggle. One of the most urgent, if daunting, methodological challenges that flows from the preceding discussion is to develop an appropriately nuanced mapping of this "transformational Time Space"—one that can inform theory and research on the space of the world, as well as the ongoing practice of creating a different world.[72]

Notes

This contribution draws extensively upon chapter 2 of my book, *New State Spaces: Urban Governance and the Rescaling of Statehood* (New York: Oxford University Press, 2004). The arguments developed herein are elaborated at greater length and more concretely in that context.

1. *Unthinking Social Science*. See also Agnew and Corbridge, *Mastering Space*.
2. Wallerstein, *The Essential Wallerstein*, 129.
3. Taylor, "Embedded Statism, 1923.
4. See Lefebvre, *State, Space, World*.
5. Elden, "Missing the Point."
6. See, for instance, Hardt and Negri, *Empire*.
7. Lefebvre, *State, Space, World*; Brenner and Elden, "State, Space, World."
8. For some initial efforts toward this end, see Brenner, Jessop, Jones, and Mac-Leod, eds., *State/Space: A Reader*.

9. Rosenberg, *Follies of Globalisation Theory*.

10. Jessop, "Globalization and Its (Il)logics."

11. Rosenberg, *Follies of Globalisation Theory*, 2.

12. Jessop, "Globalization and Its (Il)logics." In an effort to circumvent such confusions, the remainder of this chapter adopts the terminology of "global restructuring" rather than referring simply to "globalization." In contrast to the notion of globalization, which implies the existence of a singular, unified mega-trend, the notion of restructuring implies an uneven, multifaceted, polymorphic, and open-ended process of change (Soja 2000). However, when discussing the work of authors who deploy the notion of globalization, I shall continue to use this generic term.

In addition to the danger of conflating causes and effects in studies of globalization, it is equally important to recognize the politically contested character of popular and academic discourse on this theme. Notions of globalization have been deployed strategically by diverse actors and organizations—including transnational corporations, state institutions, nongovernmental organizations (NGOs), and oppositional social movements—in order to pursue specific political and ideological agendas. This politico-strategic aspect of globalization has played a hugely powerful role in influencing popular understandings of contemporary capitalism, whether as a means to naturalize neoliberal policy prescriptions, to promote state institutional restructuring, to reorient corporate strategies, to reinterpret social identities or to rally anticapitalist resistance (Kelly, "Geographies and Politics"; Bourdieu, *Acts of Resistance*).

13. Lefebvre, *Production of Space*; *State, Space, World*; Massey, "Politics in Space/time."

14. Sheppard, "Spaces and Times of Globalization."

15. Harvey, "Geopolitics of Capitalism."

16. Marx, *Grundrisse*, 539.

17. Harvey, "Geopolitics of Capitalism," 146.

18. Harvey, "Limits to Capital," 416.

19. Harvey, "Geopolitics of Capitalism," 150.

20. Harvey, "Geopolitics of Capitalism."

21. Harvey, *The Urban Experience*, 192–94.

22. Giddens, *Consequences of Modernity*.

23. Harvey, "Geopolitics of Capitalism."

24. Cameron and Palan, "Imagined Economy."

25. See, for instance, Panitch, "Globalization and the State"; Helleiner, *States and the Reemergence of Global Finance*; Sassen, *Losing Control?*

26. Lefebvre, *De L'État*; Brenner, *New State Spaces*.

27. Goswami, *Producing India*.

28. Walker, *Inside/Outside*.

29. As Taylor ("Embedded Statism") notes, until relatively recently even the discipline of human geography has replicated this territorialized, state-centric conceptual

THE SPACE OF THE WORLD   135

orientation, either with reference to the urban scale (urban ecology and the study of urban systems), the national scale (political geography), or the transnational scale (geopolitics). Due to its anarchist, anti-statist roots in the work of theorists such as Elisée Reclus and Peter Kropotkin, classical regional geography provides an exception to this tendency insofar as regions were viewed as ecologically delimited, contextually specific environments, rather than as territorial subunits of the state. Likewise, in major strands of the discipline of history, an idiographic notion of space-as-context provided an important alternative to the conception of space-as-container that dominated the other, more nomothetically oriented social sciences (1922–23).

30. Sack, *Human Territoriality*.

31. Spruyt, *The Sovereign State and Its Competitors*.

32. Taylor, *Metageographical Moments*, 6. This is not the place to analyze the complex institutional histories through which this state-centric epistemology gradually became hegemonic as a mode of social-scientific inquiry, particularly in the postwar United States but also in Europe, the Soviet Union, and much of the Third World. My concern here is less to examine the institutional consolidation of state-centrism than to characterize analytically its main geographical and epistemological presuppositions.

In this context, it is also crucial to note that these state-centric tendencies in the classical social sciences co-existed uneasily with an opposing, if largely subterranean, "globalist" strand of theory and research. This globalist mode of analysis was elaborated during the nineteenth and early twentieth centuries, above all in Marx's theory of capital accumulation and in the theories of imperialism developed by Lenin, Luxemburg, and Bukharin. Although major strands of Marxian social theory were also eventually infused with state-centric assumptions (such as the notion that the national scale was the main strategic locus of class struggle), this intellectual tradition was arguably the most important alternative to state-centrism within classical sociological discourse. Following the Second World War, various non-Marxist alternatives to state-centrism also emerged, including the *Annales* school of historiography and the figurational sociology of Norbert Elias. In addition to these strands of research, Taylor ("Embedded Statism," 1918–19) detects various late nineteenth-century contextualist alternatives to state-centric conceptions of space, such as idiographic approaches to historiography and Marshallian-inspired economic analyses focused on the problem of urban-regional agglomeration.

33. Mann, *Sources of Social Power*; Maier, "Consigning the Twentieth Century to History."

34. Taylor, "Embedded Statism,"1920.

35. Collinge, *Spatial Articulation of the State*.

36. See Swyngedouw, "The Mammon Quest." According to Robertson ("Globalisation or Glocalisation," 36), the term "glocalization" originated in Japanese business discourse, where it was used in the 1980s as a marketing buzzword to describe

the adaptation of global corporate strategies to locally specific conditions. This term is not unproblematic, however, not least because of its apparent implication that *two* geographical scales, the global and the local, dominate contemporary rescaling processes. Like Swyngedouw, I reject this limited view of contemporary spatial transformations and insist upon their fundamentally multiscalar character. For, in addition to the global and the local, a variety of other scales—including the body, the urban, the regional, the national, and the supranational—are likewise key arenas and targets of currently unfolding rescaling processes. Moreover, the political, institutional, and cultural expressions of each of these scales are being significantly redefined under contemporary conditions, thereby undermining any conceptual grammar that treats scales as if they were stable, fixed entities or platforms. Despite these analytical dangers, the notion of glocalization is useful because, like the concept of the relativization of scales, it underscores the ways in which inherited scalar hierarchies are being shaken up and re-jigged under contemporary capitalism.

37. Dicken, Tickell, and Peck, "Unpacking Globalization," 159–60.

38. Sassen, *Losing Control*.

39. See Brenner, *New State Spaces*.

40. *Globalization, Knowledge, and Society*, 9.

41. Waters, *Globalization*, 3.

42. See Lipschutz "Restructuring World Politics"; Spybey, *Globalization and World Society*; Robertson, *Globalization*.

43. See Wallerstein, *Historical Capitalism*, 13–19; "The Rise and Future Demise of the World Capitalist System," 7–19; *The Modern World-System I*, 37–38, 348.

44. Wallerstein, "The Rise and Future Demise," 6 (emphasis mine); see also Wallerstein, *The Modern World-System I*, 67, 348–49.

45. Wallerstein, *The Modern World-System I*, 348.

46. Wallerstein, *The Politics of the World Economy*, 39, 27–36; and *Historical Capitalism*.

47. See Walker, *Inside/Outside*.

48. Scholte, *Globalization*.

49. O'Brien, *Global Financial Integration*, 1–2.

50. Hardt and Negri, *Empire*, 336.

51. Scholte, *Globalization*, 1968.

52. Castells, *Rise of the Network Society*; Jameson, *Postmodernism*; Appadurai, *Modernity at Large*.

53. Hardt and Negri, *Empire*, 335.

54. Sack, *Human Territoriality*.

55. Smith, "Remaking Scale."

56. Agnew and Corbridge, *Mastering Space*.

57. Yeung, "Capital, State, and Space," 291.

58. Swyngedouw, "Mammon Quest."

59. Storper, *The Regional World*; Scott, *Regions and the World Economy*.

60. Hardt and Negri, *Empire*.

61. Castells, *The Rise of the Network Society*.

62. Radice, "The National Economy," 274.

63. Smith, "Spaces of Vulnerability," 72; emphasis original.

64. Swyngedouw, "The Heart of the Place."

65. Cox, *Spaces of Globalization*.

66. Brenner, *New State Spaces*.

67. Gill, "New Constitutionalism."

68. Newman and Paasi, "Fences and Neighbors."

69. See Wallerstein, *Unthinking Social Science*.

70. Lefebvre, *Production of Space*.

71. Lefebvre, *State, Space, World*.

72. Wallerstein, *Unthinking Social Science*, 147.

Cartographies of Connection

Ocean Maps as Metaphors for Inter-Area History

KÄREN WIGEN

Wallerstein's opus was required reading at many history graduate programs in the 1980s, when I was a student. The grandeur of the work's sweeping vistas, and the power of its comprehensive categories, made a major impression on my generation. Yet most academic historians, trained in national fields and typically mentored by enthusiastic fans of "all things original, spare, strange," were never entirely comfortable with the model-building impulses of world-systems theory.[1] Much of the work that Wallerstein inspired took up his theory less as a model than as a foil for nuanced local studies, where archival findings often challenged the model's overarching claims.[2] By the 1990s, a countervailing turn toward micro-history, a widespread linguistic turn, and the rise of identity, meaning, and cultural logic to the forefront of American historians' analytical concerns combined to pull the field away from macro-history altogether.

Yet the past two decades have witnessed a slow sea-change in the practice of history in the United States, one that has gradually forced attention back on large-scale movements and processes, albeit in more plastic and pluralistic ways. Instead of studying a putatively stable national core, more and more historians today find themselves drawn to the mobile and the marginal. Impatient with the space-time grid of their professional training, a growing group of scholars identifies with a thematically defined agenda, one concerned with the global circulation of people and ideas, money and microbes, social movements and institutional responses. What all these phenomena have in common is their unconventional, expansive geography. None can be satisfactorily investigated within the bounds of a single state, and most spill across even the macro-regions of area studies.

Collectively, the ascendancy of such topics has begun to configure new fields of inquiry, variously termed international, world, global, or inter-area history. As the editors note in introducing this collection of essays, historians have joined in "the hunt for large transnational configurations that a focus on the local or national scale had left invisible."[3] Yet as they also rightly point out, the new visions of planetarity that compete for attention and resources across the humanities have yet to come fully into focus in this field. Part of the reason for this lack of attention may be that, in fundamental ways, transregional histories trouble the foundational categories of the discipline. Areas and states have long constituted not only the intellectual apparatus through which we think about the world, but also the units in which we organize our curriculum and train our students. Investigating far-flung connections is thus a daunting project, both professionally and conceptually, and has prompted a searching conversation about the origins, uses, and limits of received geographies.[4]

If participating in that conversation has taught me anything, it is that ours is not the first generation to confront a bewildering new world with an outmoded map. As historians today set about bending, bridging, and otherwise improvising on inherited categories to accommodate new findings and new questions, we might do well to look to an earlier moment of cartographic improvisation, when another group of thinkers was forced to bend and stretch their inherited meta-geographical framework to accommodate new findings and new questions. The precedent that I have in mind is the mapping of the world's oceans in the early modern era. Starting in the late fifteenth century, as every school-child learns, European navigators discovered continents that had been previously uncharted. But they also made simultaneous discoveries of vast sea-spaces. The process of mapping water-bodies may not have drawn as much attention as the assimilation of new landmasses into the medieval continental scheme. But conceptually, the challenge of maritime cartography was more complex—for reasons that go to the heart of our current predicament.

Like the global connections that draw our attention today, the ocean is a crossroads, a site of interaction—a space of passage, rather than a place to settle and control. By its nature, sea-space has to be shared. This in turn makes its geographical identity hard to fix; the usual rules of geopolitical nomenclature—naming by claiming—do not readily apply. Moreover, ocean-space has few clear boundaries. Winds and currents might organize the earth's waters into various subsystems, but all of them are connected, and fixing their limits in any durable, objective way has proved impossible. As a result, oceans have posed a conceptual challenge very similar to that of transnational history: neither one can be carved up definitively into discrete, bounded domains. Atlas makers since the early modern period have thus faced a conundrum similar to our own: how does one go about mapping a global commons? By what principles might areas be delimited in an inter-connected, interstitial, inter-area domain?

The answers to those questions have been a long time coming. As Martin Lewis has documented, European maritime geography effectively remained in flux for almost half a millennium. Between 1450 and 1950, western cartographers experimented with four fundamentally different models for mapping ocean space: national seas, maritime arcs, bounded basins, and a single global ocean.[5] It is my contention that each of these four ocean schemes constitutes a useful metaphor for a specific paradigm in the emerging field of inter-area history. To the extent that scholars of transnational phenomena can be thought of as explorers in a similarly borderless, interstitial domain, revisiting these early oceanic geographies might help us to see broader patterns in the way that new scholarship is mapping inter-area history. The remainder of this essay fleshes out these four paradigms, drawing on an earlier cartography of interactive sea-space to shed light on the emerging geographies of connective history.

National Seas

The first way that European cartographers attempted to apprehend ocean-space was by carving it up into national seas. In this early model, maritime territory was essentially appropriated as an extension of national territory; coastal waters were simply named after the states that abutted them. Thus maps of the North Atlantic might show a "British Ocean" and a "Scottish Ocean;" the Western Pacific was typically labeled a "Chinese Sea"; and the waters off the coast of South America were routinely segmented into a "Sea of Peru," a "Sea of Chile," a "Sea of Brazil," and so on. Not surprisingly, enterprising map makers in western Europe tended to extend European national claims conspicuously farther than the rest. A map from 1553 by Pierre Desceliers, for instance, represents the North Atlantic as a striking succession of horizontal bands, projecting a "Sea of France," a "Sea of Spain," and a "Sea of the Antilles" thousands of miles into open waters.[6]

This kind of cartography serves as a useful metaphor for the discipline's most venerable inter-area fields: *diplomatic* and *imperial history*. Operating in the same way as the toponyms on Desceliers's map, labels like "Spanish Em-

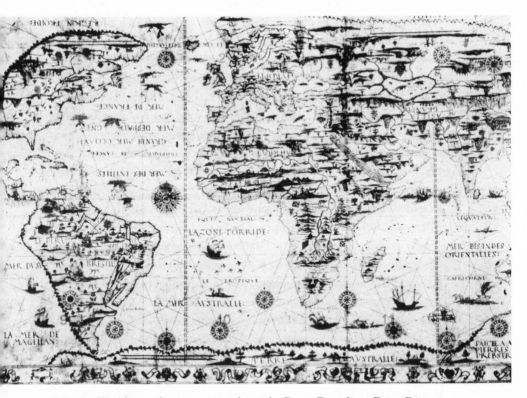

Figure 1. World map showing national seas, by Pierre Desceliers. From *Die Weltkarte des Pierre Desceliers von 1553*, reproduction published in 1924 by the Vienna Geographical Society. From the American Geographical Society Library, University of Wisconsin, Milwaukee Libraries.

pire" or "American diplomacy" effectively extend a national claim over a big swath of transnational space. The resilience of this kind of categorization can be seen not only in higher education but also in the publishing industry that supports it. Consider the organization of a recent catalogue from Penguin Books. According to Penguin, the spice wars in the Indian Ocean—featured in Giles Milton's recent paperback, *Nathaniel's Nutmeg*—constitute an episode in British history. Likewise, a reprint of *The Voyages of Captain Cook* is also identified as a book about Britain, rather than, say, as a work of Pacific studies (a category that Penguin does not yet recognize) or "world history" (a category that appears to include only developments in Asia and Africa). These cases reveal a common paradigm, one where transnational entanglements are framed in national terms.

A third approach that falls under this rubric—and one that has, to some extent, grown out of diplomatic and imperial histories—is *international* history, an area of the discipline that has taken off since the end of the Cold War. Although the field is a broad one, and loosely defined, international history fundamentally centers on the study of international institutions (from the Olympics to NGOs), the evolution of the interstate system (from Westphalia to the United Nations), and the role of transnational movements (such as the struggle for human rights or native land claims) in international politics. While its objects of inquiry have a potentially global and transhistorical reach, in practice the subfield's temporal focus is the twentieth century, and its spatial center of gravity lies clearly in the Atlantic world.[7]

This model obviously has its limits, and many historians in the past few years have made a powerful case for the need to go beyond the nation-state framework that dominates imperial, diplomatic, and international historiographies alike. Yet not only do states remain important actors on the world stage, but the habit of identifying great swaths of world history as de facto "national seas" has its uses. If nothing else, this habit can serve to alert national historians to transnational concerns. Such is the case in British history, where the late twentieth century gave rise to a whole new body of scholarship, focusing less on the British empire than on imperial Britain. Bringing imperial history back home, as it were, this scholarship documents in case after case how developments in the metropole were profoundly shaped by the needs, the resources, and the lessons of the colonization project.[8]

Similar stirrings are afoot in East Asian history. In new work on China, Korea, and Japan, diplomatic and imperial relations are being recast, not as peripheral concerns suitable for separate specialties, but as central concerns and crucial preconditions for the assertion of state legitimacy.[9] The same is true for the pre-modern era. Where comparative sociologists argued in the 1980s for "bringing the state back in,"[10] Tokugawa and Qing historians in the same years began bringing the world back in to the history of the nation-state.[11] To be sure, many textbooks still reflect an older perspective (describing the Tokugawa period as "an era of seclusion," for instance, and segregating discussions of empire from chapters on domestic development). But a new emphasis on the interconnectedness of East Asia has already begun to reshape the materials through which historians teach about this region.[12]

Ocean Arcs

Just as diplomatic and imperial paradigms are not the only way to approach inter-area studies, however, so national seas are not the only way to conceptualize sea-space. During the European Enlightenment, French cartographers developed a new model, embedding national seas in long ribbons of water that might wrap around or between whole continents. The result was a two-tier configuration, incorporating local seas into longer *ocean arcs*. (A 1719 map by Nicolas Sanson shows this new principle at work. See figure 2.)

Like his predecessors, Sanson identified a dozen national seas, bordering the coastlines of every continent. But farther from shore he demarcated a single "Occidental Ocean," curving from northern Europe around the horn of Africa; its counterpart, the "Indian or Oriental Ocean," was shown as flowing from the Bay of Bengal to the Banda Sea. Between these two, he identified a "Meridional or Ethiopian Ocean" that wrapped around the entire southern half of Africa. Similar ribbon-like arcs (some with the same names) can be seen on a 1696 map by Jacques-Dominique Cassini (see figure 3).

Cassini also added a dramatic, sinuous "Sea of the North," extending from the Caribbean Sea to the North Pole and beyond, linking up with the Pacific in the vicinity of Kamchatka.

While it is not entirely clear how these ocean arcs were derived, it appears that they were meant to mark pathways of interaction. Both Cassini's and Sanson's "oceans" roughly denote trading circuits in the age of sail. Their Indian or Oriental Ocean, for instance, corresponds to the old segmentary trading system that extended from the Swahili coast to the South China Sea. Likewise, their Occidental arc approximates the first leg of the triangular trade in the North Atlantic, which was already well established when their maps were published at the turn of the eighteenth century. Finally, their Meridional or Ethiopian Ocean denotes the hazardous passage around the Cape of Storms, where European ships braved the Agulles Current to forge a direct link between the Indian Ocean and the Atlantic world.[13] Cassini's "Sea of the North" is a more fanciful projection, but the intended implication may be that this stretch of sea, too, marks a potential pathway of interaction (the elusive northwest passage that the French, in particular, were so eager to find).

For whatever reason, ocean arcs had a relatively brief life on European maps, and their very existence is mostly forgotten. Yet their contours remain

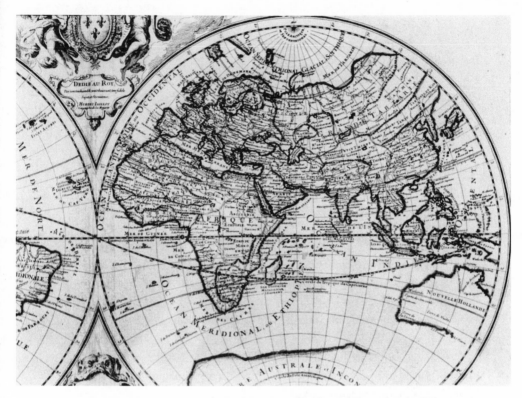

Figure 2. World map showing ocean arcs, by Nicolas Sanson. From Sanson's "Mappe-monde géohydrographie, ou description générale du globe terrestre et aquatique, en deux plans-hémisphèriques" (Paris: Hubert Iaillot, 1719). From the American Geographical Society Library, University of Wisconsin, Milwaukee Libraries.

provocative, inviting us to think about pathways of connection as demarcating meaningful "areas" within the wider expanse of the sea. That sensibility, I would argue, has a clear counterpart in inter-area history today: the study of *trans-local networks*.[14] Like Cassini, the network historian starts from the geography of interaction, framing an area on the basis of historical human linkages. Such an approach can illuminate an enormous variety of associations: from feminist sisterhoods to Sufi brotherhoods, from governmental bodies like the East India Company to nongovernmental bodies like the Red Cross.[15] But of all the transnational networks on the planet, the one with the greatest grip on our profession's imagination at the moment is undoubtedly the diaspora.

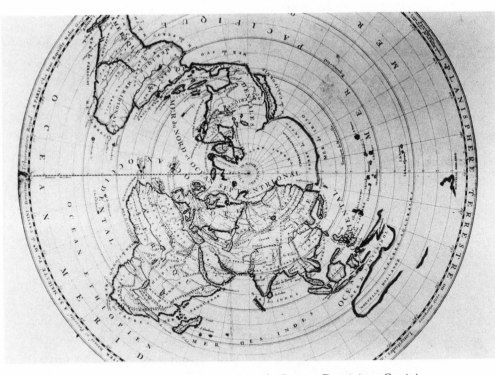

Figure 3. Polar projection showing ocean arcs, by Jacques-Dominique Cassini. Detail from Cassini world map of 1696. From the American Geographical Society Library, University of Wisconsin, Milwaukee Libraries.

Considered from a geographical standpoint, diaspora scholarship has a compelling feature: it effectively creates new domains for historical research. In methodological terms, what is novel about this approach is the way it has allowed scholars to frame fields on an ad hoc basis, crossing conventional borders in pursuit of particular patterns of interaction. The prototype here is Paul Gilroy's *Black Atlantic*. Notably, Gilroy did not propose to study one empire; nor did he tackle all of Atlantic history; nor did he posit an "African Atlantic" (a colonial inversion of the national seas paradigm). Instead, Gilroy identified a cultural archipelago as his area, stretching his frame to include all black people and their cultural forms, on whatever side of the Atlantic he might find them.

This is a fascinating way to think about areas, and one that has clearly struck a deep chord. In the last few years, diaspora scholarship has rocked the academic world. Its burgeoning scholarship, headlined in the journal *Diaspora* (but spilling over into area- and discipline-specific journals as well), propelled a five-year Ford Foundation initiative called "Crossing Borders," and has issued a profound challenge to the institutional and pedagogical segregation of ethnic and area studies.[16] Indeed, it is worth pondering why this approach has gained such a following at this historical moment. What social forces might be converging to make the diaspora paradigm so compelling to Anglo-American academics in the late twentieth century? Certainly, the reactivation of global diasporas as important economic and political forces in our time, following the liberalization of U.S. immigration laws in the 1960s and the tremendous surge of migration world-wide in subsequent years, has played a role.[17] The growing power of diasporic identities in our own classrooms has unsettled our mental maps of the past.

For all their power, however, networks and diasporas are not the only new principles for mapping world history, just as ocean arcs were not the final answer for mapping the world's seas. Over the course of the twentieth century, both national seas and ocean arcs largely gave way to a third paradigm: that of the discrete ocean basin.

Ocean Basins

By the 1950s, most atlases and geography textbooks recognized only three "true" oceans: the Atlantic, Pacific, and Indian. These labels were not new in themselves; all three toponyms had appeared on European maps since at least the 1400s. What was novel was the way they were deployed. Rather than sharing space with national seas and maritime arcs, the Atlantic, Indian, and Pacific oceans now extended right up to the shoreline. A true ocean had come to be defined as a bounded body of water, vast in scale, abutting the surrounding land masses on most sides. This remains our normative ocean prototype today.

For those who seek to reconfigure areas in history, the basin paradigm might at first seem retrograde. After all, discrete, bounded oceans are the conceptual counterpart of discrete, bounded land areas—the very grid that inter-area history is trying to transcend. But I would submit that, when extended to sea-space, this paradigm undergoes a subtle but important shift. At sea, it functions to frame interstitial spaces of passage as autonomous

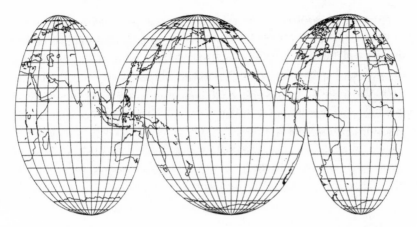

Figure 4. World map showing one global ocean, by Athelstan Spilhaus. From *Atlas of the World with Geophysical Boundaries, Showing Oceans, Continents, and Tectonic Plates in Their Entirety* (1991). Reprinted with permission of the American Philosophical Society, Philadelphia.

places with their own names. Giving such spaces an independent identity marks them as worthy of study in their own right.

In this sense, the basin model is a useful metaphor for yet a third approach to inter-area studies: the study of contact zones, frontiers, and borderlands. The essence of this approach is to focus on interstitial places: zones of particularly intensive cross-cultural exchange, whether in the form of conquest or creolization. What makes this approach distinctive is that, while shifting attention away from national cores, it retains a primary emphasis on place. Empires and diasporas, fortune-seekers and pilgrims, germs and ideas might pass through, but in this approach, the geographical frame is fixed, and the perspective is resolutely regional.[18]

A recent interdisciplinary conference on "Interactions in History," to take one example, featured three different manifestations of the contact-zone approach, which together help convey its breadth. John Mears, reflecting on borderlands as a comparative analytical category, made the important point that borderlands have been historically made into "bordered lands" by the actions of nearby states. Stephen Rapp, focusing on the Caucasus, turned the same point around, insisting that, if we want to understand places like Caucasia in their own terms, we must view them through local eyes as a "crossroads" rather than as someone else's frontier or periphery. Finally, geographers Palmira Brummett and Lydia Pulsipher showed that maritime cities serve simultaneously as nodes in a wider system of exchange and as the locus of complex, cosmopolitan communities in their own right, with distinctive and durable identities that mark them off (sometimes starkly) from the nations that surround them.[19] Together, these papers not only demonstrate the promise of crossroads and border studies, but make an important methodological point: namely, that scale of analysis is not a given that can be read off from historical processes, but a critical scholarly choice. Since inter-area interactions manifest themselves at every scale, from the micro to the macro, inquiring into the history of intercultural contact calls for innovative choices in geohistorical frameworks.[20]

The Global Ocean

The final metaphor for inter-area studies might be seen as either a refutation or a transcendence of the earlier models. This is the approach where national seas, ocean arcs, and maritime basins are subsumed into a single global ocean. Both Elisée Reclus and Carl Ritter, two of the nineteenth century's most systematic geographical thinkers, insisted that the earth's oceans were really one great, globe-girdling water-mass, dominating the southern hemisphere (just as the bulk of Eurasia and North America dominated the northern hemisphere). From this perspective, the Atlantic, Pacific, and Indian oceans are merely giant embayments of a single, interconnected sea.

The vision of a single ocean in figure 4 readily serves as a metaphor for a fourth paradigm in transnational history, the global approach. This can take a number of forms. On the one hand, global historians can trace the path of a particular mobile entity, whether a germ, an idea, or a commodity. This biography-of-things approach has given world history some of its most powerful, vivid material for classroom use, bringing home to students in a concrete way the extent to which globalization pervades their daily life.[21] But globalists can also take other tacks. Some focus on responses to mobility: attempts by situated actors (whether workers or consumers, states or local communities) to regulate, channel, or disrupt global flows. French historian Matt Matsuda, for instance, has drawn attention to the tremendous levels of energy that modern European states had to invest in a system of identification designed to keep track of the movements of their increasingly mobile citizens, workers, and outlaws.[22] Adam McKeown adopts a similar focus, documenting the enormous and unwieldy institutions designed to regulate and to facilitate Chinese immigration across the Pacific.[23] Both of

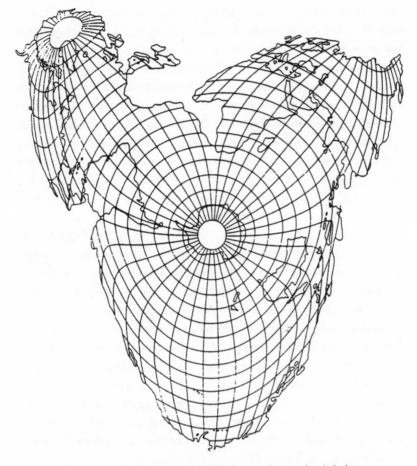

Figure 5. World map highlighting individual ocean basins, by Athelstan Spilhaus. From *Atlas of the World with Geophysical Boundaries, Showing Oceans, Continents, and Tectonic Plates in Their Entirety* (1991). Reprinted with permission of the American Philosophical Society, Philadelphia.

these recent works effectively answer Lauren Benton's call for a new "institutional world history."[24]

Nor does this exhaust the possibilities of the global paradigm. A third way to do global history is to identify a moment in time and take a truly catholic interest in everything that happened in the world during that moment. The temporal slice might be as wide as a century, or as narrow as a single year.[25] While a narrow slice may be the only manageable one to tackle in scholarly writing, more expansive units of time can clearly be productive frameworks within which to organize courses, conferences, and scholarly journals.[26] And for those who desire a truly panoptical view across eras as well as areas, there is yet another way to do global history: namely, to analyze the shifting kinds, degrees, and registers of globalization over time.[27]

This brief inventory suggests at least four ways to do global history: tracking specific flows, analyzing responses to flows, taking a slice of time, and narrating successive modalities of globalization. Admittedly, these are disparate studies to group under one paradigm. But what unites them is their truly global reach. To the extent that historians working in this vein are analyzing processes rather than places, and dealing with truly globe-spanning regimes, they effectively take us beyond inter-area to "pan-area" history.

In short, just as cartographers after 1492 conceptualized sea-space from four very different perspectives, so historians are approaching inter-area connections in four corresponding ways: as extensions of national history, through transnational networks, by focusing on contact-zones, and by analyzing global flows or processes. Each of these approaches generates a different meta-geography for inter-area history, so that in a sense we have four competing models for organizing this emerging subfield. But I would argue that there is no need to privilege one of these approaches over another. All four models can and should be retained and deployed simultaneously for different sorts of projects. To go back to the ocean metaphor, national seas are useful frameworks of analysis for some purposes; grouping them into ocean arcs or basins will reveal other sorts of processes and dynamics; and these in turn need to be conceptually combined for still other analytical purposes into a single global framework.

Bringing the World to Students

The foregoing discussion has highlighted developments in historical research, citing recent articles and monographs that circulate primarily among professional academics. This begs the question, how is the new inter-area perspective being incorporated in curricular materials? How are historians bringing trans-local perspectives into the university classroom?

One answer is to incorporate inter-area perspectives into the national surveys that constitute most historians' bread-and-butter courses. This is being done in a wide variety of ways across the discipline, often through subtle but powerful shifts in the nature of textbooks and assigned readings.[28] A bolder option, being explored on many campuses, is to develop new courses that tackle a wider canvas: diasporic spheres, ocean basins, or world history as a whole. Spurred by the creation of an Advanced Placement test for world history in American high schools, the past decade has seen a burgeoning of such courses across the United States—and a parallel profusion of textbooks and teaching aids.[29]

One hallmark of this new literature is a new historical atlas, published in London by Dorling Kindersley as the *Atlas of World History*.[30] The atlas's general editor, Jeremy Black, has previously published sharp critiques of the ethnocentric world views represented in national atlases.[31] That background has served him well here, judging from the remarkably even-handed way in which the Dorling Kindersley *Atlas* represents the globe. Every regional section, for instance, follows the same sequence, beginning with a two-page spread on "Exploration and Mapping." This reveals exploration to have been a truly global project, placing the familiar charts of European discovery alongside equally detailed treatment of non-European voyages, and showing a tantalizing sample of pre-modern maps from every world region. More generally, the atlas is organized around themes that correspond closely to the various paradigms of inter-area history discussed above. Prominently featured are transnational flows (whether of peoples, languages, religions, or biota), commercial and social networks (including criminal syndicates), and transoceanic diaspora (including a variety of slave migration streams).

Taken together, the maps in the atlas drive home a major lesson of the new trans-local history: that while locations on the globe may endure, the human configurations that we call places effectively come and go. If thriving centers can be turned into backwaters under a new regime, peripheries too are subject to inversion; and a cultural "middle ground" of the kind identified by Richard White is highly vulnerable to chance and change.[32] These examples bear out geographer Doreen Massey's point that the localities we inhabit are temporally as well as spatially delimited; all places, at whatever scale, are temporary "envelopes of space-time."[33] By my reading, this message increasingly underlies college-level history pedagogy across the United States, in virtually every subfield of the discipline.

Inevitably, however, the turn to inter-area history raises challenges for historical practice. To paraphrase Jeffrey Wasserstrom's recent manifesto in *Perspectives Online*, historians may increasingly want to "read globally," but we still need to "write locally."[34] One question this raises is, how do we train the next generation? What configuration of fields best prepares an apprentice historian for pursuing archivally grounded yet globally minded research? A second question has to do with incorporating indigenous voices into our work. Inasmuch as "one person's periphery is another person's homeland," part of the project of inter-area studies must be a critical analysis of location from many different perspectives. After all, "world regions" are also "regional worlds": places from which local people articulate their own world views. In other words, "areas" are not just objects but also active participants in knowledge production. Taking this insight seriously will entail changing the way we work; in particular, it points toward collaborative research with scholars in the areas we study. But this in turn raises logistical questions: how can such collaborative work be supported? What are its difficulties? And, if it is indeed worthwhile, how can we get it recognized by tenure and promotion committees?

A final challenge is that of making world history truly inclusive. By dint of their training and professional pressures, practitioners of U.S. and European history tend to focus their lenses more narrowly than do historians of Asia, Africa, and Latin America. Perhaps as a result, Americanists and Europeanists tend to be underrepresented in conversations about global history. Yet historians who operate at a micro-scale are everywhere revealing local evidence of hybridity and multiculturalism—the outcomes and engines of the very global interactions charted in works like the Dorling Kindersley *Atlas*. Surely, historians working near home and those studying distant lands are both viewing similar processes, just at a different scale of resolution; we may be using different ends of the telescope, but we are all looking at the same interactive world. Both perspectives are needed, and specialists from all areas must be in on the conversation, if the field is to move forward. Otherwise, the "world" of world history may end up rather like the world of world music: a truncated category produced by the marketing department, rather than an inclusive intellectual domain.

Notes

1. Quote from the George Herbert poem, "In praise of dappled things."
2. For example, Stern, "Feudalism, Capitalism, and the World-System in the Perspective of Latin America and the Caribbean."
3. Palumbo-Liu, Robbins, and Tanoukhi, "The Most Important Thing Happening," this book, 3–4.
4. Lewis and Wigen, *The Myth of Continents*.

5. Lewis, "Dividing the Ocean Sea."

6. For reproductions of these and other maps discussed in this essay, see Lewis, "Dividing the Ocean Sea."

7. These observations are based on an analysis of recent issues of *The International History Review*, published by Simon Fraser University since 1979. Representative works include Borstelmann, *Apartheid's Reluctant Uncle*; Benton, *Law and Colonial Cultures*; Gaddis, *The Cold War*.

8. For examples, see parts I and II of Cooper and Stoler, eds., *Tensions of Empire*.

9. For a review of this literature, see Wigen, "Culture, Power, and Place." See also Katzenstein and Shiraishi, eds., *Network Power*, and Schmidt, "Colonialism and the 'Korea Problem' in the Historiography of Modern Japan."

10. Evans, Rueschemeyer, and Skocpol, eds., *Bringing the State Back In*.

11. See Wigen, "Japanese Perspectives on the Time/Space of Early Modernity."

12. Two excellent works that synthesize the new perspectives include Hudson, *Ruins of Identity*, and Morris-Suzuki, *Reinventing Japan*.

13. For information on the difficulties of navigating in this region (and much else on oceans and seafarers in the early modern period), see the "Latitude" website created by Patricia Seed of Rice University: http://www.ruf.rice.edu/~feegi.

14. As Dirlik argues, "trans-local" is a better term than transnational to describe these spaces, being both more grounded and more flexible. Adopting a trans-local perspective also signals an important analytical move, inasmuch as "it carries us from one conceptual realm—that of nations and civilizations—to another—that of places" ("Performing the World," 397).

15. Papers on these and other network topics were presented at an "Interactions" conference, 1–3 February 2001, at the Library of Congress. Select contributions were published in Bentley, Bridenthal, and Yang, eds., *Interactions*. The complete program, with abstracts, is available on the Web at www.theaha.org/grs/phase2/phase2.html.

16. For how these trends have affected Asian-American studies, see *positions: east asia cultures critique* 7, no. 3, (winter 1999), a special issue on "Asian Transnationalities." On related developments in African-American studies, see Shea, "A Blacker Shade of Yale."

17. Luibheid, "The 1965 Immigration and Nationality Act." More broadly, see Appadurai, *Modernity at Large*, and Anderson, "Exodus."

18. An important subfield where this perspective has been worked out is the new Western history of the United States. See Limerick, *The Legacy of Conquest*. Equally influential is White's *The Middle Ground*. The Chinese historian Peter Perdue sees the closing of the North American frontier as but one act in a ubiquitous early-modern process, whereby centralizing states throughout the northern hemisphere gobbled up the territory of nomadic pastoralists, permanently eliminating "the strongest alternative to settled agrarian society since the second millennium BCE" (*China Marches West*, 10–11).

19. Rapp, "Chronology, Crossroads, and Commonwealths: World-Regional Schemes and the Lessons of Caucasia."

20. There is now a considerable body of historical work on borderlands where these and other issues are examined at length. A seminal work for the new bottom-up (or margin-in) perspective is Sahlins, *Boundaries*. For a conceptual overview, see Donnan and Wilson, *Borders*; for a systematic exploration of border models and their applicability to Japan, see Batten, *To The Ends of Japan*.

21. See, for instance, Crosby, *Ecological Imperialism*; Appadurai, ed., *The Social Life of Things*; and Clunas, "Modernity Global and Local."

22. Matsuda, "Doctor, Judge, Vagabond." A revised version is reprinted, with illustrations, as chapter 6 of Matsuda's later book, *The Memory of the Modern* (Oxford: Oxford University Press, 1996).

23. McKeown, *Chinese Migrant Networks and Cultural Change*.

24. Benton, "From the World-Systems Perspective to Institutional World History." See also Geyer and Bright, "World History in a Global Age."

25. For a lively example of the latter, see Wills, *1688*.

26. On the latter point, see the journals *Eighteenth Century Studies* and *Early Modern History*, both of which strive for global representation within a temporal frame.

27. This is the approach taken by C. A. Bayly in "From Archaic Globalization to International Networks, circa 1600–2000."

28. For example, Thomas Bender—editor of an important collection entitled *Rethinking American History in a Global Age*—has since written a textbook that aims to deprovincialize U.S. history. See Bender, *A Nation Among Nations*.

29. An excellent gateway to these resources is the world history webpage maintained by George Mason University's Center for History and New Media, at http://chnm.gmu.edu/worldhistorysources/index.html. Another clearinghouse is H-World, http://www.h-net.msu.edu/~world.

30. Black, ed., *Atlas of World History*.

31. Black, *Maps and History*.

32. White, *The Middle Ground*.

33. Massey, "Places and Their Pasts."

34. Wasserstrom, in *Perspectives Online*, January 2001, on the Web at www.theaha.org.

What Is a Poem?

The Event of Women and the Modern Girl
as Problems in Global or World History

TANI E. BARLOW

The prominent Asia historians Mark Elvin, Andre Gunder-Frank, Philip Huang, Victor Lieberman, Ken Pomeranz, and Bin Wang have repeatedly criticized and rewritten Wallersteinian world-systems theory through the prism of regional history. In a staged debate intended to clarify a related dispute, *The Journal of Asian Studies* pitted a neo-Marxist China historian against a leading proponent of the regionalist idea that a "great divide" between Chinese and European advanced sectors had opened after 1800, and then only on the basis of historically contingent factors. Philip Huang accused regionalist historians of substituting environmental factors for long-term processes of historical relations of production, Malthusian pressures, and stagnant labor involution.[1] Pomeranz, a leading regionalist, argued that China's suddenly weakened position vis-à-vis England in the nineteenth century was due to England's accelerated coal industry and its colonial control of North America, and not to endogamous, Chinese rural proletarianization, core-periphery relations, or involuted strategies of capital accumulation.[2] So, on the question of underlying causes of England's industrial capitalist world dominance and China's catastrophic nineteenth and twentieth centuries, one side privileged slow-developing, substructural features of a national economy within a system of unequal global capitalist exchange, while the other attributed England's relative advantage to a sudden, late-emerging, contingent take-off in an asystematic surge in a cultural, political continuum called "Eurasia."

Pomeranz made regular reference to the space of Eurasia during the debate, and the significance of this line of regionalist opinion will help me illustrate why the "event of women" provokes such a useful crisis in thinking about global history. Regionalist Asia historians, including Pomeranz, hold that the political economies of pre-modern Europe and China were basically similar. Not only did they form two ends of a continuous land mass, in fact, their contiguities gave them an elemental similitude in their very substance. This postulated equivalence meant that historical Eurasia was isomorphic, not just with a continental land mass as such, but with an entire, continental political economy; so Africa, the Americas, and Australia notwithstanding, Eurasia—*the West in Asia, not the West as such*—stood as the fulcrum of the modern world. Whether the precise subset of Asia implied is Central Asia, China, or Southeast Asia, regionalists like Pomeranz, implicitly and at times explicitly, rest their case on this framing device. Difference is subordinated to similitude and what in a world-systems approach were two unequal substances becomes, in the work of Eurasia regionalists, a single substance laid out in a continuum. One now finds Eurasia-focused studies ritually scolding Wallerstein on the ground that world-systems theory peripheralizes Asia conceptually, and that the resulting Eurocentrism or "European exceptionalism" of the theory invents spurious causes for China's underdevelopment, such as its static imperial political despotism, its alleged ethnic homogeneity, and supposed social uniformity.[3]

Victor Lieberman, for instance, sharply rebukes Wallerstein's work on world-systems and has explored exhaustively what is at stake for regionalists like himself who are striving to center attention on Eurasia.[4] Citing "antiformalist trends in European historiography" (69) he argues, first, that even *avant-garde* Europeanists now reject the idea that Europe took off from a better rationalized economy or superior cultural heritage; second, that Wallerstein naturalizes European economic and social dynamism (a maneuver Japan historians also undertook during the Japan-dominated 1980s); and most centrally, because historical contingency will prevail over Wallersteinian systems analysis, Eurasia historians are best positioned to reveal an empirical, historical record of alternative pathways to modernity. Lieberman's test case is Southeast Asia and its centrality in a ten-century, common framework shared by all of Eurasia, including France, Russia, Japan, China at crucial moments, and the Indian subcontinent. Drawing on "a more generous, less adversarial calculus of Eurasian difference" (73) than Euroexceptionalist or core-periphery systems, he asks the question why, despite geographic and other internal differences, Eurasian-wide similarities are so visible in the record.

Lieberman stresses "global synchronicity" (77), all right. But he pos-

tulates in addition to capital (i.e., "goods and bullion"), two equally important, long-distance exchange factors: ecological (technology, diseases,
crops) regimes and cultural, religious, political, and administrative ideas.
He then sets out to illustrate why these similarly weighted causal factors
oscillated in importance, contingently, during the thousand years under consideration. His "Eurasian thesis" consists of seven ensuing claims. One, Eurasia is divided geographically into exposed heartlands and protected rimlands, including parts of Southeast Asia, where original or "charter states"
formed in the era of c. 900–1300. Two, territorial consolidation under characteristically Eurasian administrative regimes followed on the disintegration
of charter states. Three, remaining subregions obeyed common patterns of
irregular political centralization and collapse, contributing to an evolutionary accumulation of Eurasian cultural forms. Four, the paradoxical era of
the sixteenth through the nineteenth centuries saw pan-Eurasian cultural
integration lead to "bounded cultural identities," or differentially marked,
proto-nations. Five, 1450–1800 marks a Eurasia-wide "early modern period."
Six, a stasis of local elites and their populations (states and societies) stabi-
lized Eurasia in this era. Seven, Europe's surge is the consequence of a process integral to the *Asian* end of Eurasia, not to Europe's singularity. That is,
while the protected rimlands of Eurasia remained intact, China, Southwest
Asia, the Indian subcontinent and island Asia all simultaneously fell prey
to "conquest elites" whom Lieberman names as "Turkic peoples, Afghans,
Persians, Manchu, Dutch, or Iberians," who interrupted regional synchronic
relations of elites and masses and imposed violent, colonial state formations
(73–84; 457–60). This event gave Europe the contingent opening to industrial revolution.[5]

In Lieberman's hands, the idea of an isomorphic, categorical Eurasia
achieves full expression. Because the balance of my remarks focus on how
the singular universal of women was launched in a contested part of Asia,
I want to rehearse the reasons why regionalism is not a strategy I can pursue, since it cannot provide a true alternative to world-systems theories.
And why, from my perspective, the regionalists have tended to reiterate
core problems in world-systems historiography that a history of the event
of women might help to illuminate.

The core predicament of the regionalist position is that it displaces a
critique of world-systems *theory* onto an *evidentiary* debate. In this regard,
Lieberman's study mobilizes empirical evidence to highlight endogenous,
localized, singular forms of human political agency. Concerned to avoid

a naive assertion that the category Eurasia appears "in the data," Lieberman invokes Ernesto Laclau and Chantal Mouffe's *Hegemony and Socialist
Strategy* to support his generalized evidentiary argument.[6] The book's value
to Lieberman appears to lie in its assertion of contingency and identity in
theoretical terms. On that basis he puts forward local historical agents who
creatively work their part of the larger Eurasian heritage. These pre-colonial
elites articulated "a political *type of relation, a form*, if one so wishes, of politics," in the millennial project of founding Southeast Asian charter states,
administrative states, early modern states, and so on at both ends of the continuous space.[7] Lieberman's bona fide local political agents, saturated with
regional knowledge, are thus decisively not automatons in a general world
system. It is not clear that this strategy avoids the trap, however. Laclau
and Mouffe are actually political philosophers who postulate hegemony as a
strategic project undertaken from the position of the political actor working toward a preferred outcome. Future anteriority and a high degree of
self-consciousness are built into the political agent's vision, and, in any case,
indeterminacy in political theory may not be the same thing as interpreting
ambiguous historical evidence (8–19).

A related issue is the theoretical ambiguity of "Eurasia itself as a unified, interactive zone" (22). There actually can be no ignoring the system
quality of what is not just localized history here but, in fact, Lieberman's
general argument about pre-capitalist politics and regional political formations. Worrying aloud on the problem of whether his fascination with Eurasian parallels has amounted to anything more than a neo-modernization
project, Lieberman declares that his is in fact a "Darwinian project" (82). The
"larger genus" is Eurasia and the "early modern political/cultural animals"
all belong to it; as a Darwinian historian his project then is to anatomize
countries that have the "strongest evolutionary affinities." Which is to say
that the systemic qualities obvious in Lieberman's work come out of evolutionary biology, where the objective analytically is "to isolate variables responsible" for diverse outcomes; this is a highly theoreticized project about
genetic selection (82–83). I do not care to dispute Lieberman's half-facetious
claim. I raise it only to draw attention to the difficult task confronting self-
styled regionalist historians. Critique of world-systems through the prism
of region—by redrawing the globe on the basis of topography, climate, circulation of disease vectors, coal, lumber, styles of womanhood, and so on—
draws our attention to the need to recognize how events of global impact
have been launched from the complex societies of Asia's regions, subregions,

its circuits of trade, and its political cultures. But what regionalists have risked is to invert Wallerstein's core-periphery system and rearticulate its systematicity in culturalist, developmental, and social evolutionary terms.

The Conditions of Context-Dependency and Historicity as Such

But what about an event in history that is both not regional, since it is a universal, and yet launched in a region, Asia, that has not generally been considered an origin point in the story of globalization or capitalism? I am going to suggest that women's emergence as categorical subject on the horizon of history provides such a useful event. Against the background of problems that the critique of world-systems from a regional perspective gives us, I raise several concerns, beginning from the question that Laclau has voiced best: "What are the conditions of context-dependency and historicity as such. . . . [and] how has an object to be constituted in order to be truly historical?"[8] Taking up, secondly, Badiou's question, "what is a poem?," shifts my discussion from historicity per se to the analytic problem of the event. At issue is the case history of the "modern girl" phenomenon, which erupted globally in the interwar years, 1919–41. Part of the larger global event of women, modern girl history, like any apprehension of truth, has its generic truth procedures and evental qualities. The stake for me is that the modern girl episode and its historical event of woman exceeds the surplus of local (or "regional," in language of the new regional histories) signification that the term "women" calls up. Claims to feminine specificity cannot hinge on regional topographies, and yet, the singular universal event of the subject women is, in fact, what Ernesto Laclau calls a concrete abstract or worldwide event and Badiou, an "event." In the modernist visual order and the capitalist commodity culture that it lavishly illustrated, the event of "woman" is expressed as an anatomical, physiological, aesthetic, narcissistic, juridical event, as well as an element in governmentality.

Both singular and multiple, this event of women fits Badiou's description of a universal singular.[9] The immediate stake, for me, then is to suggest how this integral element of the global phenomenon of modernity, the event of women, was constructed precisely with world-scale ambitions that at the same time had to acknowledge (if not submit to) the protocols of the "global" to even be articulated. Badiou's philosophic framework thus helps me to question further world-scale attempts that do reiterate familiar patterns—including the new Eurasia world-scale regionalisms. In a dialog with

Czeslaw Milosz over poetry, Badiou wrote, "The poem teaches us that the world does not present itself as a collection of objects. . . . The poem must arrange an oblique operation of capture" of the world and its object, for one enters into the poem "not in order to know what it means, but rather to think what happens in it."[10] Drawing from the analogy of the poem (and I will suggest below reasons why this is a useful strategy), I will ask what will prove historically not useful, what is more noticeable, what is invented in thinking a launch of "woman" from the geopolitical and cultural space of "Asia"?

Ernesto Laclau posed to Judith Butler the question, "What are the conditions of context-dependency and historicity as such. . . . [and] how has an object to be constituted in order to be truly historical?" during their debate over the philosophic question of contingency and universality. In another manuscript I have examined Laclau's point that, while Butler can ground her philosophy in American-style sociology, she cannot arrive at history, and that this compromises her concept about genders and sexualities being universally, *historically* contingent.[11] The reason I return to Laclau's initial indictment is the efficient way it deals with the question of what a so-called context of analysis is and thus how it might compromise understanding of subjects like the global modern girl. Laclau's fundamental concern is that Butler cannot commit to any universalism at all, "any rule whose tentative validity extends beyond a certain cultural context" (285). Historicity actually has nothing to do with cultural contexts, Laclau argues. His remark is useful in the context of world-scale analysis seen through the problematic of the event of women. This is because, as I suggested in the analysis of the regionalists, the analyst finds it necessary to return time and again in order to redefine the context around its particularities. And it is a telling critique of Butler's position, since for her there is no way to address the subject except through the question of "context" of a space (region) or sexual community.

But even if context and historicity were the same substance, eventually Butler would have to admit that no theory and no theoretician can "operate without some categories wider than those which apply to a particular context." Staying with the debate between philosophers for a moment longer, the problem is that when she confounds "history" with "context" and attempts to "specify contexts" historically, Butler ends up in a logical error. She can only specify difference, that is, context "through a metacontextual discourse which would have to have transcendental aprioristic validity." Her claim to historicity would be necessarily belied in the last instance. Now Laclau himself promotes the need to historicize, and includes himself within the category of philosophical historicists. His criticism of Slavoj Žižek is the inverse of his critique of Butler; for example, Žižek tarries a little too long with the negative and too uncritically embraces the ancient cliché that the Real interminably upsets the apple cart of the Symbolic. But Laclau's point is significant. "Either," he argues, "we historicize the place of enunciation—which says nothing about the degree of 'universality' attributed to the statements—or we legislate about that degree," which he adds, "can be done only by transcendentalizing the position of enunciation" (285–86).[12]

Historicity is about variability. But when a limit is placed on variation (to specify, for instance, regional variables that characterize Eurasia and also make it not-Africa *as a region*), we automatically face an "ontic" question, a question of ontology. The problem is that history must be true no matter what locale or context it is written from; so to invoke "context" in relation to history is to enter the double bind that Laclau shows inhabiting Butler's philosophic assertions. If I say that Eurasia is a space carved out of a universally recognizable set of variables that can be positively counted or affirmatively specified, then I have established a positive limit that potentially undermines my claim to legible history. While I may argue that such a strategy provides "different perspectives" on a single problem or truth, I have in fact risked making knowledge contextual, illegible, and inapplicable outside its place of origin. If, on the other hand, and this is what Laclau accuses Butler of doing, we define variability as always necessarily partial and always in flux, we get a condition that is useful but not historical. Its usefulness is that it posits a theory of social change or flux, which is great for strategic social theories of political justice, but is not, in fact, context dependent in a historical sense. A universal is historically qualified or conditioned "only at that price can one assert the nonhistoricity of the structural limit" (184). Because for Laclau the project is to scrutinize the game in play in order to capitalize on signifiers that have "no necessary attachment to any precise content, signifiers which simply name the positive reverse of an experience of historical limitation: 'justice,' as against a feeling of widespread unfairness," for instance, the claim to historicity is not the foremost problem for him (185).

What Laclau is objecting to in Butler's position is, in part, the systematicity residing in her notion of history and the way that she presumes that there will be a reconciliation between the historical and the abstract. He accuses her of implicit Hegelian thinking for this reason. And he is pleased in their debate when he can in fact find purchase for his own thinking in her notion of "cultural translation," because, in his view, it means that she draws back from discarding abstraction in the name of a historical specificity. In her translation paradigm she has embarked on a project that Laclau understands, in his own language, to be congruent with his concept of the concrete abstract, and his discussions of the logic of equivalence and hegemonic universality. But here is where questions of historicity are exhausted. In this valuable debate, two political philosophers take questions of historicity to an endpoint. It becomes clear in their exchange there is nowhere else to turn. A political project of hegemony which intends to think again about critical alternatives to a current, global, political crisis cannot be tortured into a theory of history that provides a way out of world-systems theory's European fixation or the aporia that open up in Eurasia centered projects.

Poetics of the Modern Girl

As stated previously, Badiou's question, "what is a poem?," shifts my discussion from historicity per se to the question and status of the event.[13] Immediately at issue is the case history of the "modern girl" phenomenon, which erupted globally in the inter-war years, 1919–41.[14] After surveying the way this modern girl figure was represented, the Modern Girl Around the World research project concluded that each rendering "combined and reconfigured aesthetic elements drawn from disparate national, colonial and racial regimes to create a 'cosmopolitan' look. These characteristics," it seemed to follow, "make the modern girl a valuable heuristic category that enables us to analyze how global processes intersected with and were reconfigured by gendered and racialized global hierarchies and political and economic inequalities in specific locales" (246). The "structures of common difference" that the Africanist Richard Wilk had alluded to in his work on beauty contests became in this collaborative project a significant constituent element of what the agenda termed "gendered modernity," which the group sought to situate in ongoing debates over how to characterize modernity, including my own line of argument regarding colonial modernity.[15] This particular emphasis materialized because the collaborative project targeted as its areas of particular concern, "how a commodified Modern Girl became recognizable, consumable and locally intelligible. . . . what the Modern Girl conveyed to contemporaries about the possibilities and dangers of modern life and how she figured in the modern political formations of nationalism, fascism and communism" (248).

The project did not seek an explicit world-scale theoretic or critique, however, since the rules of collaboration required us to take seriously knowledge production in each of the specific regional and area studies that made up the members' expertise. This decision did resolve one outstanding problem in large scale research by shifting the burden of expertise from one onto many shoulders, which means that thorough grounding in each regional archive was assured. However, the consensus that collaborative courtesy imposes cannot help but leave other problems unresolved. For instance, while in some regional specializations there has been discernable movement toward world-scale critiques, others have moved to take up a problematics of the colonial periphery, or have dealt primarily with entrenched antimonies such as "cosmopolitan National Socialism" and U.S. racial multiculturalism.

The modern-girl phenomenon is one programmatic instance of a world-scale event of woman, an event which has not been fully thought through in world systems theory and which, by its absence and again in its presence, opens a useful lacuna in the systematics of globalist theories. By "the event of women" I mean the specific historical revelation taking place across the colonial modern world during the period of imperialist and anti-imperialist political regimes, when it was declared that a newly recognized political form—women—had a name, was nameable, and thus formed a totality; and that the name "women" specified a subject equally the same and also different from men. The singularity or novelty of this event of the declaration of women has been well documented in the work of Lila Abu-Lughod, Antoinette Burton, Billie Melman, Meng Yue, Dai Jinhua, Gayatri Chakravorty Spivak, and Kumari Jayawardena, among many regional specialists and archival researchers, compilers, and historians.[16] Each scholar has in one way or another commented on the simultaneity of the discovery that no word was adequate locally to name the universal subject, that figure that tied all nations, all peoples, all political modernities together. The truth of the event of women is, finally, "diagonal relative to every communitarian subset," which is simply to say that the declaration by a Kang Yuwei or a Tan Sitong or Mary Wollstonecraft or Qiu Jin of the truth of women was not a claim to a pre-existing identity (since women came as a shock among thinkers for whom "women" was either a non-issue or a kin term) or to an exclusive category since none other than Gandhi alleged himself to be or contain within himself a woman.[17]

Having pursued the case of Chinese progressive feminist discourse over the course of the twentieth century, I have little doubt that women as discursive category and women as subject are (or, more accurately, is) a building block of Chinese colonial modernity. Philip Corrigan's and Derek Sayers's initial insight into the cultural production of English modernity in their Maoist-inspired classic, *The Great Arch*, suggested as much. My older work has proposed a similar incident but launches the event from the location of intellectuals, political operatives, and social theorists in Chinese treaty port cities. Yet even possessing a large archive of Chinese-authored writing on what I ended up calling progressive feminism, and despite having documented the obvious coeval or simultaneous launching of the feminist subject "women" as a discursive subject, I confront a substantial analytical obstacle. How is it possible to reconcile the relation of singularity (the modern emergence of a subject, women, as such) and multiplicity (that this subject in many instantiations, emerged at the same time, in similar anti-imperialists projects all over the globe)? How do we understand the ways that the concrete abstraction of women, in political theories like Chinese feminism, but also in advertising and sociological writing, is both abstractly described in internationally circulating theory and also a framework of personalized, experiential authenticity? Why do names like the "modern girl" or "new woman" present historians with a situation where the name as such, a universal, exceeds the surplus of local ("regional," the new regional histories') signification that the sociological category of women calls up? [18]

One way to address the problematic is to amass evidentiary arguments. For instance, it is feasible to illustrate what the techniques of imperialist or colonial capitalist expansion were and to link the emergence of new markets in industrially produced commodity to the figure of woman, a "commodity girl." [19] Advertising images that appeared in colonially occupied sectors of China, such as Tianjin, Shanghai, and particularly in Japanese-occupied Manchuria provide a good example of such an argument. Take for instance this undated calendar poster advertising chemical fertilizer (figure 1). In it an elegant woman wearing a velour wrap with faux fur lapel and cuffs over her high neck gown and pearls, what might be a Lalique corsage on her shoulder, stands in front of a lily pond on a rocky overhang.

A spray of quince or plum blossoms frame her beautifully made-up face and brow as she gazes steadily out at a spot just beyond the potential customer. Along the sides of the scene are legends reading "Moth eyebrows calendar poster's sulpheric ammonium (liusuanya) fertilizer (feitianmen) will

Figure 1. Undated Brunner Mond fertilizer girl calendar poster, circa 1926.

improve every kind of plant. Using this marvelous fertilizer will make the harvest plentiful and bountiful and make a sizeable profit (huoli youhou)." Around the borders appear scenes of agricultural labor farmers drawn in a neo-traditional style, shouldering their muckrakers and swabbing their brows as they hump large baskets of animal fertilizer out to spread on fields as water buffalo wait in front of wooden plows. Painted onto the wall of the wealthy rural dacha on the far shore of the pond is an advertising trademark and slogan. Over the top of the ad runs the invitation "Please use Bu'nei'men chemical fertilizer." Two plump bags of the commodity complete the scenario and their cheery trademark of the upturned thumb is repeated elsewhere in the graphic. That was circa 1926.[20]

Who this girl is, what body she has under those fine, up-to-date clothes, what region her fabulous landscape is allegedly a part of, the relation of new generic commercial arts to her body morphology: these are relatively uncomplicated questions and traditional research about place and times can address most of them. For instance, figures wearing the same Frenchified designer coat over a high Manchurian collar (figures 2 and 3) appear in *Shanhai nichinichi shimbun*, the Japanese language Shanghai newspaper *Shengjing shibao*, a Chinese language Manchurian paper published in Shenyang, Manchuria; even in the Tianjin-based *Beiyang huabao* of 1927, which kept readers up-to-date with high society dames in Beijing, Tianjin, Shenyang, Europe, and the United States.

Bu'nei'men girl bears more than a passing resemblance to allegedly Parisian fashion illustrations in Anne Rittenhouse's daily column, "Dress," in the Shanghai, American-owned, tabloid *Evening Star* (figure 4), and in illustrations for "Potpourri of Fashion's Hints," in the sedate, China-oriented, English language *Shanghai Times*. These images of the European or Japanese-inspired, Chinese new or civilized woman are historically legible in the social, political, categorical order that was colonial modern China. An inter-Asian cosmopolitan image of the fashion mannequin is an explicit illustration of a constituent part of what made colonialism a modernist project.

The question of what makes a space into a region, an "Asia," is also a question that historical research can be coerced into addressing without reference to isomorphy or symbolic political terrains such as Eurasia. Bu'nei'men is the Chinese name for Imperial Chemical Industries (ICI) Ltd., established in 1926 when John Brunner and Ludwig Mond merged their soda ash chemical production company, Brunner Mond Co., (est. 1873) with Nobel Industries, Ltd., Limited Alkali Company, Ltd., and British Dyestuffs Corpo-

Figure 2. (*right*) U. J. Soskin
furrier, *Shanghai nichinichi
shimbun*, 4 September 1932, 4.

Figure 3. (*below*) Fengxin clothier,
Shanghai nichinichi shimbun,
10 December 1932, 2.

御婦人方よ
此の機會を逸し給ふな

弊店では八月廿二日月曜から毛皮、
諸製品毛皮オーバーコートなど實
際に原價の半値で皆様に提
供致します

LEIPZIGの系本店から一九三三年型の毛皮
品が新しく到着致しました 又一九三三年型
のオーバーコートの諸品が入荷致しました

すべて毛皮品の御誂文や 直しや作りかへ
には 極上で其の唯一専門家として知られた
U. J. Soskin 氏が親しく指圖に携へるのです

さあ御來店あつて 秋の來ぬうちにお作りあ
つて 新しいもの同様になさいませ

御參觀 大いに歡迎致します

U. J. SOSKIN

THE SIBERIAN FURRIERS CO.,
ザ サイビーリアン フアーリアース 會社
御安寺路一一三七、
(同じ様な名前の店がありますから御注意下さい)
電話三二二一一

冬！、
御婦人方のオーバーの御用意は今から……
三三年の柄合が揃つて居ります

豊信洋行洋裝店
電話四、三七七四

Figure 4. Anne Rittenhouse,
"Dress," *Evening Star*,
28 September 1922, 1.

DRESS

By ANNE RITTENHOUSE

Will Our Waistlines Go Back to Normal or Will They Rise Higher and Take the Position Fashionable in the First Empire?

Paris.—"The waist line is getting back to normal," says one American in Paris.

"It doesn't seem to be stopping at normal," remarks another, "for seemingly it is rapidly mounting to the high waist line of the Directoire and Empire mode."

Some one with a talent for statistics counted seven strikingly short-waisted frocks in one day at the races. And those seven, like the biblical lost sheep, got a great deal more attention than the ninety and nine that remained in the position to which we have become accustomed.

It is really a very interesting conjecture, isn't it?

First, are we ready actually to abandon the extreme long waist?

And if you answer "yes" to that question: "Are we going to stop with the normal waist line or go up to the high waist line that France adopted at the time of the Revolution and retained for the next thirty years?"

It was the waist line of Josephine, and of Empress Maria Louise, the waist line of Madame Recamier, of Madame Le Brun, and the charming characters of Jane Austen.

It has been much railed at—this high waist line—especially by critics who lived in the generation that followed. Fashions in the whole shortwaisted period have been judged among the most outrageous that ever appealed to vain womankind.

The Directoire mode is the one that has hitherto been most spoken of as a source of possible inspiration at the present time. Paris now seems to be hankering after the more formal period of the Empire. The ankle length straight skirts, and the straight hanging overskirt or tunic, the fairly high round neck line, the silver embroidery—these things are more characteristic of the Empire than they were of the Directoire.

The frock in the sketch shows a tendency toward Empire modes rather than those of the Directoire. It is of black crepe de chine over a gray slip. The frock is embroidered in silver threads and the coat of the black crepe de chine with collar and lining of the gray.

One thing that you should remember in predicting the passing of the very low-swung waist line, is that in these essentials fashion does not change swiftly. It took thirty years for the high waist line of the Directoire-Empire period to spend itself, and that though there were railings against it almost from the start. Then it took a half century more or less to add a little bit more length to the Victorian waist line that called itself normal but was higher than the waist that prevailed in the nineties.

No, waist lines are not things that change over night. If you are one of the women who simply cannot take an interest in clothes so long as these exaggeratedly long waists prevail, don't be over-confident. One swallow does not make it summer, and seven short-waisted frocks at one race do not establish a new fashion.

This high waisted frock is of black crepe de chine embroidered in silver and worn over gray slip. The matching coat has large gray collar.

ration, Ltd., to compete with Germany's IG Farben cartel, formed a year earlier. Brunner Mond is the semiotic or transliterative element in the Chinese brand name, Bu'nei'men. Both before and after the ICI merger, colonial expansion was integral to its business strategy. Pre-merger "Brunner Mond" entered the China market in 1899, just as Nakayama Taiyodo or Club Cosmetics Company of Osaka, (founded 1903) would in 1911. Brunner Mond's unusually flexible managerial structure, and the fact that for nearly forty years it dominated the Chinese market in soda ash sales and distribution while steering clear of the comprador system, made it the envy of other corporate imperialists. The "Please Use Bu'nei'men" poster girl probably dates from the late 1920s when nationalist entrepreneur Fan Xudong forced ICI into renewed advertising campaigns. Fan put Brunner Mond on the defensive using Yongli-Jiuda Chemical Conglomerate, which he established 1914–17. Of course, to squeeze Brunner Mond, Fan had to strike deals with the Chinese state, various warlord cliques, Mitsui Corporation (for Japanese homeland markets), and ICI itself. Indeed, Yongli-Jiuda had inched toward majority 55 percent market share by 1937, thanks for the most part to its participation in Japanese imperialist expansionism.

In the political semiotics at work here, corporate imperialism and colonial modernity are the logics structuring a sense of region. The Bu'nei'men girl standing amidst commodity images in a cultivated field, wearing elegant clothes, and affecting a pose, is a signifier of "Asian" colonial modernity and one, though a highly complex instance, of many similar images. Another example of how a modern female image signifies Asian colonial modernity through ephemeral forms like the advertising calendar poster or repeating newspaper advert, is this banal ad for Utena skin products (figure 5), which routinely appeared in the Japanese-owned, Chinese language newspaper, Shenjing *Daily News*, published in Shenyang, a city known during the Japanese colonial era as Mukden.

The date on the newspaper reads, "July 30, the year Kangde [Koutoku], 5." Kangde, the Chinese pronunciation, or Koutoku, is the reign name of Manchuria's puppet emperor, former Qing dynasty, Manchu ruler Puyi; this newspaper measured political time using a faux national system based on Puyi's ascension to the puppet throne. The Utena ad interestingly underlines the ambiguities of the contemporary political calendar when it calls Utena cream or powder a high quality "national product," yet leaves indefinite which nation, Manchuria, China, or Japan is indicated by introducing its "national product" in three languages.

Figure 5. Utena Creme, *Shenjing shibao*, 30 July 1939, 6.

Similar logics are at work in a calendar poster—which I will discuss in greater detail shortly—for the Kobe based Nakayama Taiyodo Club Cosmetics Company (CCC), incorporated in 1903 (figure 6). But this poster is "Chinese," only in the sense that it is peddling products in the China market.

By the 1920s, CCC, monopolizing a third of the Japanese islands' cosmetics market had, like Brunner Mond, already begun to develop what became, with the Japanese occupation of Manchuria (1931), Tianjin and Shanghai (1938), outright colonial markets. Immediately following the success of its first product, "Club Araiko, the toilet washing powder," CCC had contracted Dongya gongse or East Asia, Co., branches in Shanghai and Hankow, to market CCC's full range of products—tooth powder, toothpaste, face powder, cosmetic soap, and makeup—under the Chinese brand name "Shuangmeiren" or Two Gorgeous Girls.

The calendar poster element of the CCC ad campaign was insignificant compared to the years' long duration of its black and white, drawn or cartoon image newspaper advertising blitz. A Japanese language, China based, paper *Manshu nippo*, targeted Japanese language readers with already established brand loyalty. The Chinese language newspaper *Shenjing shibao* mounted a persistent, varied, and sustained advertising campaigns second

Figure 6. Undated CCC cosmetic girl calendar poster.

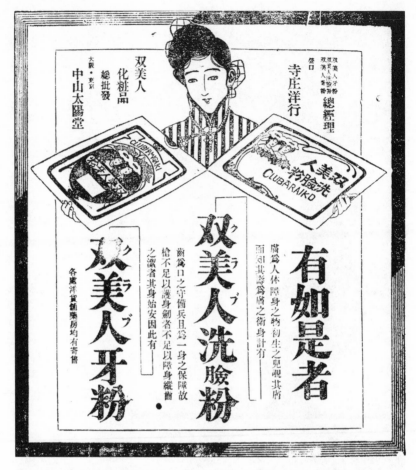

Figure 7. Club Araiko, *Shengjing shibao*, 1 February 1937, 3.

only to British American Tobacco for its innovation, duration, and variety, as in the figures appearing here targeting Japanese reading consumers.

The logics of colonial modernity and corporate capital are most prominent in the feminized sign of a Japanese-style, pan-Asian regionality (see figure 6, 171). In this Nakayama poster ad a rather Asian-looking girl with bobbed hair, wearing an Italianate, Japanese-style Europeanized dress and South Seas coral beads sits smiling like the Mona Lisa and gazing outward, holding a musical instrument in her lap. Japanese, Russian, North American, and Chinese texts draw attention to "Japanese fashion Club Cosmetics Company products (CCC)" and its famous sobijin logo of two women. The elements of her style are coherent in the colonial everyday material culture

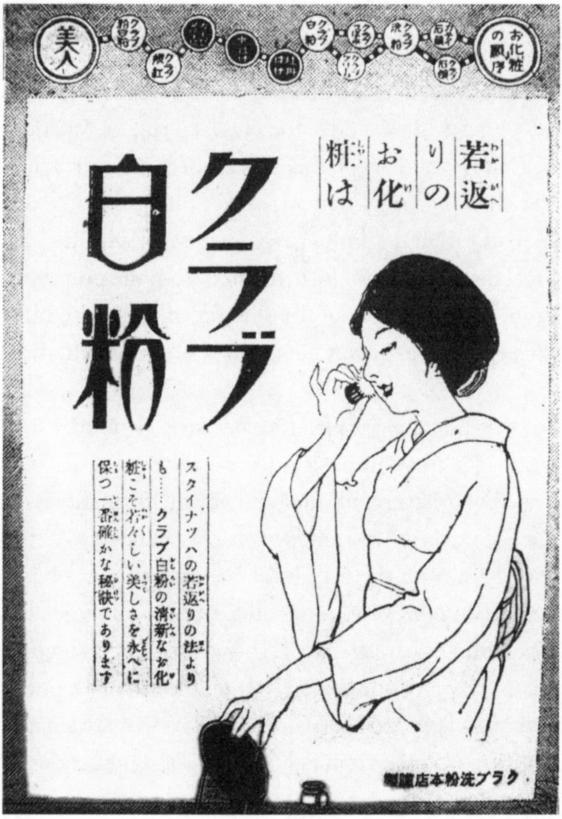

Figure 8. (*left*)
Powder puff girl,
Shengjing shibao,
19 March 1928.

Figure 9. (*below*)
Powder puff girl,
Shengjing shibao,
29 March 1929.

of Chinese advanced sector modernity, which was advanced in part because colonial capital had occupied it. I do not think it is an exaggeration to suggest that this CCC girl is a condensed figure of what the Korean, Chinese, or Manchurian subject had yet to achieve under the civilized rule of Japanese colonial administration. That is why I allege that this modernized, advanced Japanese prototype of the worldly Asian woman, freed of the yoke of Western imperialism and the bad oriental family, perhaps in-sync with the developmental time of global history, cannot be extricated from the politics of colonial re-regionalization, and the imperialism of modern corporate capitalism, which present this ephemeral advertising image as a representation of a Chinese women.

But the complexity of this CCC poster girl does not stop with its reality as a saturated visual image, for the composition is decidedly poetic. It is poetic in the sense that the little picture, like a poem, is an "affirmation and delectation" which "does not traverse" a boundary or space alluded to in the composition, but, rather, "speaks on the threshold."[21] The image is oblivious to extradiegetic referentiality or even indirect reference in a predictable pattern. This poster is not a mimetic image at all. It does not directly represent anything; or more correctly any one thing. Rather, the ad, like a poem "dissolve[s] the referent that adheres" to the historical terms that are already in play—colonial modernity, corporate capital, Nakayama Taiyodo, modern girl—"in the crucible of naming so as to give timeless existence to the temporal disappearance of the sensible" (22). So while it is undoubtedly the case, as Lacanian theorists delight in pointing out, that "every regime of truth is grounded in the Real by its own unnamable," what forms the unnamable in this poetic advertising image is "woman." Why else create a generic feminine image that is flexible enough to stand in relation to any commodity, from soap powder to fertilizer? In Badiou's exegesis on the poem, he discloses the need to distinguish between "unnamables." That is because his generic truth of poetics takes shape in the distinction he draws between mathematics (where consistency of language is valued above all else) and poetics (where what is at issue is actually the power of language without the pressure of consistency or rigid referentiality). Both regimes are capable of truth, but each possesses distinct protocols.

The visual image of the modern, pan-Asian, commodity girl is not, of course, a real poem, nor does it operate within the problematic of language as such. Where the analogy of advertising image and poem or, more capaciously, art, is useful, however, is its reminder that a visual image, like a poetic utterance—or choreographed movement, cinematic frame, staged enactment—is not extradiegetic. There is nothing in the genre of the advertising that would suggest it is referential. Grasping its power to move us does not require or rest on an extradiegetic reading. Like other kinds of modernist drawing, commercial art may in fact be an organized experience of the self-referentiality of the women image and the commodity image. A reason to adapt a poetics to a beautiful commercial image like this one is, however, the injunction that "to enter the poem" involves giving up the question of what it means, in order "to think what happens in it" (29). And here is where I think the modern girl is a significant place for thinking what happens in visual art that evokes the event of women. There is something happening in this advertising image and in the Brunner Mond posters. In the language of contemporary philosophy these images are heteronymous; they are pictorial versions of poetic heteronymy.[22]

That being said, I have no qualms about using these examples of commercial modern girl advertising campaigns to focus attention on the historical question of capital (a universal value) and its local instantiation. The posters do illustrate how a linked series of images of modern femininity appeared at precisely the same juncture that similar images arose in commodity advertising in other markets, emerging markets, and imaginary markets, in the ephemera of an inter-Asian, and global advertising project. What occurs to me, nonetheless, is that the heteronymy of these remarkably consistent bodily presentations of an anatomically accurate pin-up girl and the "other scenes of use value" where they appear, do ground the Real in a mystery, which is given the name of Women in modernist thought. These commercial women images are indeed similar in different places, just as the category "women" in modern nationalism, modernist governmentality, modernist civil discourses of citizenship, and subjectivity is present in anti-imperialist and imperialist projects from Egypt and the Middle East to the Japanese colonies, India, and China. Yet the repetitive quality of the images and their consequent power to present a heteronymy or inexhaustibly heterogeneous and polyvocal image, present historians a visual poetics in which the feminine character of the global modern girl is both singular and universal, a "coextension of the sensible and of the Idea but conceding nothing to the transcendence of the One. . . . [and denying] anything that would resemble empiricism."[23] To put it bluntly, the more heteronymous these images are the more universal and substantial they appear to us. They eventually become the very substance "woman." They cease to be a *subject effect* of nation, ethnicity, region, race, patriarchy, or caste.

How to understand "women" as a substantial or elemental subject is related to the question of what these ephemera are and what modernist commercial advertising images do. Heteronymic images are not, in my view, representations, and this is where the conventional tactics of reading historically falter. The Brunner Mond girl image, like others of its kind, is not a representation because it cannot be said to represent anything in particular; it is associative and evocative, so unless a context is historically, retrospectively constructed around it, the image refers most potently to itself. Fertilizer or toothpaste, the woman image is all about the femininity of the modern woman and her accoutrement. Images of women in inter-Asian markets are self-referential in the sense that they divulge a modernist feminine body to public sight. To this degree the Brunner Mond Corporation advertising image of the girl in the fertile field participates in a modernist visual politics of the modern girl heuristic. But it also highlights the fact that this modernist feminine body resembles the commodity form that appears with it in the frame (in other places I have suggested how this works in a commodity world of cosmetics and soaps). The central image associates the feminine body to a brand of chemical fertilizer, suggesting that it is the commodity-body relation and not the relation of women and cosmetics (or the relation of men and women) that is at stake in advertising images considered generically.

My overarching points in this section are not so complicated. It is first that the Brunner Mond image particularly cannot be read off in a one-to-one relation to a culture or region lying somewhere adjacent to the drawings. In part that is because, as I have argued here, the power of the image derives historically from what we know about its multipart, corporate, nationalist origins, and in part from its complex generic qualities of contemporary advertising image, the history of Chinese commercial art in the first third of the twentieth century, the poetics of its generic visuality, the re-coalescing morphology of this modern, colonial female body and so on.[24]

In the language of social science, these images cannot be contained within either a *cultural* regionalism (no matter how flexible or "soft" its borders are said to be), given the British branding of the product, or an origin point called "the West" since, for the most part, the ambiguities that pattern its coherence are legible in the context of Japan's aggressive pan-Asia colonial ideology asserted in Korea, Taiwan, Okinawa, the main islands, and other parts of the Japanese empire. In other words, this ephemeral visual image is neither securely and singularly "Asian," nor obviously a derivative project, as for instance long-running Pond's, Kodak, and Ford Motor car company campaigns in Shanghai are. And it is, second, that the power and the importance of the evidence do not lie in their potential to illustrate fashion or the existence of people in the world of Asian modernity, but rather in the way that this commercial, mechanical repetition of images of bodies like these present a mysterious substantiality and name it women.

Philosophy and the Event of Women

The fact that the more heteronymous these advertising images become the more universal they appear is why, in the end, I preferred to turn toward a theory of the event and away from polemics over the universal and the particular, the region and its subregions, the heuristic and its examples, the international and the national, the cultural and the meta-cultural, and so on. Alain Badiou's philosophy of the event is complex and it is a philosophy, as defined by himself in his own enormous body of work. Nor am I pretending to be a philosopher or to do philosophy in any sense. I am drawn by the content of the assertions that Badiou makes about truth and thinking, and by what I see as his essentially historical problematic. In this regard Badiou takes up where Walter Benjamin, a poet, had left off, at the question of how acts proper to history must blast the truth out of a flow of time. "Philosophy does not itself produce any effective truth," Badiou has asserted. "It," he argues, "seizes truths, shows them, exposes them, announces that they exist."[25] This is the respect in which philosophy today is, in his view, a complex form of systematic and axiomatic thought: modern philosophy "is an axiomatic conviction, a modern conviction," which begins from the event of "our times."[26] After a long period in which theory or philosophy had started from the assumption of finitude, boundedness, and substance, Badiou proposes that in our moment, while "it is very difficult to reduce a situation to finite parameters" since this difficulty and the problem of heteronymy positively characterize our time as such, and since we think in our time, thought must become infinite and open itself up to time. This is partly the reason I argue that to give the event of women its proper historical due it is necessary to confront directly the double binds of culturalist, regionalist, systems theories.

As in his concept of "inaesthetics" ("a relation of philosophy to art that, maintaining that art is itself a producer of truths, makes no claim to turn art into an object for philosophy. . . . [and] describes the strictly intraphilosophical effects produced by the independent existence of some works of art"[27]), Badiou argues in general that contemporary philosophy is a "kind of thinking [that] never defines what it thinks" or founds itself as an object, but "*grasps the disposition of undefined terms*" (my emphasis). As I pointed out explicitly in considering Badiou's question, "what is a poem?" undefined terms are encountered in poetic work, since that is a condition of poetics as a truth procedure. But implicitly, I have also been arguing that the modern girl, for instance, is an undefined term that makes sense only in relation to a categorical "women," itself a modernist category that can be historically described; as historical category, women is a subject of truth, is a subject in relation to a historical event in which what had not existed before was declared to exist. This raises two points. First, as Badiou posits in relation to the position of "proletarian" in Marxist thought, i.e., it forms "the central void of early bourgeois society," *women* is the name that twentieth-century thinkers— feminists, demographers, census takers, poets, and biologists—gave to the "central void" of modern citizenship and consequently of nation and nationalism. The central antagonism of modern middle-class men and women was precisely the deficient ground of Enlightenment refusal to grant citizenship and thus subjective fullness to women as women.[28] This is the value to me of Badiou's position that when contemporary philosophic thinking does encounter a term, "women," for instance, "it is not in the sense of *a naming whose referent would need to be represented*, but rather in the sense of being laid out in a series wherein the term subsists only through the ordered play of its founding connections."[29] (This turn in Badiou's philosophy is rooted in his dogma that, philosophically speaking, ontology is mathematical, a point I will not pursue.)[30]

Central to my concern, rather, is the question that has brought Badiou to prominence in recent social theory and that is problematic of the event. In Badiou's view, when philosophy seizes truths, shows them, exposes them, and announces that they exist, it also "turns time toward eternity—since every truth, as a generic infinity, is eternal. . . . [Thus] philosophy makes disparate truths compossible, and, on this basis, *it states the being of the time in which it operates as the time of the truths that arise within it*."[31] This term, "compossible," or "philosophic compossibility," refers to Badiou's growing effort to demonstrate how philosophy can "put together in some kind of systematic shape those contemporary truths it is able to recognize and affirm." This move of compossibilization, which is, to repeat, the proper of philosophy, proper to contemporary philosophy as axiomatic thinking, in essence seeks to show the inseparability of the time and its universal truths, the times and its generic, infinite thought.[32]

What I have implied in my discussion of the commercial images of females in the Brunner Mond and Nakayama Taiyodo campaigns is that the event of women is a constituent part of modernity and that compossibility, the historical relation that obtains between axiomatic thinking and our times. I have of course suggested in the examples I have chosen how the "global" phenomenon of women as a category of modernity was constructed precisely with world-scale ambitions at the same time it had to acknowledge (if not submit to) the protocols of the "global" to even be articulated. But I have further argued that in the event of its articulation—and I will provide further historical examples in later revisions of this essay—the singular was launched from the multiple. The key terms for my purposes here are "generic infinity" and compossibility because what I need to show now is how the global works in this regime. Badiou's well known division of truth into four conditions, "the matheme, the poem, political invention and love," and his argument that it is the job of philosophy to develop "generic procedures" for fixing the eventual site has proven useful in my analysis.[33]

I have suggested that women is singular to, and a marker of, modernity, just like the categories of society, worker, student, and youth. The central problem is that systems theories, and regionalists as much as systems theorists, are not, with all their emphasis on continuities and continua, able to see the event. Ernesto Laclau's regard for the question of how history recognizes its own subjects, and particularly Badiou's requirement that we ask historical knowledge to specify its proper relation to irreducible or universal human inventions, usefully complicate world-scale analysis. This paper has posed the question of how the event of women, an integral element of what defines the modern as such, could be so absolutely absent in world-scale analysis in both pre-capitalist and capitalist take-off studies, and its inverted form, the Eurasia paradigm. And it has suggested in its attention to corporate colonial aggression on the China mainland why an event of woman was launched from a regime that was neither a core nor a periphery. This is not a call to "gender" history. Rather the essay has, in fact, raised several problems that cannot be resolved in the paradigms in play, but would require a world scale to address and resolve. For instance, how would the new globalist or regional histories accommodate the global event of women? Does this event of women rest on exclusively cultural factors that neo-globalism would, in the end, consider epiphenomenal? Is the event as such primarily cultural or is it also reflected in the historical changes in the sexed division of labor in China, a history that Francesca Bray has convincingly argued? How can world-systems theory exclude the sexual division of labor as a cause or an indicator of modernity? But can it include it? Alternatively, Žižek's question about the "infinite multiple" of women in feminism draws attention to the fact that while much feminist scholarship claims that there is no woman as such, it supplies as proof of its own assertion a reference to infinite numbers of specific or historical women. Actually, "women" is neither an impossible category nor asserted through infinite multiples, but rather is, instead, an event inherent in modernity, which is to say that the evental quality of women cannot be addressed by changing the "scale" or "units" of analysis in play.

Notes

1. Huang, "Development or Involution in Eighteenth-Century Britain and China?" "China's (or the Yangzi delta's) delayed industrialization, in other words, cannot be explained by the lack of availability of coal as Pomeranz asserts; rather, it is the lack of industrial demand that explains the nondevelopment of China's coal industry" (533).

2. Pomeranz, "Beyond the East-West Binary." See pages 546 for critique of the land–labor ratio, 552 for discussion of the weight of proletarianization as developmental factor, and 553–54 for questions related to the relation of capital accumulation, development, and industrial breakthrough strategies.

3. Perdue, *China Marches West*, 525 and 662, nn. 9 and 10.

4. Lieberman, *Strange Parallels*.

5. Lieberman had (by the time this chapter was written) published only the first of these two volumes. Volume 1 stresses the themes of similitude, contingency, and the Eurasian regionalism.

6. Laclau and Mouffe, *Hegemony and Social Strategy*, 37. Lieberman seems most drawn to the thesis regarding "the general field of the emergence of hegemony" (Eurasia appears to be the emergent hegemonic category for Lieberman) because Laclau and Mouffe describe hegemony as creative activity "of articulatory practices, that is, a field where the 'elements' have not crystallized into 'moments'" (134). In other words, Laclau and Mouffe's value to Lieberman would appear to lie in their assertion of contingency and identity in theoretical terms.

7. Laclau and Mouffe, *Hegemony and Social Strategy*, 139; emphasis in original.

8. Butler, Laclau, and Žižek, eds, *Contingency, Hegemony, Universality*, 183.

9. See Badiou, *Saint Paul*.

10. Badiou, *Handbook of Inaesthetics*, 29.

11. Barlow, "Gender and Region."

12. In other words, in Butler's way of thinking we would have to give up the project of linking universalizing theory to historical specificity, or we can opt for Marxist, liberal, or in her case, Hegelian, meta-theory that rests for its authority on the scholar's position, the privilege of reason. I will argue shortly that when historians (and Laclau is not interested in history or in writing history) insist on remaining in the historiographic problem of contingency vs. universality we are prey to similar problems. We will either declare one element or another to be universal (core-periphery exchange, labor involution, state building evolution) and legislate from the position of universality, or risk a strategy based on "contingency," which is another way of saying, context. That is why I am going to propose beginning from the event of women, and its generic procedures, rather than reading the women into the record. That is also why I would prefer to investigate the event, not in order to know what it means as one element of a system, but rather to think what happens in it and perhaps after it.

13. Badiou, *Saint Paul*, for a discussion of "the event." Badiou declares that "Truth is diagonal relative to every communitarian subset; it neither claims authority from nor (this is obviously the most delicate point) constitutes any identity" (14). Here as elsewhere in his work Badiou excludes from possibility any "event of women" since, first, he classifies "women" as an identity, and, second, he presumes that any identity of women would be predicated out of communitarianism. Obviously, I do not subscribe to either of these notions. For me the "event of women" is neither sexuation, nor is it a communitarian event. It is a something "other than" the condition or situation of sexuation, the foundational feminine, the philosophic woman, and so on. It is also, most definitively an event to which fidelity has been paid, and thus a Truth. While I do not produce a scriptural event, I also do not need to. Obviously my distance from Badiou is on the question of historicity and, to use his and Lazarus' language, the problem of the evental site. "The evental site," according to Badiou, "is that datum that is immanent to a situation and enters into the composition of the event itself, addressing it to *this* singular situation, rather than another" (70). While I generally agree on a problematic of the composition of the event I draw the relation in a different way.

14. Barlow, et. al., eds, "The Modern Girl Around the World." The Modern Girl Around the World collaborative research project founded in 2000 at the University of Washington has documented in detail the emergence of an identifiable, global phenomenon in China, India, Japan, Australia, France, South Africa, Europe, and the United States. I am a co-founder of the project along with colleagues Alys Weinbaum, Priti Ramamurthy, Lynn Thomas, Uta Poiger, and Madeleine Dong. We

set out to establish that, as our published research agenda puts it, "the modern girl emerged quite literally around the world in the first half of the twentieth century." Thus the project was inherently world-scale in its structure. The book, *The Modern Girl Around the World* (Weinbaum, Thomas, Ramamurthy, Poiger, Dong, and Barlow, eds.) illustrates the local concerns associated with this figure and particularly the racial formation structuring what, in the Agenda is called "the context." I have problematized the question of "context" in this essay. A second collaborative research group, The Modern Girl, Colonial Modernity and East Asia, was headquartered in Tokyo at the Institute of Gender Studies at Ochanomizu University. This group focused on the Japanese imperial project, the modern woman, and the modern girl phenomenon in colonial region making. See Ito, Barlow, and Sakamoto, eds. What follows in this section is rooted in my work with both collaborative groups but is not a position shared by either of them.

15. Wilk, "The Local and the Global in the Political Economy of Beauty," 124.

16. Abu-Lughod, ed., *Remaking Women*; Burton, *Burdens of History: British Feminists, Indian Women, and Imperial Culture*; Melman, *Women's Orients*; Yue and Jinhua, *Surfacing onto the Horizon of History*; Spivak, *In Other Worlds: Essays in Cultural Politics*.

17. Badiou, *Saint Paul*, 14–15. I am putting into my own words Badiou's stricture on why Saint Paul illustrates the "universal singularity" that he is as a subject of the truth of the event of Christ's arising. This relation of the event and subject in Badiou's philosophy is discussed in detailed, accessible language in Peter Hallward's exposition, *Badiou: A Subject to Truth*, 114–22.

18. I have been influenced in this concern by Žižek's critique of mainstream feminism. He points out correctly, I think, that no matter how many deconstructions are carried out against the "woman subject," each part recombines automatically because the iterations are bound together as a set. Or at least, that is my rethinking of his concern. What he offers instead is the old saw that the subject women cannot be deconstructed because it structures the symbolic. See Žižek, "Psychoanalysis in Post-Marxism: The Case of Alain Badiou."

19. My thanks to Wang Yiman for inventing this term in an off-the-cuff remark.

20. In an earlier version of this essay, "History and the Border," I use this same case of the Brunner Mond advertising campaign to illustrate why the concept of "beyond borders" is not feasible. Here I am, in essence, using the same empirical case to illustrate the historical grounds on which a universal signifier, the global modern girl, is an event in Badiou's sense. The idea of "border" is analytically insupportable. For a discussion of this problem in the context of the history of Chinese feminism, please see the conclusion to Barlow, *The Question of Women in Chinese Feminism*.

21. Badiou, *Handbook of Inaesthetics*, 17.

22. Ibid., 40.

23. Ibid., 44.

24. See Ellen Laing, *Selling Happiness*.

25. Badiou, *Handbook of Inaesthetics*, 14.

26. Badiou, *Infinite Thought*, 169–93. Professor Badiou has recently clarified what he means by "our times" in *Logics of Worlds*.

27. Badiou, *Handbook of Inaesthetics*, xvi.

28. I use antagonism in the sense of Laclau and Mouffe, "a relation wherein the limits of everyday objectivity are *shown* — in the sense in which Wittgenstein used to say that what cannot be *said* can be shown. . . . [since] the social only exists as a partial effort for constructing society . . . antagonism, as a witness of the impossibility of a final suture, is the 'experience' of the limit of the social. Strictly speaking, antagonisms are not *internal* but *external* to society; or rather, they constitute the limits of society, the latter's impossibility of fully constituting itself" (Laclau and Mouffe, *Hegemony and Socialist Strategy*, 125).

29. Badiou, *Theoretical Writings*, "The Question of Being Today," 43.

30. Where I agree with Badiou without reservation is in his critique of human rights. See Alain Badiou, *Ethics: An Essay on the Understanding of Evil*. This puts me in the camp of feminist scholars like Gayatri Chakravorty Spivak who do not presume that "women's rights are human rights," and who discourage the common assumption that the woman question is a question of liberal human rights.

31. Badiou, *Handbook of Inaesthetics*, 14.

32. See Hallward, *Badiou: A Subject to Truth*, 244–47.

33. Badiou, *Manifesto for Philosophy*, 35.

PART FOUR

Ethics, Otherness, System

The Legal System of
International Human Rights

HELEN STACY

International human rights are a unique subset of international law—one that has massively expanded over the last decades—that international lawyers describe as the quintessential product of late twentieth-century globalization. Within the legal profession, international human rights law as a specialized component of international law is viewed as new and innovative, a relatively world-scale juridical phenomenon produced by post–Second World War institutions such as the United Nations, gaining momentum in the West during the economic boom times of the 1960s, and burgeoning anew with the slew of new nations and constitutions created at the end of the Cold War when the Soviet Union collapsed. This perspective sees international human rights as a project of the courts and the legal profession, newly connecting the world in one global human rights legal system, one global human rights culture, one cosmopolitan universe.

This short-range view of the law of international human rights forgets the longer-term historical, intellectual, economic, and political forces of prior chapters of history.[1] It overlooks earlier world-scale projects that emerged from European ideas about the role of civilized governments, ideas that profoundly shaped the international legal system. Utilizing Immanuel Wallerstein's insight that all analysis should be simultaneously historic and systemic, this chapter describes the legalization of human rights as simply the most recent version of several prior world-scale phases. Despite international law's ostensible foundations in the equality of nation-states and the equality of all people, the development of international law tells a more complicated story. From its earliest beginnings, international law has emerged from assumptions about the intellectual superiority of some people over other people. These understandings are a constitutive part of legal regulation from the earliest moments of the Enlightenment period. They continue to shape today's international legal system.

I look to the lineage of international law and human rights from the early European colonization of the New World to trace the systemic features of this historic trajectory. In a train of events commencing with Western Europe's colonization of the Americas, Africa, and the Pacific, the idea of law and rights as inherently "international" grew from ideas about religion, territory, trade, and governance. The first phase of "world-scale" thinking about the legal power of governments abroad, that of colonial expansionism, was consolidated in a second nodal point in the late nineteenth-century when legal professional identity produced the new phenomenon of the "international lawyer." Despite its appellation, this professional body reflected iconoclastic European intellectual trends about human nature and legal regulation. In each historical phase I draw out the persistent assumption of superiority of some people over others that has been at the center of legal regulation, an assumption at odds with the ambitions of contemporary international human rights discourse as a discourse of human equality.

Colonization and legal professionalization carried inherent assumptions of inferiority and superiority, of religious, civilizational, and national difference that are enmeshed in today's discourse of international human rights. These first and second stages subsequently merged with the liberal ideals of "universal humanity" that crystallized in the 1946 United Nations Charter and the 1948 Declaration of Human Rights. The U.N. system established today's international legal arrangements, legalizing the concepts of national sovereignty and individualism as the twin foundations of international human rights. International human rights law now has an explicitly transformative agenda, connecting political virtues and their broader applications across national borders. Understanding the flawed history of the legalization of rights as both historic and systemic need not undermine the best intentions of international human rights. Instead, a deeper knowledge of the earliest beginnings of international law might help contribute to greater humility in its contemporary applications.

First Stage "Civilizing"

International law and human rights as a world-scale system began in the fifteenth century, when Europe's "discovery" of the New World used law as a mechanism to legitimize Europe's annexation of the Americas. Trade within

Europe had already led to the steady increase in the number of law treaties *between* European rulers. Europe's rule abroad expanded its laws mechanism so as to regulate radical religious and cultural difference. When a Papal command of 1495 divided the world beyond Europe into an exclusive duopoly between the Portuguese and the Spanish, the first truly global empires in history were created, more global in their reach than the contiguous territories of either Rome or Islam. Portugal, through colonizing Africa, Brazil, India, and Malaysia, and Spain, through its colonization of the Americas and parts of East Asia, each extended their power across continents and oceans with a network of legal treaties, commissions of authority, and gazetted regulations. The steady assimilation of overseas territories radiating outward from Europe was a legal juggernaut that by the seventeenth century had added the empires of England, France, and the Netherlands to an ever-more intricate network of legal arrangements.[2]

An understudied feature of Europe's colonization over this period was the defining role of Islam as a regulatory bulwark against which the European sovereigns defined their legal powers. By the sixteenth century, the Ottoman Empire ruled thirty-six provinces that spanned Europe, Asia, and Africa under a complex Islamic jurisprudence that sought to bind only Muslims. Europeans, on the other hand, who regarded their national laws binding upon every person within their national borders, simply applied their laws to the geographic territory of their colonies. The European powers increasingly developed the laws of their colonial rule based upon their individual and singular national identities—one that was English, or French or Spanish—which implied highly particular traits and legal relationships within that colonial territory. For example, Spanish and Portuguese colonies were ruled through their national civil "inquisitorial" legal system, whereas British colonies were ruled through English "common law" legal system. Islamic scholars, on the other hand, regard the Ottoman sultan as the sole and absolute sovereign of all Muslim people, irrespective of local characteristics and political arrangements.[3] What mattered was a Muslim's attachment to a faith rather than their geographic placement within territory. These differences between European and Islamic jurisprudence were constitutive of the European imagination about an international system of laws. Religions like Islam that were obdurately different to Christianity were seen as obstacles to the full expansion of world-scale law. The incompatibility of religious and secular versions of law were linked by Europeans not only to the definition of "civilization," but also to what it meant to be fully human.

This was ironic, given that religion was the first rationale for overseas European rule. The Papal *Inter caetera* commanded Spain "to instruct the . . . inhabitants and residents and dwellers therein in the Catholic faith, and train them in good morals."[4] Catholic missionaries instructed indigent Indians in Christianity under rudimentary notions of Europe's religious obligation to "educate" disbelievers. The legal justification for European rule over America's indigents flowed directly from this religious justification. An instruction by Papal Bull to spread Christian divinity was regarded by the conquistadores as an expression of "natural law." By that logic, European sovereigns, ruling their own European populations by natural law, were justified in their enslavement of the Indians because they were "slaves, sinners, heathens, barbarians, minors, lunatics and animals."[5]

When Christianity's civilizing missions in the Americas morphed into wholesale slaughter, some back in Spain wrote about the moral problems produced by the subjugation of distant lands and peoples. Salamanca scholar Francisco de Vitoria (1485–1546) was the first to question the legal authority behind Europe's colonial expansionism. Vitoria argued against forced religious conversion. He gave an eloquent defense of Indian rights in his *De Indis* lecture (1532), arguing that the indigenes

> are not of unsound mind, but have, according to their kind, the use of reason. . . . They have polities which are orderly arranged and they have definite marriages and magistrates, overlords, laws and workshops, and a system of exchange, all of which call for the use of reason; they also have a kind of religion.[6]

Although his approach was still rooted in Christian assumptions about God's divinity, Vitoria cautioned Europe's sovereigns about their religious justifications for bringing non-Christians into the European legal system. He reformulated the concept of natural law to argue that all humans, even colonial indigents, shared the same nature, manifested by the Indian's evolving systems of law and order that demonstrated they had the human characteristic of reason. This required, Vitoria argued, that Europe allow them a lawful right to exercise their own religion.

However, in a paradoxical, even cruel, twist of fate, Vitoria's compassionate argument of ascribing European-like rationality to the Indians served only to hasten their subjugation. His moral argument for the freedom to practice non-Christian worship could not counteract the doctrine of international law which then (as now) grants unfettered freedom of movement to travelers and traders of the "highways and the high seas." Vitoria's plea to include the Indians within the scope of universal reason meant the Indians were also subject to the European customary law of unabridged travel and trade over foreign lands. This enmeshed the Indians in European governance because any resistance to Spanish travel and trade was interpreted as a hostile act under international law. European traders thus had legal justification to retaliate against such "hostility," often by seizing "resistant" natives and taking over their lands.

Vitoria's argument against universal Catholicism was quickly replaced with a much more potent world-scale force: that of universal economic behavior, put into service of European empire.[7] Either the Pope's universal law of Christianity delivered indigenous South Americans into proselytizing hands of the men of the Church, or the universal law of economic expansion delivered them into the hands of European governments who punished their resistance to European trading activities. The economic requirements of world-system empire trumped the prior world-system of natural law.

World-Scale Sovereignty: The Law of Nations

European sovereigns who claimed large swaths of the New World in the name of religion, secularism, and science were challenging Rome's universal claims of jurisdiction over the peoples of Europe. This had a profound effect on reshaping the idea of sovereignty, which in turn sparked a new phase of thinking on the world scale. Whereas Vitoria's treatise had been mostly intended to establish principles for the European conquistadores as they colonized the new world, religious differences *within* Europe were lessening the power of Rome and increasing the power of the governments of nation-states. Trenchant critiques of religious intolerance took root in England over the next century as the right to freedom of conscience when the struggle between Catholics and Protestants in England led ultimately to the establishment of parliamentary sovereignty after the Glorious Revolution in 1688.

Eighteenth-century legal scholarship in continental Europe articulated a normative vision about sovereignty, one of global society divided into sovereign states rule by national legislative structures and grouped into regional alliances. And yet secularism's ascent did not dislodge colonialism in the New World. The weakening of religious absolutism in the Old World did not displace the paradigm of global governance through the civilizing force of European empire. Whether by the crafty strategies of Machiavelli's *Prince*,

Hobbes's all-powerful *Leviathan*, or Locke's more modulated political bargain, secular governance was the new faith that challenged the power of the Church.

The new hierarchy of the nation-state was as just as potent as the old hierarchy of religion. The German philosopher Christian Wolff wrote *The Law of Nations* in 1749, defining the "law of nations" as an immutable feature of the natural law that binds all nations together in one shared conscience.[8] Wolff wrote that nations are like free persons—just as people are equal before the law, nations states are equal before one another. For Wolff, the world was made up of many individual nations that are bound together in their common wish to promote the common international good. In 1758, Swiss jurist Emmerich de Vattel echoed Wolff and argued that sovereigns ought to increase human happiness through promoting political liberty, mutual aid among nations, and the diminution and mitigation of wars, writing:

> The end or aim of civil society is to procure for its citizens the necessities, the comforts, and the pleasures of life, and in general their happiness; to secure to each the peaceful enjoyment of his property and a sure means of obtaining justice; and finally to defend the whole body against all external violence.[9]

The philosophical capstone of the initial world-scale phase of civilizing people came with Immanuel Kant's theory of individual rights. Kant argued at the turn of the nineteenth century that individual human well-being, what today we call individual human rights, should form the corpus of international law. Worldwide peace could emerge only if states ruled their people with "republican" principles and then joined with all other nations in a voluntary league of all nations. Kant's global organization of nation states was premised upon "cosmopolitanism" described as a single moral community to which all humanity belonged.[10]

Like Vitoria, Kant criticized Europe's colonizing activities abroad, describing them as

> the inhospitable actions of the civilized and especially of the commercial states of our part of the world. The injustice which they show to lands and peoples they visit (which is equivalent to conquering them) is carried by them to terrifying lengths. America, the lands inhabited by the Negro, the Spice Islands, the Cape, etc., were at the time of their discovery considered by these civilized intruders as lands without owners,

for they counted the inhabitants as nothing. In East India (Hindustan), under the pretense of establishing economic undertakings, they brought in foreign soldiers and used them to oppress the natives, excited widespread wars among the various states, spread famine, rebellion, perfidy, and the whole litany of evils which afflict mankind.[11]

However, while Kant's world-view differed from that of the missionaries and the new zealots of national sovereign autonomy, his methods were still substantially the same. For Kant, law was the tool of justification and the mechanism of implementation. Kant understood that law was central to making any world-scale claim: "The principle of universality demands that our social and political relations should be governed and our public conflicts settled in a universal manner. This requires the existence of law."[12] He was a century ahead of his time in advocating the institutionalization of universal principles, anticipating the late nineteenth century's evolution of international law as a discipline, separate from philosophy, diplomatic relations, and public law.

Professionalizing International Law

When the next stage in world-scale international law finally took place, it came as the standardization of particular international legal practices and ideologies. This took two forms: first, through the nineteenth century's professionalization of international law; and second, with the creation over the twentieth century of international institutions. Both phases sought to rectify the failures of the two prior epochs through refashioning the discourse of international solidarity about shared values and beliefs. The linchpin in the last phase has been the creation of professional identity by lawyers themselves.

Until the late nineteenth century, legal agreements between nation-states were ad hoc, mostly transacted by delegates of monarchs and senior government officials. Laws and treaties were expressed as the preferences of the sovereign, dealing with the expediencies of each new situation. Although lawyering at home in European towns and cities was influenced by local lawyers' guilds, lawyering abroad was attached to the activities of governments and had no external monitoring body, either formal or inchoate. There was no universal ideology in lawyering of inter-governmental transactions. When lawyers became involved in regional or international matters, they acted as handmaidens of their government, without any particular allegiance to external professional ethics or values.

This changed in the late nineteenth century, in Europe at least, and this transformation had a profound effect on the evolution of international human rights discourse. Galvanized in their opposition to European nationalism, a small handful of European lawyers established the first professional organization for lawyers who were interested in the new field of "public international law"—the law of conduct between nation-states. The new face of international law from the late nineteenth century went from a loose grouping of philosophers, political theorists, and even religious thinkers to a new breed of public international lawyers. They were practicing or academic lawyers who saw Europe as a political organization of independent states moving inexorably forward in Enlightenment liberal progress. Appalled by the brutal nationalism that had both sides in the Franco-Prussian war failing to honor the 1864 Geneva Convention, they instead promoted European nationalism with their values of paternal humanism as their European brand of liberal rationality.[13] This first generation of lawyers saw "international law [as] social and cultural in a deep sense: not as a mere succession of treaties or wars but as part of the political progress of European societies."[14] The first professional journal of international law, the *Revue de droit international et de législation comparée*, published at the end of 1868, was a professional mouthpiece that advocated liberal legislative reform in European nations. The initial volumes focused on the reform of penal law—particularly the abolition of capital punishment—as well as on new social legislation, including laws on child labor, education, and public assistance. These lawyers strove to become the legal conscience of the civilized world through claiming that international law articulated the popular conscience of civilized peoples.[15]

In fact, very few European governments implemented their reforming suggestions. And what had been framed as a critical response to European nationalism was still at heart an ideology of universalization, only this time through projecting European bourgeois ideals on a world scale. Ideologies of European conquest and taming of uncivilized people and places now competed with ideologies of bourgeois liberalism as the foundation for international human rights. As the nineteenth century ended and European liberalism faltered in the face of aggressive colonial economic expansion, the organization and the men who promoted its values were less and less relevant. One key factor remained, however: international law as a subset of legal disciplinary practice, motivated by normative visions, had been established.

Human Rights Go International

The period that followed—from the turn of the century to the mid-1930s—was determined by the outcome of the First World War. The League of Nations, established by the Treaty of Versailles following the First World War, was Kant's vision of an international government of governments. Two factors prevented Kant's cosmopolitan dream from materializing in the League. First, only a small number of relatively impotent non-Western states joined the family of nations within the League. Second, the success of the Bolshevik Revolution and the establishment of the Soviet Union, with its starkly different political and social ideology, challenged the universality of the West's system. Then, when in the late 1930s the League of Nations failed to prevent another world war, it seemed that any world-scale ambitions of international law were doomed to failure.

Two major developments following the end of the Second World War signaled a new departure in the evolution of international human rights as a world-scale phenomenon. First, under the 1945 United Nations Charter and different from the League of Nations, the new international legal order was based upon universal membership and free association among *all* nation-states. Second, the United Nations Charter voiced the bedrock belief that wars would not be waged if all nations respected the sovereignty of other nations. Equal national sovereignty was formally instituted in the international system of law.

International institutionalization proceeded apace. The United Nations, its specialized agencies, and other international organizations, became the coordination device to ensure Kant's perpetual peace through respect for national sovereignty. There was a massive expansion of international organizations, some at the international level and others on a regional level, marking the transition of international law from a system of formal rules to an embryonic system of co-coordinated programs.

Since then, the number of international human rights treaties has grown exponentially. For example, the 1948 Convention Against Torture transposed the Nuremberg Judgment into international law and articulated a universal human right against state-sponsored torture. The 1966 International Covenants on Civil and Political Rights and Social, Economic, and

Cultural Rights articulated "negative" and "positive" freedoms, respectively. The 1979 Covenant on the Elimination of Discrimination Against Women and the 1989 Covenant on the Rights of the Child each articulate particular human rights of particular categories.

Old and New World-Scale Problems

Law's role in the world-scale phenomena of international human rights is a story of successive worldviews, each universalizing in its approach. Originally, Europe had sent its civilization around the globe in grand colonizing sweeps, first using law as a tool of religion. Expansion to the New World began initially in the name of religious authority—laws administered by those with political power but justified as earthly incantations of heavenly scripture. But in the course of bringing the "heathens" under Rome's jurisdiction, the nature of legal authority altered. Religious divisions in Europe between Catholics and Protestants demonstrated there was no single, fixed version of religious authority. Ideas of religious tolerance in Europe spawned new philosophical justifications for human nature that rested more in ideas about human rationality and shared humanity. Finally, intellectual crosscurrents that took hold in Europe after the Treaty of Westphalia in 1648 established strong national claims to sovereign autonomy that are today expressed in the U.N. Charter as the primacy of the nation-state. As secularism became more accepted, the role of science grew. Wallerstein comments:

> We must remember that at least until the late eighteenth century, there was no sharp distinction between science and philosophy in the ways in which knowledge was defined. At that time, Immanuel Kant found it perfectly appropriate to lecture on astronomy and poetry as well as on metaphysics. . . . Knowledge was still considered a unitary field.[16]

Naturally, as Wallerstein notes, these world-scale movements were constituted through inequality. It is hardly surprising therefore that a belief in religion as all encompassing was simply replaced by equally disparate world-scale alternatives. Arguments for both Kantian universal humanity on the one hand, and very particular indigenous identity on the other, were deployed instrumentally. Universalism was the rationale behind replacing indigenous institutions with European-style institutions; paternal particularism was the rationale for withholding individual human rights from indigenous people as these were too advanced for primitive peoples. Colonial paternalism was rationalized by Darwinian arguments that portrayed the colonizers as intellectually superior precisely because they had subjugated the indigenous population. Anthropologists drew a clear distinction between "savage," "barbarian," and "civilized" peoples. For instance, in 1877 in the opening pages of his book *Ancient Society*, the lawyer and anthropologist Lewis Henry Morgan wrote: "It can now be asserted upon convincing evidence that savagery preceded barbarism in all tribes of mankind, as barbarism is known to have preceded civilization [and that these] three distinct conditions are connected with each other in a natural as well as necessary sequence of progress."[17]

Each stage had a new use for, and rationalization of, legal authority. The world-scale idea of "civilization" was epitomized by the regulatory state, administered through secular government and individual rights. Some nations were "free" and "civilized" while others were "backward" and "uncivilized." The norm was for Europe to view colonialism as beneficial for the colonized people who were not yet ready for the political equality and individual human rights that were animating European political discourse. While the new civil and political rights emerging in Europe and North America were couched in terms of universal rights, "uncivilized" nations needed to first be taught how to properly take advantage of such rights. Of course, those who judged the standards of civilization were those with economic and military power—England's Pax Britannica, for example, was vast. Similarly, the scale and reach of the empires of the Netherlands, Germany, and Belgium created legal, economic, and military networks all over the world. God had been replaced by the nation-state. The new credo—exemplified by the behavior of very particular European nations—was "civilized society." It involved, in other words:

> Exclusion in terms of a cultural argument about the otherness of the non-European that made it impossible to extend European rights to the native, inclusion in terms of the native's similarity with the European, the native otherness having been erased by a universal humanitarianism under which [Europe] sought to replace native institutions by European sovereignty.[18]

The outcome, however, was the same, no matter if universalism or particularity were argued: the end result was always increased colonial control over natives, and their lands, through legal regulation. It is a pattern that continues today.

Today

Since the end of the Second World War and accelerating with the demise of the Cold War, human rights have become the ultimate expression of law and international relations. Contemporary human rights language and culture today is a complex mix of political claims and legal entitlements, fought out in front of the "world community" of United Nations committees, national governments, international nongovernmental organizations, the media, and transnational corporate interests.

The reigning perception about international human rights is that they are a new world-scale phenomenon, a political and legal creation of the twentieth century, the turning point of post-Holocaust European-American humanist ideals, the happier face of globalization. This view holds that the genocide trials at Nuremberg inaugurated international human rights—rights that had previously been featured in particular nation-states such as France and Britain and the United States, but were termed "universal" in the 1948 U.N. Declaration of Human Rights because they applied to all people in all nations. The spate of national constitution-making that took place around the world after Nuremberg incorporated these human rights in bills of rights of nation-states, an international trend that accelerated over the decolonization period of the 1960s. Sweeping universal human rights were then incorporated into the flurry of new constitutions of the former Soviet satellites, in South Africa's post-apartheid constitution, and in post-authoritarian Latin American nations.

The great universalist aspirations of the United Nations are today critiqued from both the political right and the political left. Conservatives claim that international law and the international community are illusory and that the war of all nations against all nations is a permanent state of human affairs.[19] International law, they argue, is merely a pawn of international politics. The very idea of an international system of government is normatively flawed and empirically wrong.[20] Conservatives point also to the voluntary nature of treaties and the lack of international enforcement powers, claiming that international human rights law is merely feel-good rhetoric, an instrumental exercise in international public relations. On this analysis, nations enter into treaties and other international legal institutions when it serves their broader national interests. Any adoption of international human rights law into domestic legislation simply reflects that interest rather than any deep commitment to the principles of international human rights. Any cooperation among states on human rights issues is the seren-dipitous byproduct of that rational act of national self-preservation. And weaker states, the realists and the anti-globalists argue, simply express inter-national human rights commitment because they have little else to negotiate with: weak states simply "trade" sovereignty in obeisant necessity for eco-nomic advantages from stronger states.

Nothing captures the disagreement about international human rights more starkly than the pragmatic, unilateralist vision of the United States and the utopian and multilateralist vision of Europe. The classical philosophic roots of American doctrine create the belief that only a sovereign state can make and enforce law reliably. Some in the U.S. claim that international human rights law generates a cloud of rhetoric that does little to actually secure human rights, and others go further and say that international human rights, in fact, are at odds with American principles.[21] The European Union, in contrast with the American experience, has merged national legal systems with supranational schemes. Not only are the visions incompatible, but they also construct different institutions to pursue those visions. Yet despite little ideological agreement about the substance of the international vision, inter-national human rights are the battleground on which they are fought. The lineage of world-scale revolutions is essentially unaltered: from Church, to State, to human rights.

Conclusion

We live today in an international human rights culture. Together with its baggage of cultural imperialism, the period between the publication of Vat-tel's treatise on international law and the creation of the United Nations Declaration of Human Rights of 1948 was one of phenomenal growth of international law as the diplomatic and commercial relations between na-tions multiplied and intensified. Despite the many institutional changes wrought by the United Nations, the post–Second World War international human rights regime is a consequence of these earlier historical, intellectual, and economic developments.

A better view of international human rights is one informed by world-scale analysis. Of course, the realities of human rights around the world are far from homogeneous. "International law" as a term of art was first coined when Europe expanded to the New World. Law was the incubus for new secular theories about nationhood, governance, and human identity. Colonization required a form of schizoid extraterritorial supervision in the colonial satellites—one that demonstrated enough similarity to European political power that it could be asserted against other greedy European powers competing for the same territory, and yet enough difference from European political power that it clearly trumped any power of the indigenous colonized populations. At the same time, victory over Islam and the Ottoman Empire required a triumphal account of the all-encompassing competency of European governments relative to the Caliphate.

The analysis of human rights offered here illustrates that international community as an ideology has emerged from great inequalities over several centuries, inequalities that today are reflected in today's debates about the content of human rights and the role of the international community in enforcing them. Today, as in the previous world-scale phases, law is the oil and the glue in spreading and resisting inequality. An inherent feature of the international system of law is that it claims one single vision of the good life as universally preferable, and relies on different mechanisms of force to pursue that vision. There are huge differences in culture, politics, and economic power. These differences are not being leveled as the international human rights system evolves, but rather are a feature of the system itself.

Notes

1. I offer a more complete argument in *Human Rights for the Twenty-First Century: Sovereignty, Civil Society, Culture* (Stanford: Stanford University Press, 2009).

2. For a beautifully crafted history of the Western Enlightenment discourse of human rights, from an historical, literary, and gendered perspective, see Hunt, *Inventing Human Rights,* Early Spanish and Portuguese colonization was competing with the world-scale ambitions of the Ottoman Empire. European public law in the sixteenth and seventeenth centuries "rejected the Ottoman state and all it embodied," and while some scholars like Grotius said it was possible to make treaties with non-Christian states, the grandfather of British jurisprudence, Sir Edward Coke, said any legal traffic with the Islamic state was unlawful.

3. Imber, *The Ottoman Empire, 1300–1650*.

4. Davenport, *European Treaties*.

5. This is Anghie's summary of fifteenth-century perceptions of non-Europeans, *Imperialism, Sovereignty, and the Making of International Law*, 19.

6. Francisco de Vitoria, *De Indis et de Ivre Belli Relectiones* (1532), 127. Quoted in Anghie, *Imperialism, Sovereignty, and the Making of International Law*, 20.

7. I am indebted to Anghie's treatment (chap. 2 of *Imperialism, Sovereignty, and the Making of International Law*) of Vitoria.

8. Christian von Wolff, *The Law of Nations Treated According to a Scientific Method*.

9. Emmerich de Vattel, *The Law of Nations* (1758).

10. The term derives from Greek meaning world + πολις (*polis*) meaning city, people, citizenry, and was widely used by ancient philosophers, such as the Stoics and Cynics to describe a universal love of humankind as a whole, regardless of nation.

11. Kant, "Perpetual Peace."

12. Kant, *Kant's Political Writings*, 20.

13. Koskenniemi, *The Gentle Civilizer of Nations*, 39.

14. Ibid., 93.

15. Ibid., 41.

16. The Harvard legal historian Mary Anne Glendon credits the U.N. Declaration of Human Rights with "confirming the worst fears held in 1948 by the Soviet Union and South Africa [by] providing a rallying point for the freedom movements that spurred the collapse of totalitarian regimes in Eastern Europe and the demise of apartheid" (*A World Made New*, xvi).

17. Morgan, *Ancient Society* [1877], 5–11.

18. Koskenniemi, *The Gentle Civilizer of Nations*, 130.

19. Goldsmith and Posner, *The Limits of International Law*, 13, 21–78. In their recent short, sharp book, the law professors Goldsmith and Posner argue that there are no principles of international legality that are larger than any specific treaty that binds states, sometimes even against their will. Neither treaties, nor customary international law, nor human rights norms, have a moral force that that binds states even if those states never explicitly agreed to them. International law, they argue, is a part of international politics. States enter into treaties and other international legal institutions when doing so serves their interests. Any cooperation among states is a by-product of that rational act.

20. Ibid., 21–78.

21. See ibid. A superb critique of this position can be found in Jason G. Ralph, *Defending the Society of States*.

Rationality and World-Systems Analysis

Fanon and the Impact of the Ethico-Historical

DAVID PALUMBO-LIU

Up until the twentieth century, it seems that the finitude of the earthly sphere served primarily to facilitate the explorations and exploitation demanded by progress, and to make practical and realizable Western aspirations to dominion. In the twentieth century, as terrestrial distances began to shrink to a level that seemed to be constraining, the limitations of the earth could even be invoked as added incentive for the ever more upward and outward explorations needed to enlarge that sphere of dominance still further. In short, the abode of our present and past habitation came to look less like a home base and more like a launching pad, the place from which we, as men (and a few women) of science, could soar into space, establishing a position of mastery over an ever more cosmic unity.

—Immanuel Wallerstein, *Open the Social Sciences*, 4.

Any attempt to launch a world-scale analysis must invent an overarching grid or framework, usually secured by a key word. My essay will argue that one such framework, central to Wallerstein's world-systems analysis, is secured by a revised notion of rationality. This revision is intimately connected to a political and ethically informed rethinking of the disciplines. Coterminous with the expansion of the unit of analysis in world-systems analysis was a moral and ethical rationale—the endeavor to view historical, political, and more recently, cultural phenomena in both spatially and temporally broader and differently systematized manners brought with it an ethical question as to how knowledge was produced about others who were now drawn into a different epistemological frame. What could world-systems analysis bring to disciplinary knowledge that would differ qualitatively, and politically, from its predecessors in the social sciences? World-systems analysis found that certain methodologies, models, and assumptions—founded on a notion of rationality—obfuscated issues of morality and politics, of being with others in a substantively rational way. The knowledge produced by the reigning paradigm of the social sciences could only ultimately reproduce the status quo of the world and its distribution of labor, goods, resources, et cetera.

In this essay I use Wallerstein's world-systems analysis as a counterexample to the systematic ordering of the world based on a particular kind of understanding and formulation of human behavior. That brand of knowing is characterized by an assessment of the proximity or distance the behavior of others holds to a particularly located notion of rationality. World-systems analysis puts that point of reference into question. I use the historical case of Fanon, and Wallerstein's use of Fanon's work, to animate that questioning. I argue that in making the move to the world scale, we cannot ignore the particularities of race, nation, and location. Such particularities do not necessarily defeat the ambitions of world-systems analysis, but they do demand some rethinking of how the system is secured. In the case I will address here, this means rethinking reason. I want, however, at the outset to carefully delineate the scope of my essay. I have no real ambition to extrapolate from the empirical case of Fanon a broadside against "rationality" writ large—the burden placed on this particular historical case would simply be too great. If, on the other hand, this essay is used as an instance upon which to launch specific inquiries into other case histories, or even in the hands of some, a broad theorization of rationality, then I should be pleased.

In setting forth this investigation, I present the critical interconnection of two key elements of world-systems analysis's historical development: first, its sense of ethical obligation to go beyond the disciplinary assumptions of the time; and second, the "counter-knowledge" of Franz Fanon, a mode of rationality deeply informed by race and history that came precisely from "the other side" of what was presumed to be rational. I will set the historical frame for the launch onto the world scale, considering particularly the issue of the "two cultures" of the sciences and the humanities that influenced Wallerstein. I then sketch out Wallerstein's approach to the idea of "two cultures" and his outline of the development of the social sciences and their distribution of intellectual labor and areas of activity, specifically aligning rationality and truth with the sciences, and the beautiful with the humanities, and noting the particular intervention of world-systems analysis, both in terms of disciplines and in terms of ethics and politics.

I then discuss his specific approach to notions of rationality and in particular the ideological charge of rationality, and consider the role Freudian psychoanalysis played in the reassessments of rationality undertaken by both the social scientist Wallerstein and the analytic philosopher Donald Davidson. Finally, I examine Wallerstein's citation of Franz Fanon and focus on the way Fanon's historical example triangulates the project of world-systems analysis in critical and worldly ways. It is in Fanon (and Wallerstein's engagement with Fanon) that we discover a critical revision of the notion of rationality as imbricated in revolutionary politics and issues of race. This formed a fundamental cornerstone for world-systems analysis and continues to be critical for its application today, as it speaks to global, world-scale notions of culture. Harking back to the introduction to this collection, Wallerstein's understanding and appreciation of Fanon had everything to do with what Wallerstein considered "the most important thing happening" at that critical period in his intellectual development: "the struggle to overcome the control by the West of the rest of the world."

Dividing the World: A Crisis of Language and Knowing

Since the 1950s was a critical period in Wallerstein's thought, it is important to consider what was then going on in the world in terms of knowledge, and how aspirations toward "taking dominion" actually took flight. Let us therefore consider the precise moment when the world indeed became a launching pad. That launch provided an entirely new vantage point, and the world appeared in a different light, and in a different language. That linguistic turn, I will emphasize, valorized rationality and divided the ways in which we would speak about, and know, this new world.

In 1952, the International Council of Scientific Unions (ICSU) proposed a comprehensive series of global geophysical activities to span the period July 1957 through December 1958. The International Geophysical Year (IGY), as it was called, was timed to coincide with the high point of the eleven-year cycle of sunspot activity. In March of 1953, the National Academy of Sciences appointed a national committee to oversee U.S. participation in the IGY. According to the National Academy of Sciences, the U.S. program included "investigations of aurora and airglow, cosmic rays, geomagnetism, glaciology, gravity, the ionosphere, determinations of longitude and latitude, meteorology, oceanography, seismology, solar activity, and the upper atmosphere."[1] In connection with upper atmosphere research, the United States undertook to develop an orbiting satellite program. However, the

USSR reached that goal first, launching Sputnik in 1957, and immediately the Cold War ramifications of this supposedly "cosmically" driven scientific enterprise became known as the "race for space."

Hannah Arendt chose precisely the launching of Sputnik to emblematize a new and troubling global situation in her classic work, *The Human Condition* (1958). Aside from its international political and military consequences, which she abhorred, Arendt noted that the launching of Sputnik ushered in a crisis of language, and of politics. For her, this launch into space marked a deeply troubling step further in humankind's alienation from the world itself:

> The trouble concerns the fact that the "truths" of the modern scientific world view, though they can be demonstrated in mathematical formulas and proved technologically, will no longer lend themselves to normal expression in speech and thought. . . . We who are earth-bound creatures and have begun to act as though we were dwellers of the universe, will forever be unable to understand, that is, to think and speak about the things which nevertheless we are able to do. . . . Wherever the relevance of speech is at stake, matters become political by definition, for speech is what makes man a political being.[2]

We can still do things, but "normal" language now has fallen behind in its descriptive power—common language can no longer adequately capture the realities that the space age has opened up. In short, we can no longer really talk about the world in which we live and act; though we are unlikely to stop speaking in the face of this inadequacy, "worldly" language now seems mundane, prosaic, irrational, alienated. The separation between the world we inhabit and that which a few scientific specialists have "seen" or "captured" colors our speech with futility. We can now only speak *as if* we understood what we were doing. Critically, what Arendt laments is not only a new linguistic incapacity, but also a profound impasse for political articulation and practice. According to Arendt, the historical moment of the late 1950s that intimated such a political crisis was not the first time that humans attempted to rationalize the world, to make it tractable through instruments of scientific language and representation:

> Prior to the shrinkage of space and the abolition of distance through the railroads, steamships, and airplanes, there is the infinitely greater and more effective shrinkage which comes about through the surveying ca-

pacity of the human mind, whose use of numbers, symbols, and models can condense and scale earthly physical distance down to the size of a human body's natural sense and understanding. Before we knew how to circle the earth, how to circumscribe the sphere of human habitation in days and hours, we had brought the globe into our living rooms to be touched by our hands and swirled before our eyes. (251)

On the one hand, in this regard Sputnik was merely the latest assertion of the human will to rescale the world, to make it manageable and intelligible by means of a new set of surveying tools. Human beings, Arendt informs us, had already conceived of semiotic systems to make the immensity of the universe graspable by way of the imagination. According to her, the human capacity to translate the grandeur of Nature into a practical idiom, in a strong sense a willful repudiation of the Sublime, has been with us for ages. On the other hand, Sputnik ushered in the era when knowledge by scientific "surveying" performed a much more radical feat—it made the body's natural sense of the universe irrelevant. "It is the nature of the human [scientific] surveying capacity" says Arendt, "that it can function only if man disentangles himself from all involvement in and concern with the close at hand and withdraws himself to a distance from everything near him. The greater the distance between himself and his surroundings, world or earth, the more he will be able to survey and to measure and the less will worldly, earth-bound space be left to him" (228).

This time, science actually offered us something far beyond the capacity to shrink time and space laterally across the world's surface; it finally became possible (and therefore necessary) to launch vertically into space and appraise the world afresh from that delinked perspective. We now were compelled out of our "living rooms" and the world delivered to us in "numbers, symbols and models." Mankind's apparatuses for space travel blasted into space armed with an entirely new set of figurations. And again, this resulted in a weird and unprecedented situation wherein ordinary human language became passé, inappropriate to the way the world looked now: "[Man] has been forced to renounce normal language, which even in its most sophisticated conceptual refinements remains inextricably bound to the world of the senses and to our common sense . . . it could be argued that the layman and the humanist, still trusting their common sense and communicating in everyday language, are out of touch with reality."[3] If, as Arendt notes above, "speech is what makes man a political being," then what kind of politics are available to us now, across this huge divide? The ardent and passionate championing of science (over and against the humanities) as the likely savior of modern humankind, crystallized a few years after Arendt's text in the famous Snow-Leavis "two cultures" debate, inaugurated in 1959.[4] I will return to this debate and Wallerstein's particular take on it further on in this essay. For now, it is important to follow history, as it places new and critical demands on both the sciences and humanities to know a new world in the postwar era.

Two Cultures and Area Studies: Disjuncture and Consolidation

We should not lose sight of the fact that immediately after the end of the Second World War, a decade before the "two cultures" divide was invented, pragmatists saw the need to breech the divide between science and the humanities under the imperatives of national and international security. This drive toward "total knowledge" was the founding spirit behind area studies. I want to juxtapose these two models—the disjunctive "two cultures" model, and the re-combinative model of area studies: both attempted to foster new knowledge about the new postwar world; both were driven by the exigencies of the Cold War to "think" the New World Order.

One of the primary documents for the birth of area studies is Robert Hall's *Area Studies: With Special Reference to Their Implications for Research in the Social Sciences* (1948).[5] Hall precisely advocated "bringing about the cross-fertilization within the social sciences and of bridging the gap between the social sciences and the humanistic disciplines" for the sole purpose of achieving "the fundamental totality of all knowledge."[6] As Vicente Rafael explains, "Through area studies, then, the 'integration' of differences—between disciplines, global regions, and nation-states—could be accomplished."[7] Nevertheless, the subject matter itself manifested differences that resisted easy "integration," intellectually, politically, and strategically. In fact, this totalizing move was joined to its contradiction in practice. Wallerstein places the rise of area studies within a trajectory of disciplinary unraveling: "The cold war concerns of the United States led to the funding and encouragement of 'area studies,' which led the four 'Western disciplines' to do research for the first time in the Third World. This in turn both ended the territorial monopolies of and undermined the traditional justifications for both anthropology and Oriental studies." Furthermore, "the world revolution of 1968 dealt a further blow to the traditional divisions of the disciplines by fostering a general questioning of the liberal verities and thereby created the social space for the flourishing of studies of and by the 'forgotten' groups— women, people of color, gays and lesbians, and so on—as well as permitting the rise of 'cultural studies.' All of this together led to an immense blurring of the boundaries, to the irrelevance of most of the historic justifications for the boundaries as they were constructed between 1850 and 1945, and to widespread intellectual confusion."[8]

Thus the end of the Cold War may have left some "areas" intact, but badly in need of rethinking. Their boundaries were less clear, but more urgently the entire relation between "areas" and the metropolitan West had to be re-thought, both academically and generally. On the one hand, the confidence of the absolute and indeed "natural" hegemony of the West was shaken; on the other hand, the autonomy and more importantly the power of "others" was hardly to be assumed. It is in this context of increased pressure on the "two cultures" concept that we find Wallerstein addressing the notion of rationality as something that has to be rethought. If we are seeking ways to conceive of a world system, what kinds of basic characteristics bind human beings across space? Could rationality serve as a common trait? This was an especially difficult question to answer, once one factored in the emergent Third World, whose actions, and, coincidentally, skin color, seemed to place it outside that purview. How would "the West" see "the rest?" Through which optics would "dominion" be secured? How would knowledge deploy both the humanities and the natural sciences to that end, and how would the social sciences offer an alternative?

Rationality, Its Other, and World-Systems

World-systems analysis is intimately connected with disciplinary issues, which are in turn connected to moral and political ones. It is attentive to the contradictions of liberalism, particularly when liberalism is applied to those deemed to be specifically "minor," or "particular." Specifically, it notes that certain methodologies, models, and assumptions, founded on a notion of rationality, have obfuscated issues of morality and politics, of being with others in a substantively rational way.

Indeed, Wallerstein locates his study of the modern invention of academic disciplines with the invention of "two cultures" and their respective episte-mologies.[9] The first, the humanities, "used what was called an idiographic epistemology. They emphasized the particularity of all social phenomena, the limited utility of all generalizations, and the need for empathetic under-standing."[10] The second, the natural sciences, "used what was called a nomo-thetic epistemology. They emphasized the logical parallel between human processes and all other material processes. They sought therefore to join physics in the search for simple universal laws that held true across time and space." In relation to these two cultures, social science was "like someone tied to two horses galloping in opposite directions."[11] Most important for any discussion of the moral and political aims of world-systems analysis, "What the concept of the two cultures had achieved was the radical separa-tion, for the first time in the history of humanity, in the world of knowledge between the true, the good, and the beautiful." Wallerstein draws the con-clusion that "the great methodological debates that illustrated the historical construction of the social sciences were sham debates, which distracted us from realizing the degree to which the 'divorce' between philosophy and sci-ence effectively eliminated the search for the good from the realm of knowl-edge and circumscribed the search for truth into the form of microscopic positivism that took on many guises."[12]

Given this disciplinary divide, one that brought with it a parceling out of ethical responsibilities, the newly formed social sciences had a choice (so to speak). Wallerstein tips the balance toward a more holistic approach, one that would bring the social sciences and the humanities together in a com-mon pursuit of the good and the beautiful. This pursuit is to take place, emphatically, in the world: "World-systems analysis is primarily a protest against the ways in which social science is done, including the area of theo-rizing. I continue to believe that we must somehow find modes of descrip-tion that dismiss the very idea of the separation of the three arenas of social action [moral, intellectual, political]. I continue to believe that the historic categorizations of the disciplines of the social sciences make no intellectual sense any more."[13] Crucially, the embrace of the pursuit of the good and the beautiful is not done for mere speculation or contemplation, but to af-fect social change: "[Social science] constitutes an interpretation of social reality that at once reflects this social reality and affects it. . . . Social science is an arena of social struggle, but it is not the only one, and probably not the central one. Its form will be conditioned by the outcomes of future social struggles as its historic form was conditioned by previous social struggles."[14] Simply put, world-systems analysis sought to remove "the heavy hand of sci-entism" and "incorporate utopistics."[15]

The "heavy hand of scientism" is characterized by, among other things, a firm belief in positivistic rationality and the ability of science to capture and explain human action. Its success was in no small part thought to be attributable to its discrete distance from prejudice or subjectivity. And yet such a notion of rationality may be seen not as removed from the world, but rather precisely as a sublated form of politics, one that translates human action into numbers and statistics and then transforms those numbers and statistics into alibis for certain kinds of practices and decisions.

Wallerstein begins his 1995 lecture "Social Science and Contemporary Society: The Vanishing Guarantees of Rationality" with a quote from Gramsci: "What is 'politics' for the productive class becomes 'rationality' for the intellectual class. What is strange is that some Marxists believe 'rationality' to be superior to 'politics,' ideological abstraction superior to economic concreteness."[16] Wallerstein observes: "It is not only that intellectuals transformed politics into rationality but that this proclamation of the virtue of rationality constituted an expression of optimism on their part and served to fuel the optimism of everyone else. Their credo was: 'As we proceed towards a truer understanding of the real world, we proceed thereby to a better governance of the real society, ergo towards a greater fulfillment of human potential. Social science as a mode of constructing knowledge was not merely built on this premise; it offered itself as the surest method of realizing the rational quest.'"[17] This optimism was particularly seductive when it refused to be involved (explicitly) in substantive issues in the material world, preferring instead the elegant abstraction of human action into mathematical ciphers.

But this move was possible only by first separating "rationality" into two different kinds. According to Weber: "The term 'formal rationality of economic action' will be used to designate the extent of quantitative calculation or accounting which is technically possible and which is actually applied. The 'substantive rationality,' on the other hand, is the degree to which the provisioning of given groups of persons (no matter how delimited) with goods is shaped by economically oriented social action under some criterion (past, present, or potential) of ultimate values (*wertende Postulate*), regardless of the nature of these ends."[18]

Wallerstein applies Weber's distinction to Gramsci, "By calling the 'political' the 'rational,' are we not implying that issues of substantive rationality should be put in the background so that issues of formal rationality be the only ones that remain under discussion? And if we do so, is this not because issues of formal rationality in fact involve unadmitted but quite clear commitments to value-rational social action of a particular kind, the kind that takes conflicting ends, in Weber's words, 'as given subjective wants and arrange(s) them in a scale of assessed relative urgency.' To talk of rationality is to obscure the political, the value-rational choices, and to tilt the process against the demands of substantive rationality."[19] In this move we find exactly the separation of science, in its formalism, from the substantive issues of the good and the beautiful, in short, from issues of ethics. Thus, within the very division between formal and substantive reason, we find the logic that divides the two cultures. However, critically, this is but a "sham" division, in Wallerstein's word, for scientific rationality is shot through and through with politics. The true political charge of rationality thus resides doubly—in its totalizing positivistic claims and in its masking of the politics of that move.

Given this situation, Wallerstein appreciates deeply the significance of the radical intervention Freud makes into such a pure notion of rationality:

> Freud led us down a path whose logical conclusion is that nothing is irrational from the point of view of the actor. And who is any outsider to say that they are right and the patient is wrong? . . . But if nothing is irrational, as seen from someone's point of view, whence the hosannas for modernity, for civilization, for rationality? Formal rationality is always someone's formal rationality. How then can there be a universal formal rationality? Formal rationality is usually presented as the utilization of the most effective means to an end. But ends are not so easy to define. They invite a Geertzian 'thick description.' And once given that, Freud is hinting, everyone is formally rational. Substantive rationality is precisely the attempt to come to terms with this irreducible subjectivity, and to suggest that nonetheless we can make intelligent, meaningful choices, social choices.[20]

Davidson: Paradox and Charity: Rethinking Rationality

At this point I would like to bring in another voice, this time from outside the social sciences, to complement, in a different way, Wallerstein's use of Freud. Donald Davidson's extensive and provocative writings on rationality and irrationality refer in similar ways to the critical importance of Freud. Freudian analysis refigures rationality as consistency. Individual agents cannot be deemed to be acting irrationally if their actions can be considered consistent and therefore inferred to be following some reasonable pattern in their minds. A second element from Davidson that I would bring forward is the "paradox of irrationality," a paradox that abides in the fact that even when we try to impute inconsistency to an actor we can only do so by using the procedures of rationality. Our efforts to explain irrational behavior unwittingly bend it to rationalization. If we abandon that frame, and let the irrational be, we have in effect retreated from the task and admitted defeat—the rational has met something that cannot be reasoned, and we lose at that instant "the background of rationality needed to justify any diagnosis at all." Again, it is psychoanalysis that has facilitated this insight into the dynamics of rationality:

> The underlying paradox of irrationality, from which no theory can entirely escape, is this: if we explain it too well, we turn it into a concealed form of rationality; while if we assign incoherence too glibly, we merely compromise our ability to diagnose irrationality by withdrawing the background of rationality needed to justify any diagnosis at all.
>
> What I have tried to show, then, is that the very general features of psychoanalytic theory that I listed as having puzzled philosophers and others are, if I am right, features that will be found in any theory that sets itself to explain irrationality.[21]

That is to say, Freud's psychoanalytic critique posits rationality in even seemingly irrational behavior by discovering the logic that informs the consistent workings out of the patient's behavior. Moving too quickly to a simple diagnosis of "irrationality" abrogates the responsibility for the rigorous exercise of rationality, or therapy.

I will return to this passage later; here let me mention one other element in Davidson's writings that is essential to our discussion of Wallerstein and Fanon. It is the element of intersubjectivity. In this same essay ("Paradoxes of Irrationality"), Davidson writes: "We start out assuming that others have, in the basic and largest matters, beliefs and values similar to ours. We are bound to suppose someone we want to understand inhabits our world of macroscopic, more or less enduring, physical objects with familiar causal dispositions; that his world, like ours, contains people with minds and motives; and that he shares with us the desire to find warmth, love, security, and success, and the desire to avoid pain and distress."[22] In another essay, "The Second Person," Davidson makes this baseline even more emphatic: "Belief, intuition, and the other propositional attitudes are all social in that they are states a creature cannot be in without having the concept of intersubjective truth, and this is a concept one cannot have without sharing, and knowing that one shares, a world, and a way of thinking about the world, with someone else."[23] Hence, all propositional attitudes require some sense of being together with others, of assuming a common set of knowledges of the world, and preferences and needs. Let us now take two insights together, leaving aside for the moment the issue of rationality as consistency.

Rationality cannot impute irrationality without either inadvertently endowing the irrational with rationality through its discursive actions (explaining the irrational) or giving up rationality altogether (withdrawing the background of rationality). This paradox will be important in relation to a paradox Fanon feels captured within—as he reasons the white man's unreasonableness, his reason is rendered irrational by the white man because his is the reason of a black man. I will argue that Davidson's paradox can be applied logically to at least partially neutralize that paradox. For if reason always endows unreason with its own character, then the white man's imputing unreason to the black man must endow this unreason with reason too. And yet we will see the obdurateness of unreason when coupled with racism, politics, and power, and this fact deeply informs Fanon's revolutionary politics. Secondly, and intimately connected to the previous point, the intersubjective nature of knowing the world and making propositions about it will be a cornerstone of Fanon's work, but it will also be an emphatically politicized and historicized one.

Up to now we have five critical elements: first, the ethical imperative to knowledge beyond the parameters of normative rationality, an imperative that takes Wallerstein beyond the standing boundaries of the social sciences; second, the important insights of Freud, whose psychoanalytic intervention opens the door to new perspectives on rationality; third, the notion of rationality redefined as consistency; fourth, the paradox of irrationality that shows us how the rational, in exercising its power to rationalize, either endows the irrational with rationality or has to give up not only its hegemony but its explanatory claims altogether. Fifth, we have the centrality of intersubjectivity to all these issues. As a final and essential concept from Davidson, I would add a principle that addresses precisely the necessary openness to another's concept of truth, without which it seems to me all justification of intersubjectivity falls short. For without the predisposition to entertain other possible truths, firmly believed in by others, how can an intersubjective encounter actually take place? I am speaking of Davidson's elaboration of Quine's "Principle of Charity." Davidson explains, "[Quine's] principle directs the interpreter to translate or interpret so as to read some of his own standards of truth into the pattern of sentences held true by the speaker." He continues, "I would extend [Quine's] principle of charity to favor inter- pretations that as far as possible preserve truth: I think it makes for mutual understanding, and hence for better interpretation, to interpret what the speaker accepts as true as true when we can."[24] The "charity" here thus means to extend to the speaker some baseline assumptions of truthfulness, as found in the listener's own sense of what counts as true. It believes, if you will, in an essential will to be truthful. Most germane for my purposes, Davidson links this idea of charity and truthfulness to "rational accommodation":

> The key to the solution for simultaneously identifying the meanings, be- liefs, and values of an agent is a policy of rational accommodation, or a principle that Quine and I, following Neil Wilson, have called in the past the principle of charity. This policy calls on us to fit our own propositions (or our own sentences) to the other person's words and attitudes in such a way as to render their speech and other behavior intelligible. This nec- essarily requires us to see others as much like ourselves in point of over- all coherence and correctness—that we see them as more or less rational creatures mentally inhabiting a world much like our own.[25]

The key for me is the flexibility or "slack" charitably given—"more or less rational . . . much like our own." It is in these interstices that communica- tion can take place, bracketing for the moment the assumptions of the other being, by dint of their otherness, outside of rationality, or at least rationality that we recognize as valid and legitimate. Before we turn finally to Fanon, I would like to finish this section by making a connection between David- son's remarks on rationality and charity, and Habermas's ideas regarding otherness, a broader sense of a moral community beyond the concrete, and justice. The following passage seems to echo Davidson in important ways. We must, Habermas argues, open ourselves up to otherness, not blindly or romantically, but with the intent of communication and justice underwrit- ing the enterprise. Complementing Davidson's notion of "charity" is a cer- tain sense of responsibility. If Davidson wishes us to extend (or should we say "lend"?) to others our own sense of truth and reason, Habermas asks us to then take responsibility for translating otherness back into our idiom:

> If we interpret justice as what is equally good for all, then the "good" that has been extended step by step to the "right" forms a bridge between

justice and solidarity. For universal justice also requires that one person should take responsibility for another, and even that each person should stand in and answer for a stranger who has formed his identity in completely different circumstances and who understands himself in terms of other traditions. The remnant of the good at the core of the right reminds us that moral consciousness depends on a particular self-understanding of moral persons who recognize that they *belong* to the moral community [emphasis in original]. All individuals who have been socialized into any communicative form of life at all belong to this community. Because socialized persons can only stabilize their identities through relations of reciprocal recognition, their integrity is particularly vulnerable and they are consequently in need of special protection. They must be able to appeal to a source of authority beyond their own community. G. H. Mead speaks in this connection of the "ever wider community." Every concrete community depends on the moral community as its "better self," so to speak. As members of this community, individuals expect to be treated equally while it is assumed at the same time that each person regards every other person as "one of us." From this perspective, solidarity is simply the reverse side of justice.[26]

Nevertheless, and this is the very difficult part of realizing the aspirations of both Davidson and Habermas, we have not yet confronted the real obstacles to charity and responsibility, that is, those things that may well contaminate and corrupt such ideals. What is lacking so far in my essay is a real-world example of an ethics of knowledge founded on a notion of rationality heretofore unacceptable or invisible as such, and yet politically effective in its own right. In other words, we need an example, not a hypothesis, of a working notion of rationality that drives forward the ethics of a new knowledge informed by these critical elements. And it is here that Franz Fanon plays a critical role.

In his essay "Fanon: Reason and Violence" (1970), Wallerstein claims Fanon for the world of reason: "Franz Fanon was a man of reason and rational action, very much a product and an exemplar of the spirit of the Enlightenment in the tradition of Marx and Freud. He sought to find rational explanations for the seemingly absurdities and incongruities of social life."[27] However, Fanon's deployment of reason was precisely geared toward puzzling out different politically driven conceptions of "us" and "them" that were intimately linked to questions regarding "our reason" and "their reason." In another essay, Wallerstein makes more precise his understanding of Fanon: "In the best tradition of both Freud and Marx, Fanon sought to demonstrate that what on the surface was seemingly irrational, was beneath the surface highly rational. The book [*The Wretched of the Earth* (1961)] was therefore not merely a polemic and a call to action but a reflexive work of social science, insisting on a careful analysis of the social basis of rationality."[28] This call to action was fraught, however, with the historical legacy of racism. It is in working through that legacy to some vision of politically realistic solidarity that Fanon manifests a particular and historical notion of intersubjective rationality.

Fanon: Race, Reason, Revolution

Consider this famous and comprehensive passage from *Black Skins, White Masks*:

> The psychoanalysts say that nothing is more traumatizing for the young child than his encounters with what is rational. I would personally say that for a man whose only weapon is reason there is nothing more neurotic than contact with unreason.
>
> I felt knife blades open within me. I resolved to defend myself. As a good tactician, I intended to rationalize the world and show the white man he was mistaken. . . . With enthusiasm I set to cataloguing and probing my surroundings. As times changed, one had seen the Catholic religion at first justify and then condemn slavery and prejudices. But by referring everything to the idea of the dignity of man, one had ripped prejudice to shreds. After much reluctance, the scientists had conceded that the Negro was a human being; in vivo and in vitro the Negro had proved analogous to the white man: the same morphology, the same histology. Reason was confident on every level. I put all the parts back together. But I had to change my tune.
>
> That victory played cat and mouse; it made a fool of me. As the other put it, when I was present, it was not; when it was there, I was no longer. In the abstract there was agreement: the Negro is a human being. That is to say, amended the less firmly convinced, that like us he has a heart on the left side. But on certain points the white man remained intractable. Under no conditions did he wish any intimacy between the races [speaking of interracial sexual intercourse, eugenics].[29]

The trajectory of this passage is clear—Fanon, a man of reason, is confounded by the irrational racism of the white man and confidently confronts it armed, precisely, with reason. He "catalogues his world" in an effort to trace and discover the legacies of racism and irrationality, and yet finds that those forms have morphed and changed into various guises in the course of history, the final one being of accommodation—the Negro is found to be, after all, human. And yet, that humanity was qualified and liable to be withdrawn. Here Fanon speaks of the absolute confinement of race in terms of sexuality, but that is just the most extreme case. The point is that the designation of humanness always is open to negotiation, and for the black man it is to be always negotiated from a position of weakness. Ultimately, Fanon admits defeat, for the moment: "I had rationalized the world and the world had rejected me on the basis of color prejudice. Since no agreement was possible on the level of reason, I threw myself back toward unreason. It was up to the white man to be more irrational than I. Out of the necessities of my struggle I had chosen the method of regression, but the fact remained that it was an unfamiliar weapon; here I am at home; I am made of the irrational; I wade in the irrational" (123).

Here I wish to do two things. First is to return to Davidson's paradox. If Fanon is deemed irrational because of his race, then, following Davidson, we might assert that the white man's rationality has to endow the black man's irrationality with its own rationality, as it tries to account for or argue for this irrationality being irrational as such. But this is not how things work politically, for the fact of the matter is that the white man really makes scant effort to "rationalize" the black man's irrationality—it is seen as simply a fact that is given and beneath examination. Conversely, as Fanon notes, the more and more he is "rational," the more he is deemed to not be, because his is a black man's rationality. Again, an unexamined, naturalized assumption. The interruption of the operations of rationality by the historicized specificity and political contingencies of racism is thus disclosed, and the absence of "charity" made manifest. We therefore have to go to another argument to see how Fanon is returned from the "irrational" to the sphere of rationality, and this is done by defining rationality as consistency. In "Incoherence and Irrationality" Davidson argues: "Strictly speaking, then, the irrationality consists not in any particular belief but in inconsistency within a set of beliefs."[30] If we then switch the players' positions in this drama and examine Fanon's rational attempts to understand the irrationality of the white man, we see Fanon embarking along precisely the course outlined by Davidson's

paradox: Fanon's cataloguing of his world traces the rational, consistent unfolding of the white man's irrational racism. What might be deemed first as
simply irrational racism is discovered to be a rationalized and applied system
of consistent racist logic. This logic is traced through its transformations—
from brutal explicit racism to the "soft" racism that abides even after the
Negro is declared human, after all. To answer this persistent and consistent
rationality of racism, Fanon deploys an equally persistent and consistent
revolutionary rationality, and it is precisely within this arena of consistency
that Wallerstein's account of Fanon's political growth draws out a revolutionary rationality in Fanon, one which emphatically takes him out of the
debased, racialized state in which he must "give up" rationality and locates
him in an eminently rational and revolutionary sphere of action.

Wallerstein emphasizes the ways in which the use of reason to separate
out "us" versus "them" came to be engaged for Fanon in the political charge
to make sense of others' behavior as human action historically situated. As
such, the boundaries between "us" and "them" could shift and fuse, or separate out in different formations and alliances. Hence, what was rational had
to be constantly reevaluated, and political judgments made accordingly. In
this historically-mandated reevaluation of rationality, we find in Fanon a
consistent political project, and hence a revolutionary political rationality to
refute and disarm the rationality of racism. In this series of "explanations,"
the distinction between the "rational" and "irrational" has a central position:
"Fanon sought to explain that what appeared at first as irrational positions
of the Algerian . . . were indeed profoundly rational actions . . . Fanon insisted that it was not irrational resistance to modernity that had occurred but
rational defense against a harmful intruder."[31]

Critically, this dichotomy has to be not only localized and racialized, but
also historicized and then mapped relationally and strategically across racial
boundaries. Wallerstein writes:

> Given a Manichean world, and given Fanon's belief in uniting his roles
> of social analyst and social actor, his explanations were always in terms
> of "us" versus "them." But the intellectual problem shifted, as the world
> situation developed. Hence, the "us," was not always the same, and the
> purpose of the explanations varied accordingly. Essentially, we will argue
> that Fanon's focus of concern, his view of "us" and the purpose of his ex-
> planations evolved over time. In the beginning, he was concerned with
> explaining "us" to ourselves [and here Wallerstein means the explanation
> of the relationship between race and class in the time of revolutionary

struggle]. At a later stage, he was interested in explaining "us" to "them" [here referring to the explanation of Third World anticolonial struggles to the European left]. In his last stage, he was interested in explaining "them" to "us" [finally, the newly constituted "them"—the coupling of the colonial authorities and the betrayers of the revolution as found in the indigenous elites vs. the newly constituted "us"—the new alliance of European leftists and the anticolonial nationalist].[32]

I would argue that in deploying the term "evolution" Wallerstein aptly describes a flexible consistency of purpose that is ultimately tied to a revolutionary project of solidarity—of humanistic, non-instrumental intersubjective rationality (and, according to Davidson, there can be no other kind). And here is where I wish to tie the two threads of my essay together—rationality and intersubjectivity. If we can accept my characterization (adapting Wallerstein) of Fanon's rationality and consistency, then we have arrived at one important manner in which rationality, as a world-scale term, can be historicized and localized without losing any of its power and world-scale.[33] But this would be only one half of the picture. The other half is that this rationality has to, as Davidson argues, have an intersubjective dimension—we have to assume a common set of knowledges and desires of and in the world. This is the necessary preamble to any attempt to map rationality. In this sense, I would suggest, we have entered precisely into the realm of substantive reason and of politics. In this case, we are not so far from what Charles Taylor has called a notion of a "social imaginary": "That social imaginary is that common understanding that makes possible common practices and a widely shared sense of legitimacy."[34] The deployment of revolutionary rationality had everything to do with issues of social justice, of arguing the deconstruction of the us/them binary from both directions. To do this required the disorganization of the dehumanizing operations of rationality, and imagining a new historical starting point. This is all brought forward in the final pages of *Black Skins, White Masks*, and it is worth citing at length:

> I am my own foundation.
> And it is by going beyond the historical, instrumental hypothesis that I will initiate the cycle of my freedom.
> The disaster of the man of color lies in the fact that he was enslaved.
> The disaster and the inhumanity of the white man lie in the fact that somewhere he has killed man.

And even today they subsist, to organize this dehumanization rationally. But I as a man of color, to the extent that it becomes possible for me to exist absolutely, do not have the right to lock myself into a world of retroactive reparations.

I, the man of color, want only this:

That the tool never possesses the man. That the enslavement of man by man cease forever. That is, of one by another. That it be possible for me to discover and to love man, wherever he may be.

The Negro is not. Any more than the white man.

Both must turn their backs on the inhuman voices which were those of their respective ancestors in order that authentic communication be possible. Before it can adopt a positive voice, freedom requires an effort at disalienation . . .

Superiority? Inferiority?

Why not the quite simple attempt to touch the other, to feel the other, to explain the other to myself?

Was my freedom not given to me then in order to build the world of the You?

(231–32)

Coda

However attractive it is to simply end my essay with this powerful passage, I want to end by insisting on the hard intellectual and political labor that Fanon undertook to even be able to imagine this new historical age, to envision a time when "The Negro is not. Any more than the white man." This required the discovery and ardent deployment of a revolutionary rationality that mobilized both consistent humanizing and substantive rationality, each in turn embedded within a non-naïve yet capacious sense of being together. Simply put, Fanon could not rely on any principle of charity obtaining between the colonizer and the colonized.

The move is precisely away from "retroactive reparation," which would linger in the project to rationalize the white man's irrationality. This signals an important shift in historical thinking, and in this sense the aspirations behind world-systems analysis's reorientation of the social sciences as "an arena of social struggle" can only be fulfilled if, like Fanon, world-systems analysis bears in mind "the outcomes of future social struggles as its historic form [is] conditioned by previous social struggles."[35] The act of removing the "the heavy hand of scientism" and the act to "incorporate utopistics" in this case are one and the same.

Notes

I thank my co-editors and the press readers for their comments on my essay, and also Jürgen Habermas for our discussion on Davidson's work in relation to his own. All errors are of course mine.

1. See NASA's Web site, http://history.nasa.gov/sputnik.

2. Arendt, *The Human Condition*, 3.

3. Arendt, "The Conquest of Space and the Stature of Man," 267.

4. The idea of "two cultures" is found in positions famously articulated by C. P. Snow and his respondent F. R. Leavis. See Snow, *The Two Cultures*; Leavis, "Two Cultures? The Significance of Lord Snow"; Trilling, "The Leavis-Snow Controversy."

5. I thank Vicente Rafael for bringing this book to my attention. See Rafael's article, "The Cultures of Area Studies in the United States."

6. Hall, iii, 2, quoted in Rafael, "The Cultures of Area Studies in the United States," 94.

7. Rafael, "The Cultures of Area Studies in the United States," 95.

8. Wallerstein, *The Essential Wallerstein*, 180.

9. This resonates with, in different manners, Snow's notion of "two cultures" (literary intellectuals and scientists), and E. O. Wilson's concept of "consilience" (sciences and humanities).

10. Wallerstein, *Uncertainties*, 19.

11. Ibid.

12. Wallerstein, *Essential Wallerstein*, 195.

13. Wallerstein, *Uncertainties*, 107–8.

14. Ibid., 33. Compare with "World-Systems Analysis Was Born as a Moral, and in Its Broadest Sense, Political, Protest," *The Essential Wallerstein*, 129.

15. Wallerstein, *Uncertainties*, 15.

16. Wallerstein, "Social Science and Contemporary Society," 8, quoting Gramsci, *Prison Notebooks*, vol. 1, 231.

17. Wallerstein, "Social Science and Contemporary Society."

18. Weber, *Economy and Society*, vol 1, 85.

19. See Wallerstein's comment on the guarantees to those in power granted by rationality, at the beginning of the section of this lecture called "Social Science and Substantive Rationality."

20. Wallerstein, "The Heritage of Sociology, The Promise of Social Science," 12.

21. Davidson, *Problems*, 183.

22. Davidson, *Subjective, Intersubjective, Objective*, 121.

23. Davidson, *Problems*, 184.

24. "A Coherence Theory of Truth and Knowledge" (1983), in Davidson, *Subjective*, 148–49.

25. "Expressing Evaluations," in Davidson, *Problems*, 35.

26. Habermas, *Inclusion of the Other*, 29.

27. Wallerstein, *Uncertainties*, 85–86.

28. Wallerstein, "Fanon," 222.

29. Davidson, *Problems*, 192.

30. Wallerstein, "Fanon," 226–27.

31. Ibid., 223.

32. Ibid., 223.

33. See Breton's preface to Césaire's *Notebook on the Return to the Native Land*:

> As fundamental as Césaire's revindication appears to be, to limit its implications to the immediate would mean reducing its scope unforgivably. What I find invaluable in it is that it constantly transcends the anguish a black person associates with the fate of black people in modern society, and that, becoming one with the anguish of all poets, artists, and bona fide thinkers, but adding to it the bonus of verbal genius, it encompasses the condition allotted to man by that society even to its unbearable, but also infinitely amendable, dimensions. And here comes to the fore in bold type what surrealism has always considered as the first article of its charter: a deliberate will to deal the coup de grace to that which one calls "common sense" (which does not stop short of calling itself "reason"), and the imperious need to do away with the deadly division in the human spirit in which one component has managed to give itself complete license at the expense of the other whereas the very suppression of the latter will inevitably end up exalting it. If slave traders have physically disappeared from the world stage, their vile spirit is undoubtedly still at work. For just as their "ebony wood" became this slap dash cargo not even good enough to rot in the hold of their ships, so our dreams, that better half of our nature, become disenfranchised. "Because we hate you, you and your reason, we claim kinship with dementia praecox, with the flaming madness of persistent cannibalism. . . . Put up with me, I won't put up with you." (Breton 2001, xvii–xviii)

34. Taylor, *Modern Social Imaginaries*, 23.

35. Wallerstein, *Uncertainties*, 33.

Thinking about the "Humanities"

IMMANUEL WALLERSTEIN

This book is the fruit of a conference called to ask about the possible interface of the "humanities" and "world-systems analysis." This is a topic subject to multiple interpretations, as any reader of this book will surely notice. Allow me to develop my own views by starting with a personal reflection.

Often, when I meet someone for the first time at a social encounter, the person will ask me what I do. I usually respond by saying that I am a professor of sociology, and that I write about the modern world-system, using what I call "world-systems analysis." The usual response is to ask me what a world-system is. I explain as best I can. Most of the time, I feel that the concept seems rather strange to most people. And to the degree that it is understood, it seems to most people a vast subject, perhaps a blurry vast subject.

Now, if someone who teaches in a department of English or comparative literature gets the same question at a social gathering and responds that he or she writes about literature, I doubt very much that this person will be queried about what literature is. Any minimally educated person today will know, or thinks he or she knows, what literature is. Yet literature, too, is a vast subject, perhaps also a blurry vast subject. Of course, most people will assume that the English or comparative literature professor writes about some more limited field of literature, say English drama in the eighteenth century. But at least they will feel that this person is involved in a plausibly possible field of analysis.

Writing about literature is considered to be in the domain, or perhaps I should call it the superdomain, of the humanities. There is a small group of people in sociology departments who write about the "sociology of literature," but it is not a very large group. Writing about the modern world-system is considered to be in the domain of the social sciences. There are some people in departments of comparative literature who are writing today about something they call "world literature," but until now they too have been a rather small group.

For many people in the humanities, the social sciences are simply one branch of the sciences and attitudes toward the social sciences tend to reflect the classic divide between the two cultures. We humanists write about the concrete particular, which we seek to "understand." You social scientists pretend to write about "systems," which probably don't exist and in any case are reified versions of reality. I exaggerate the terms of this debate or conversation, but not by much.

Suppose I take a third person, a scholar who writes about religion. Where in the university system would this person be located? He or she might be in a theological faculty or a seminary, which is usually considered a "professional" school akin to schools of law or medicine. In addition, these days there are departments of religious studies in many universities, which are usually located in the faculty of humanities. Historians also feel free to write about religion. So do anthropologists and sociologists. There is even institutionalized an Association for the Sociology of Religion, which has a reasonably large number of members. I have not seen any statistics, but I would guess that if one did a survey of all scholars writing about religion, a third would be in seminaries, a third in the humanities, and a third in the social sciences.

What, then, is the difference between writing about world-systems, about literature, and about religion that should result in such a different distribution of university location for the scholars concerned with the three subject matters? Is there some acute epistemological difference between the three subject matters that makes this different distribution inevitable and correct? Or are the different patterns of distribution primarily the result of historical accidents that are hard to justify intellectually? My own inclination is to suggest the latter.

If one writes about literature, religion, or world-systems, one seeks to explain how they have become what they are and what impact their form or expression has had on the lives of people and the activities of groups. This is what I would call a "systemic" explanation, even if the word is never used. All nouns are systemic. All verbs are systemic. They all encompass a variety of instances that are summarized in the word. Of course they may be badly summarized in certain words, and scholars are constantly reviewing these summarizations and suggesting others, which they claim are better. But no statement about literature, religion, or world-systems is ever irreducibly unique. We would be totally unable to understand what the user of the statement meant. We would say he or she is talking gibberish.

On the other hand, literature, religions, and world-systems constantly evolve and change. And all statements are statements about a specific historical moment, holding true at best for that moment and not necessarily for others. The history of one moment, however, conditions the history of the next. There exists what some physicists are now calling the "arrow of time." So all scholars are forced, if they are to make intelligent statements, to be historical in their analyses.

The historical and the systemic are not opposed epistemologies. They are a linked pair with whose seemingly opposed tendencies we are condemned to wrestle. Freud said of being a parent that it is an impossible task, one that no one performs correctly. But we continue to be parents. And that is a good thing. This is what I say of scholarship. Dealing simultaneously with the systemic and the historical is an impossible task, one that no one ever performs correctly. But scholars continue to do it, even if they are often far less aware of doing it than people are of being parents.

Arnold Feldman was one of the first U.S. sociologists to write about the "development" of countries in the global South after 1945. He used to tell the story that whenever he gave a talk outlining his explanations of what was going on in these countries—that is, his tentative generalizations—there was sure to be an anthropologist in the audience who would get up and say: "But not in Pago Pago!" That is of course the traditional idiographic complaint about systemic arguments. The generalization is false because each situation is particular. And of course each situation is indeed particular. But that never means that there do not exist patterns of behavior that are more general. It is our ability to interweave the irreducibly particular with the inevitably general that is our vocation, our calling.

What we are all called upon to explain is always the world in which we are living. This is so, no matter how abstruse or remote our empirical focus seems to be, how little it seems to connect with the world in which we are living. After all, why do we want to know about matters that are abstruse or remote from our world? In the end, I challenge you to find any scholar who thinks that the matters about which he or she writes are totally irrelevant to our world. Why read Beowulf? Why try to understand trade in Sumer? Why study the Burgess shale? In each case, it tells us something about the world in which we are living now.

Well, the world in which we are living is, I contend, a capitalist world-economy. It has its history, its structure, its contradictions, its prospects. I try to study this directly. Others study it implicitly. I think it might help us all if the latter reflected more openly on what it is they are really doing.

The Twilight of Capital?

GOPAL BALAKRISHNAN

Only a few years after the end of the Cold War, world-systems theory already seemed to belong to a bygone era of upheaval. A bemused sociologist re-called a period piece scene from an academic conference held in the mid-1970s: "When Wallerstein went on to lay out 'an agenda of intellectual work for those who are seeking to understand the *world systemic transition from capitalism to socialism in which we are living*,' he literally brought the younger members of the audience to their feet."[1]

The tone of this recollection conveys how unbelievable the very idea of such a transition had become for the mainstream of academic opinion twenty years later. It was apparently hard to remember that the future of the world capitalist system had once seemed uncertain, when setbacks for America from Saigon to Managua unfolded in a context of global stagflation and labor revolts. Of course, instead of leading to any breakthroughs to a new order, the crisis of the seventies galvanized a momentous counteroffen-sive, a new phase of capitalism taking the form of austerity and immiser-ation in some zones, and profligacy and speculative bubbles in others. It was not long before the socialist bloc and anticolonial nationalisms were over-whelmed by a resurgent America, and social democracy forced into a long retreat. Rounding out this clean sweep was a wide-ranging restoration in the world of ideas and opinion. Across the social sciences, narrative schemas of a transition to socialism were replaced with diametrically opposed ones presuming a movement away from socialism—or some other backward condition—toward a modernity of liberal democracy, markets, and human rights. In this new age of western war and commerce, older tropes of clash-ing civilizations and the rise of the Orient resurfaced, providing some room for afterthoughts on alternative versions of capitalism, and even alternative modernities. Throughout these vast changes of the post–Cold War scene,

Wallerstein consistently portrayed neoliberalism as an age, not of restored capitalist vitality, but of impending imperial decline.

All of a sudden, we seem to be in the midst of another dramatic change of historical course, broadly conforming to such predictions, and perhaps vindicating the credibility of the historical theorization of the *longue durée* that framed them. The current worldwide implosion of financial and property markets is the end of the era of neoliberal globalization, which since the 1990s appeared as some untranscendable epochal horizon. The upheavals stemming from a protracted global economic downturn may soon occasion a reappraisal of a number of post–Cold War ideological verdicts on our historical situation.

"We can no longer say anything worthwhile about culture and history without first becoming aware of our own cultural and historical situation. That all historical knowledge obtains its light and intensity from the present . . . has been said by many since Hegel, but best of all by Benedetto Croce."[2]

The epigram arguably overstates the case, but conveys the problem of grasping the specific existential situations that ground the capacity to historicize. Conversely, the challenge of understanding the historical present— the onset of a world economic downturn of roughly thirties proportions, coming twenty years after the collapse of the USSR—may open up perspectives on the outer boundaries and life spans of world-systems, of historicity itself. *Hic rhodus hic saltus* (Rhodes is here; here is the place for your jump), as Hegel would say.

Immanuel Wallerstein's work offers a compelling general framework for outlining and forecasting the epochal socio-political transformations that may emerge out of the breakdown of the latest phase of capitalism. Unfortunately, today, outside of the diminished subfield of historical sociology, world-systems theory is probably better known for its distinctive terminology of "cores," "peripheries," and "semi-peripheries" than for its account of the current age of capital, and what might lie beyond its horizon. In what follows, I consider some themes from two small books by Wallerstein, one from before the end of the Cold War (*Historical Capitalism*), and one from immediately after (*Capitalist Civilization*), now published together.[3] I remember reading an older version of the first essay in 1983. If you've ever seen it, you'll recall the unforgettable image on its cover: a leviathan, staring blankly upward, devouring a school of small fish.

Wallerstein's conception of the large-scale and long-term adopts an older motif of the rise and fall of civilizations. The center he established at SUNY Binghamton is called the Fernand Braudel Center for the Study of Economies, Historical Systems, and Civilizations. What explains the appeal of this old-fashioned term, "civilization," to the founder of the world-systems school? After all, "civilization" was never a central category in the classical tradition of sociology, while historians began to avoid it after it became firmly associated with the speculations of Spengler and Toynbee. The *Annales* School had no time for such philosophies of history, but Braudel frequently enlivened his works with a less brooding, Gallic version of this older civilizations discourse. Although he stuck to conventional definitions, the most memorable passages from his work on the Mediterranean in the age of Phillip II, or on material life and commerce in pre-modern world economies evoke the deep, quasi-natural temporalities beneath "the froth of events." The affinity of the committed sociologist for the historian of the *longue durée* might seem perplexing, but it probably allowed the former a certain distance from a Marxian analytics of capitalism, anyhow too Euro-centric, in his view, to comprehend the anti-systemic agencies of an age of decolonization.

The historicity implicit in the term "civilization" has long had a stereo-typical ring, suggestive of ruins and lost cities. If Wallerstein's conception of modern capitalism as a civilization was meant to restore an entirely plausible sense of the inevitable demise of this mode of life, it may nonetheless fail to capture the specifically contemporary historical problem of what David Harvey called "the limits of capital." Capitalism is not quite a civilization in the old sense, and the forms of its decline will likely be as unprecedented as everything else about it has been.

Wallerstein was often criticized for failing to explain the genesis of capitalism. Side-stepping the specifics, he preferred to address the problem of the transition to the modern world-system in broad strokes. As he explained in both *Historical Capitalism* and *Capitalist Civilization*, Europe's distinctive, post-feudal order of multiple states allowed merchants, landlords, and colonial adventurers to circumvent obstacles that elsewhere stood in the way of the primitive accumulation of capital. Capitalism arose in the numerous interstices of the European old regime, he proposed suggestively. In contrast to other geographical zones of advanced civilization where imperial authority and customary modes of social life held traders in thrall, post-feudal European mutated into a permanently chaotic order of war, enclosures, and commerce. Over several centuries, this expanding cosmos of accumulation generated a dynamic hierarchy of states, classes, and culturally defined peoples. Although the core of this world-system was never subsumed into a single empire, a looser enforcement of its evolving rules of rank and survival has been provided by a succession of hegemonic states, each powered by the most advanced economy of the day. Hegemonic powers have promoted historic expansions of the world-system, and faltered as they became unable to provide military, financial, and normative solutions to emerging problems of accumulation and order.

The late nineteenth-century rise of new capitalist powers eventually led to the breakdown of the British Empire over the course of two world wars, releasing a cycle of anti-systemic revolts that lasted from 1917 to the late seventies. Over the last half of the twentieth century, the United States emerged as the guardian power of the world-capitalist system, charged with the extraordinary task of rebuilding and extending its domain against an advancing wave of Communist and anticolonial state formation, and then, in a second phase, enforcing neoliberal globalization in the aftermath of the collapse and retreat of these forces. In conformity with this pattern, one might assume that the deflation of an American-led neoliberalism will open up another cycle of anti-systemic revolts. But, in the aftermath of the experience of defeat and ensuing socio-cultural transformations, what forms this would assume are presently unclear. What does the past suggest?

Wallerstein argued that in order to be effective, twentieth-century anti-systemic movements had to be statist, ruthlessly promoting industrial development in order to compete in the great game of progress. But far from breaking with the world-capitalist system, the statist path of modernization remained subject to its geopolitical, economic, and cultural compulsions. The radicalization of the struggle to catch up forced the core powers of civilization to adapt, and shed the obsolescent institutions and goals of early industrial and nationalist modernity, ceding them to lower echelons of the world-system in yet another round of restructurings within an unchanged hierarchy of core, semi-periphery, and periphery. A whole cycle of mimetic-antagonistic modernization was coming to an end in the seventies,, as a generation of anti-systemic states and movements encountered the limits of accumulation and legitimacy in this mode. Wallerstein invoked the authority of Fanon to argue that the only way to transcend this impasse of derivative modernization was through the multiplication and fusion of anti-systemic forces. He advanced this diagnosis after more than a decade of internecine wars in the Communist bloc, and long after the Bandung springtime of anticolonial nationalism. Looking back at this failed cycle of revolts, Wallerstein concluded that the state—the *telos* of all anti-systemic movements—had become the main obstacle to building new forms of autonomous collectivity. One suspects that after a couple of decades of the neoliberal hobbling and delegitimation of public authority, he might now have a different take on the problem. Arguably, it remains to be seen whether, or in what ways, the twentieth-century triad of state, movement, and people will continue to be definitive in the coming period.

Wallerstein's conception of a seamless world-system always raised the problem of what its boundaries were: at what moment did the Ottoman realm, or Qing China, for example, become part of it? In his account, any contact with the world-capitalist system entailed a sudden, near complete subsumption into its totalizing hierarchy. Marxist critics found this vision too holistic, and proposed a more open figure of combined and uneven development, of incomplete totality, of a simultaneity of the non-simultaneous, while non-Marxists proposed stories that gave more agency to non-Western peoples, leading to culturally distinctive variants of modernization, and so forth. Historical judgments regarding inside and outside, structure and agency, or beginning and end, raise philosophical problems concerning the elementary forms of our thought, but whatever answers we come to should be historical and historicized themselves, although the trivializing deconstruction of binary oppositions is of course much easier.

Wallerstein's remorseless insistence that even the most anti-systemic states remained wholly subject to its multilevel compulsion to accumulate was qualified by the claim that the system's centuries-old power to englobe was in the midst of a long-term crisis. Perhaps we are now entering into a period in which the power of these compulsions, ever more dependent on debt and public subsidy, will begin to wane, opening up new parameters for de-linking, more favorable conditions for breakthroughs in self-determination. But the cultural, subjective inclination and capacity for such political experiments may have also waned in many regions of the world system. What then should we make of Wallerstein's claim that historical capitalism will come to an end over the course of the twenty-first century? Many will still find this an incredible proposition—is it not in the very nature of capitalism to bounce back after a round or two of creative destruction?—although a note of hesitation has become audible, for the first time in thirty years.

Wallerstein argues: "But the future world order will construct itself slowly, in way we can barely imagine, never mind predict. It is therefore somewhat of a leap of faith to believe that it will be good, or even better."[4] This is a context in which we can reflect on the future of the humanities and critical social science. The first phase of the world economic downturn that we are in is already turning into a fiscal crisis of the postwar university system. Without anti-systemic reforms, large parts of the support system for the analysis and interpretation of society and culture could be eliminated, however detrimental this may be to the longer-term interests of the capitalist system. Obviously some institutions will be harder hit than others, but if the bottom gives way in the more exposed sectors, inevitably this will lead to structural adjustments of the disciplinary and divisional framework of the research university. Wallerstein was always a trenchant critic of the institutional grid of academic knowledge production, accusing it of subservience to power, money, and fashion, and going so far as to call into question its traditional epistemic ideals.

Wallerstein asks: "But how much light does this form of truth shed upon the process of decline of this historical system, or on the existence of real historical alternatives to the endless accumulation of capital? Therein lies the question."[5] Like Lacan's diagnosis of the crisis of modern university discourse[6]—or Heidegger's before it—Wallerstein's criticism of disciplinarity assumed that intellectual trends, fashions (idle talk!), and the occasional epistemic crisis would continue to unfold in the vast bureaucracies of higher education. The coming phase of structural transformation threatens to shut down the material basis of this assumption. In England, during the early phases of the primitive accumulation of capital, the monasteries were dissolved, with momentous cultural consequences. The university logic of the late phases of capitalism remains to be seen.

Notes

1. Alexander, "Modern: Anti, Post, and Neo," 64.

2. Schmitt, "The Age of Neutralizations and Depoliticizations," in *The Concept of the Political*, 80.

3. Wallerstein, *Historical Capitalism with Capitalist Civilization*.

4. Ibid., 93.

5. Ibid., 89.

6. "Let us ask how capitalist society can afford to allow itself a relaxation of university discourse . . . if we embrace this relaxation which, it has to be said, has been offered, aren't we falling into a trap?" (Lacan, *Seminar XVII*, 235).

Bibliography

Abu-Lughod, Janet. *Before European Hegemony*. Oxford: Oxford University Press, 1991.

Abu-Lughod, Lila, ed. *Remaking Women: Feminism and Modernity in the Middle East*. Princeton: Princeton University Press, 1998.

Agnew, John A., and Stuart Corbridge. *Mastering Space*. New York: Routledge, 1994.

Ahmad, Aijaz. *In Theory: Classes, Nations, Literatures*. London: Verso, 1992.

Albrow, Martin. *The Global Age*. Oxford: Polity, 1996.

———. "Introduction." In *Globalization, Knowledge and Society*, ed. Martin Albrow and Elizabeth King, 1–14. London: Sage, 1990.

Alexander, Jeffery. "Modern: Anti, Post, and Neo." *New Left Review* I/210 (1995): 63–101.

Ali, Tariq. *Conversations with Edward Said*. London: Seagull, 2006.

Anderson, Benedict. "Exodus." *Critical Inquiry* 20, no. 2 (winter 1994): 314–27.

Anderson, Perry. "Confronting Defeat," *London Review of Books* (17 October 2002), 10–17.

———. *Lineages of the Absolutist State*. London: Verso, 1974.

———. *The Origins of Postmodernity*. London: Verso, 1998.

Anghie, Anthony. *Imperialism, Sovereignty, and the Making of International Law*. Cambridge: Cambridge University Press, 2004.

Appadurai, Arjun. 1996. "Disjuncture and Difference in the Global Cultural Economy." In Appadurai, *Modernity at Large*, 27–47.

———. *Fear of Small Numbers: An Essay on the Geography of Anger*. Durham: Duke University Press, 2006.

———. *Modernity at Large: Cultural Dimensions of Globalization*. Minneapolis: University of Minnesota Press, 1996.

———, ed. *The Social Life of Things: Commodities in Cultural Perspective*. Cambridge: Cambridge University Press, 1981.

Apter, Emily. "Global *Translatio*: The 'Invention' of Comparative Literature, Istanbul, 1933." *Critical Inquiry* 29, no. 2 (winter 2003): 253–81.

———. *The Translation Zone: A New Comparative Literature*. Princeton: Princeton University Press, 2005.

Arac, Jonathan. "Anglo-Globalism?" *New Left Review* 16 (July–August 2002): 39–45.

Arendt, Hannah. "The Conquest of Space and the Stature of Man." In *Between Past and Future*, 265–82. New York: Penguin, 1968.

———. *The Human Condition* [1958]. Chicago: University of Chicago Press, 1998.

Arnold, Matthew. *Culture and Anarchy* [1869]. New Haven: Yale University Press, 1994.

Asad, Talal. *Genealogies of Religion: Discipline and Reasons of Power in Christianity and Islam*. Baltimore: Johns Hopkins University Press, 1993.

Ashcroft, Bill, Gareth Griffiths, and Helen Tiffin, eds. *The Empire Writes Back: Theory and Practice in Postcolonial Literatures*. London: Routledge, 1989.

Badiou, Alain. *Ethics: An Essay on the Understanding of Evil*. London: Verso, 2001.

———. *Handbook of Inaesthetics*. Stanford: Stanford University Press, 2005.

———. *Infinite Thought: Truth and the Return of Philosophy*. Trans. and ed. Oliver Feltham and Justin Clemens. New York: Continuum, 2003.

———. *Logics of Worlds*. New York: Continuum, 2008.

———. *Manifesto for Philosophy*. Trans. and ed. Norman Madarasz. Albany: State University of New York Press, 1999.

———. *Saint Paul: The Foundation of Universalism*. Stanford: Stanford University Press, 2003.

———. *Theoretical Writings*. Trans. and ed. Ray Brassier and Alberto Toscano. New York: Continuum, 2004.

Balibar, Etienne, and Immanuel Wallerstein. *Race, Nation, Class: Ambiguous Identities*. London: Verso, 1992.

Barlow, Tani. "Gender and Region." Unpublished keynote address, Harvard University, 2006.

———. "History and the Border." *Journal of Women's History* 18, no. 2 (summer 2006): 8–32.

———. *The Question of Women in Chinese Feminism*. Durham: Duke University Press, 2004.

Barlow, Tani, et al., eds. "The Modern Girl Around the World: A Research Agenda and Preliminary Findings." *Gender and History* 17, no. 2 (August 2005): 245–95.

Basalla, George. *The Evolution of Technology*. Cambridge: Cambridge University Press, 1988.

Batten, Bruce L. *To the Ends of Japan: Premodern Frontiers, Boundaries, and Interactions*. Honolulu: University of Hawaii Press, 2003.

Bayly, Christopher A. "From Archaic Globalization to International Networks, circa 1600–2000." In *Interactions: Transregional Perspectives on World History*, ed. Jerry H. Bentley, Renate Bridenthal, and Anand A. Yang, 14–29. Honolulu: University of Hawaii Press, 2005.

Bender, Thomas, ed. *Rethinking American History in a Global Age*. Berkeley: University of California Press, 2002.

———. *A Nation Among Nations: America's Place in World History*. New York: Hill and Wang, 2006.

Benjamin, Walter. *Understanding Brecht*. Trans. Anna Bostock. London: New Left Books, 1973.

Bentley, Jerry H., Renate Bridenthal, and Anand A. Yang, eds. *Interactions: Transregional Perspectives on World History*. Honolulu: University of Hawaii Press, 2005.

Benton, Lauren. "From the World-Systems Perspective to Institutional World History: Culture and Economy in Global Theory." *Journal of World History* 7 (1996): 261–96.

———. *Law and Colonial Cultures: Legal Regimes in World History, 1400–1900*. Cambridge: Cambridge University Press, 2002.

Black, Jeremy, ed. *Atlas of World History: Mapping the Human Journey*. London: Dorling Kindersley, 2000.

———. *Maps and History*. New Haven: Yale University Press, 1997.

Blair, Sara. "Cultural Geography and the Place of the Literary." *American Literary History* 10, no. 3 (1998): 544–67.

Boltanski, Luc. *Distant Suffering: Morality, Media and Politics*. Trans. Graham Burchell. Cambridge: Cambridge University Press, 1993.

Borstelmann, Thomas. *Apartheid's Reluctant Uncle: The United States and Southern Africa in the Early Cold War*. Oxford: Oxford University Press, 1993.

Bourdieu, Pierre. *Acts of Resistance: Against the Tyranny of the Market*. New York: New Press, 1996.

———. "Le Champ Scientifique." *Actes de la Recherche en Sciences Sociales* 8, no. 9 (June 1976): 88–104.

———. *The Field of Cultural Production: Essays on Art and Literature*. Cambridge: Polity Press, 1993.

———. *The Rules of Art: Genesis and Structure of the Literary Field*. Stanford: Stanford University Press, 1995.

Braudel, Fernand. *Civilization and Capitalism, 15th–18th century*. Vol. 3, *The Perspective of the World*. London: Collins, 1984.

———. *The Perspective of the World*. Berkeley: University of California Press, 1984.

Brenner, Neil. *New State Spaces: Urban Governance and the Rescaling of Statehood*. New York: Oxford University Press, 2004.

Brenner, Neil, Bob Jessop, Martin Jones, and Gordon MacLeod, eds. *State/Space: A Reader*. Boston: Blackwell, 2002.

Brenner, Neil, and Stuart Elden. "State, Space, World: Henri Lefebvre and the Survival of Capitalism." In N. Brenner and S. Elden, eds., *State, Space, World*, 1–41. Minneapolis: University of Minnesota Press, 2009.

Brenner, Robert. "The Origins of Capitalist Development: A Critique of Neo-Smithian Marxism." *New Left Review* 104 (July/August 1977): 25–92.

Breton, Andre. "Preface" to Aime Césaire, *Notebook on the Return to the Native Land*. Middletown, Conn.: Wesleyan University Press, 2001.

Brigham, Ann. "Productions of Geographic Scale and Capitalist-Colonialist Enterprise in Leslie Marmon Silko's *Almanac of the Dead*. *Modern Fiction Studies* 50, no. 2 (2004): 303–31.

Burton, Antoinette. *Burdens of History: British Feminists, Indian Women, and Imperial Culture, 1865–1915*. Chapel Hill: University of North Carolina Press, 1994.

Butler, Judith, Ernesto Laclau, and Slavoj Žižek, eds. *Contingency, Hegemony, Universality: Contemporary Dialogues on the Left*. London: Verso, 2000.

Cameron, A., and R. Palan. "The Imagined Economy: Mapping Transformations in the Contemporary State." *Millennium* 28, no. 2 (1999): 267–88.

Candido, Antonio. *O discurso e a cidade*. São Paulo: Livraria Duas Cidades, 1993.

Casanova, Pascale. "Literature as a World" *New Left Review* 31 (January/February 2005): 71–90.

———. *La république mondiale des lettres* [*World Republic of Letters*]. Paris: Le Seuil, 1999.

———. "Le Roman international." *Liber-Revue internationale des livres* 13 (March 1993): 12–16.

Cassirer, Ernst. *The Philosophy of Symbolic Forms* [1923–29]. 3 vols. New Haven and London: Yale University Press, 1953–57.

Castells, Manuel. *The Rise of the Network Society*. Cambridge, Mass.: Blackwell, 1996.

Cavalli-Sforza, Luigi, Paolo Menozzi, and Alberto Piazza. *The History and Geography of Human Genes*. Princeton: Princeton University Press, 1994.

Cerny, Philip. "Globalization and the Changing Logic of Collective Action." *International Organization* 49, no. 4 (1995): 595–625.

Chatterjee, Partha. *The Nation and Its Fragments*. Princeton: Princeton University Press, 1993.

Cheah, Pheng. "Grounds of Comparison." *Diacritics* 29, no. 4 (1999): 3–18.

Clunas, Craig. "Modernity Global and Local: Consumption and the Rise of the West." *American Historical Review* 104, no. 5 (December 1999): 1497–511.

Collinge, Chris. *Spatial Articulation of the State: Reworking Social Relations and Social Regulation Theory*. Centre for Urban and Regional Studies. Birmingham, U.K.: University of Birmingham, 1996.

Collini, Stefan. *Public Moralists: Political Thought and Intellectual Life in Britain, 1850–1930*. Oxford: Oxford University Press, 1991.

Cooper, Frederick, and Ann Laura Stoler, eds. *Tensions of Empire: Colonial Cultures in a Bourgeois World*. Berkeley: University of California Press, 1997.

Corrigan, Philip, and Derek Sayer. *The Great Arch: English State Formation as Cultural Revolution*. Oxford: Basil Blackwell, 1985.

Cox, Kevin, ed. *Spaces of Globalization*. New York: Guilford, 1997.

Crosby, Alfred. *Ecological Imperialism: The Biological Expansion of Europe, 900–1900*. Cambridge: Cambridge University Press, 1983.

———. *The Measure of Reality: Quantification and Western Society, 1250–1600*. Cambridge: Cambridge University Press, 1997.

Cvetkovich, Ann. *Mixed Feelings: Feminism, Mass Culture and Victorian Sensationalism*. New Brunswick: Rutgers University Press, 1992.

Damrosch, David. *What Is World Literature?* Princeton: Princeton University Press, 2003.

Davenport, Frances Gardiner. *European Treaties Bearing on the History of the United States and Its Dependencies to 1648* [1917]. Washington, D.C.: Carnegie Institution of Washington, 1967.

Davidson, Donald. *Problems of Rationality*. Oxford: Clarendon Press, 2004.

———. *Subjective, Intersubjective, Objective*. Oxford: Oxford University Press, 2001.

De Vattel, Emmerich. *The Law of Nations* [1758]. Washington, D.C.: Carnegie Institute, 1916.

De Vitoria, Francisco. *De Indis et de Ivre Belli Relectiones* [1532]. Washington, D.C.: Carnegie Institution, 1917.

Denemark, Robert A., Jonathan Friedman, Barry K. Gills, and George Modelsky. *World System History: The Social Science of Long-Term Change*. London: Routledge, 2000.

Der Derian, James. "The (S)pace of International Relations: Simulation, Surveillance and Speed." *International Studies Quarterly* 34 (1990): 295–310.

Dicken, Peter. *Global Shift*. 3rd edn. New York: Guilford Press, 1998.

Dicken, Peter, Adam Tickell, and Jamie Peck. "Unpacking Globalization." In *Geographies of Economies*, ed. Roger Lee and Jane Wills, 158–67. London: Arnold, 1997.

Dimock, Wai Chee. "Genre and World System: Epic and Novel on Four Continents" *Narrative* 14, no. 1 (2006): 85–101.

Dimock, Wai Chee, and Laurence Buell, eds. *Shades of the Planet: American Literature as World Literature*. Princeton: Princeton University Press, 2007.

Dirlik, Arif. "Performing the World: Reality and Representation in the Making of World Histor(ies)." *Journal of World History* 16, no. 4 (December 2005): 391–410.

Donnan, Hastings, and Thomas M. Wilson. *Borders: Frontiers of Identity, Nation, and State*. Oxford: Oxford International Publishers, 1999.

DuPlessis, Robert S., "The Partial Transition to World-Systems Analysis in Early Modern European History." *Radical History Review* 39 (1987): 11–27.

Eagleton, Terry. *The Eagleton Reader*. Ed. Stephen Regan. Oxford: Blackwell, 1988.

Elden, Stuart. "Missing the Point: The State of Territory Under Globalization: Empire and the Politics of Reterritorialization." In *Metaphoricity and the Politics of Mobility*, ed. Maria Margaroni and Effie Yiannopoulou, 47–66. Amsterdam: Rodopi, 2006.

Evans, Peter, Dietrich Rueschemeyer, and Theda Skocpol, eds. *Bringing the State Back In*. New York: Cambridge University Press, 1985.

Even-Zohar, Itamar. "The Laws of Literary Interference." *Poetics Today* 11, no. 1 (1990): 53–72.

Fanon, Franz. *Black Skins, White Masks*. Trans. Charles Lam Markmann. New York: Grove Weidenfeld, 1967.

Ferguson, Frances. "Comparing the Literatures: Textualism and Globalism." *English Literary History* 72, no. 2 (2004): 323–27.

Ferguson, James. "Decomposing Modernity: History and Hierarchy after Development." In *Postcolonial Studies and Beyond*, ed. Ania Loomba, Suvir Kaul, Matti Bunzl, Antoinette Burton, and Jed Esty, 166–81. Durham: Duke University Press, 2005.

Friedman, Thomas. *The Lexus and the Olive Tree*. New York: Anchor, 2000.

Gaddis, John Lewis. *The Cold War: A New History*. New York: Penguin, 2005.

Geyer, Michael, and Charles Bright. "World History in a Global Age." *American Historical Review* 100 (1995): 1034–60.

Gibson-Graham, J. K. *The End of Capitalism (As We Knew It): A Feminist Critique of Political Economy*. Oxford: Basil Blackwell, 1996.

Giddens, Anthony. *The Consequences of Modernity*. Stanford: Stanford University Press, 1990.

Gill, Stephen. "New Constitutionalism, Democratisation and Global Political Economy." *Pacifica Review* 10, no. 1 (1998): 23–38.

Gilroy, Paul. *The Black Atlantic: Modernity and Double Consciousness*. Cambridge: Harvard University Press, 1993.

Glendon, Mary Ann. *A World Made New: Eleanor Roosevelt and the Universal Declaration of Human Rights*. New York: Random House, 2001.

Globalization Project. "Area Studies, Regional Worlds: A White Paper for the Ford Foundation." The Globalization Project, University of Chicago Center for International Studies, June 1995.

Goldsmith, Jack L., and Eric A. Posner. *The Limits of International Law*. New York: Oxford University Press, 2005.

Goswami, Manu. *Producing India: From Colonial Space to National Economy*. Chicago: University of Chicago Press, 2004.

Gould, Stephen Jay. *Full House: The Spread of Excellence from Plato to Darwin*. New York: Harmony, 1996.

Gramsci, Antonio. *Prison Notebooks*. Vol. 1. New York: Columbia University Press, 1992.

Greene, Roland. "Review of Spivak, *Death of a Discipline*." *Substance* 35, no. 1 (2006): 154–59.

Gupta, Akhil, and James Ferguson, eds. *Culture, Power, Place*. Durham: Duke University Press, 1997.

Habermas, Jürgen. "A Genealogical Analysis of the Cognitive Content of Morality." In *The Inclusion of the Other: Studies in Political Theory*, ed. Ciaran Cronin and Pablo De Greiff, 3–48. Cambridge: MIT Press, 1999.

Hall, Robert. *Area Studies: With Special Reference to Their Implications for Research in the Social Sciences*. New York: Committee on World Area Research Programs, Social Science Research Council, 1948.

Hallward, Peter. *Badiou: A Subject to Truth*. Minneapolis: Minnesota University Press, 2003.

Hardt, Michael, and Antonio Negri. *Empire*. Cambridge: Harvard University Press, 2001.

Harvey, David. "The Geopolitics of Capitalism." In *Social Relations and Spatial Structures*, ed. Derek Gregory and John Urry, 128–63. London: Macmillan, 1985.

———. *The Limits to Capital*. Chicago: University of Chicago Press, 1982.

———. *The Urban Experience*. Baltimore: Johns Hopkins University Press, 1989.

Helleiner, Eric. *States and the Reemergence of Global Finance*. Ithaca: Cornell University Press, 1994.

Hopkins, Terence K., Immanuel Wallerstein, Thomas Riefer, Jamie Sudler, Satoshi Ikeda, Faruk Tabak, Sheila Pelizzon, John Casparis, Georgi Derlugian, Richard Lee. *The Age of Transition: Trajectory of the World-System 1945–2025*. London: Zed Books, 1996.

Hopkins, Terence K., Immanuel Wallerstein, et al. *World-Systems Analysis: Theory and Methodology*. Beverly Hills: Sage, 1982.

Howe, Stephen. *Empire: A Very Short Introduction*. Oxford: Oxford University Press, 2002.

Hsu, Hsuan. "Literature and Regional Production." *American Literary History* 17, no. 1 (2005): 36–69.

Huang, Philip C. C. "Development or Involution in Eighteenth-Century Britain and China?: A Review of Kenneth Pomeranz's *The Great Divergence: China, Europe, and the Making of the Modern World Economy*." *The Journal of Asian Studies* 61, no. 2 (2002): 501–38.

Hudson, Mark J. *Ruins of Identity: Ethnogenesis in the Japanese Islands*. Honolulu: University of Hawaii Press, 1999.

Hunt, Lynn. *Inventing Human Rights*. New York: W. W. Norton, 2007.

Hussein, Abdirahaman A. *Edward Said: Criticism and Society*. London: Verso, 2002.

Imber, Colin. *The Ottoman Empire, 1300–1650: The Structure of Power*. London: Palgrave Macmillan, 2002.

Ito, Ruri, Tani Barlow, and Hiroko Sakamoto, eds. *The Modern Girl, Colonial Modernity and East Asia* (in Japanese). Tokyo: Iwanami Shoten, 2009.

Jameson, Fredric. "On Literary and Cultural Import-Substitution in the Third World." *Margins* 1 (1991): 11–34.

———. *Postmodernism, or, The Cultural Logic of Late Capitalism*. Durham: Duke University Press, 1992.

Jay, Paul. "Beyond Discipline? Globalization and the Future of English," *PMLA* 116, no. 1 (2001): 32- 47.

Jayawardena, Kumari. *Feminism and Nationalism in the Third World*. London: Zed Press, 1986.

Jessop, Bob. *The Future of the Capitalist State*. London: Polity, 2002.

———. "Globalization and its (Il)logic(s)." In *Globalization and the Asia-Pacific*, ed. Kris Olds et. al., 19–38. London: Routledge, 1999.

Kant, Immanuel. "Perpetual Peace [1795]." In *Kant's Political Writings*, ed. Hans Reiss. Cambridge: Cambridge University Press, 1970.

Katzenstein, Peter J., and Takashi Shiraishi, eds. *Network Power: Japan and Asia*. Ithaca: Cornell University Press, 1997.

Kelly, Philip. "The Geographies and Politics of Globalization." *Progress in Human Geography* 23, no. 3 (1999): 379–400.

Koskenniemi, Martti. *The Gentle Civilizer of Nations: The Rise and Fall of International Law, 1870–1960*. Cambridge: Cambridge University Press, 2004.

Kristal, Efraín. "'Considering Coldly . . .': A Response to Franco Moretti," *New Left Review* 15 (May/June 2002): 61–74.

Lacan, Jacques. *Seminar XVII*. New York: W. W. Norton, 2007.

Laclau, Ernesto, and Chantal Mouffe. *Hegemony and Social Strategy: Towards a Radical Democratic Politics*. London: Verso, 1985.

Laing, Ellen. *Selling Happiness: Calendar Posters and Visual Culture in Early 20th Century Shanghai*. Honolulu: University of Hawaii Press, 2004.

Leavis, Frank Raymond. "Two Cultures? The Significance of Lord Snow [1959]." In *Nor Shall My Word: Discourses on Pluralism, Comparison and Social Hope*. New York: Barnes and Noble, 1972.

Lee, Richard. "Complexity Studies." In *Overcoming the Two Cultures: The Sciences versus the Humanities in the Modern World-System*, ed. Richard E. Lee and Immanuel Wallerstein, 107–17. New York: Paradigm, 2004.

———. *Life and Times of Cultural Studies: The Politics and Transformation of the Structures of Knowledge*. Durham: Duke University Press, 2003.

———. "Readings in the 'New Science': A Selective Annotated Bibliography." *Review* XV (1992): 113–71.

———. "Structures of Knowledge." In *The Age of Transition: Trajectory of the World-System 1945–2025*, ed. Terence K. Hopkins et al., 178–206. London: Zed Books, 1996.

———. "The 'Third' Arena: Trends and Logistics in the Geoculture of the Modern World-System." In *Emerging Issues in the 21st-Century World-System*, ed. Wilma A. Dunaway, 120–27. Westport: Greenwood, 2003.

Lee, Richard E., and Immanuel Wallerstein, eds. *Overcoming the Two Cultures: The Sciences versus the Humanities in the Modern World-System*. New York: Paradigm, 2004.

Lee, Richard E., and Immanuel Wallerstein. "Structures of Knowledge." In *The Blackwell Companion to Sociology*, ed. Judith Blau, 227–35. Cambridge: Blackwell, 2000.

Lefebvre, Henri. *De l'État: Les contradictions de l'État moderne*. Vol. 4. Paris: Union Générale d'Éditions, 1978.

———. *The Production of Space* [1974]. Cambridge: Blackwell, 1991.

———. *State, Space, World: Selected Essays*. Ed. Neil Brenner and Stuart Elden. Minneapolis: University of Minnesota Press, 2009.

Lewis, Martin. "Dividing the Ocean Sea." *Geographical Review* 89, no. 2 (April 1999): 188–214.

Lewis, Martin, and Kären Wigen. *The Myth of Continents: A Critique of Metageography*. Berkeley: University of California Press, 1997.

Lieberman, Victor. *Strange Parallels: Southeast Asia in Global Context, c. 800–1830*. Vol. 1. Cambridge: Cambridge University Press, 2003.

———. *Strange Parallels: Mainland Mirrors: Europe, Japan, China, South Asia, and the Islands*. Vol. 2. Cambridge: Cambridge University Press, 2009.

Limerick, Patricia. *The Legacy of Conquest: The Unbroken Past of the American West*. New York: W. W. Norton, 1987.

Lionnet, Françoise, and Shu-Mei Shih, eds. *Minor Transnationalism*. Durham: Duke University Press, 2005.

Lipschutz, Ronnie. "Restructuring World Politics: The Emergence of Global Civil Society." *Millennium* 21 (1992): 389–421.

Lowe, Lisa, and David Lloyd, eds. *The Politics of Culture in the Shadow of Capital*. Durham: Duke University Press, 1997.

Luibheid, Ethne. "The 1965 Immigration and Nationality Act: An 'End' to Exclusion?" *positions: east asia cultures critique* 5, no. 2 (fall 1997): 501–22.

Maier, Charles. "Consigning the Twentieth Century to History: Alternative Narratives for the Modern Era." *American Historical Review* 105, no. 3 (2000): 807–31.

Mann, Michael. *The Sources of Social Power, Volume 2: The Rise of Classes and Nation-States*. New York: Cambridge University Press, 1993.

Marx, Karl. *Grundrisse: Foundations of the Critique of Political Economy* [1857]. Trans. Martin Nicolaus. New York: Penguin, 1973.

Massey, Doreen. "Places and Their Pasts." *History Workshop Journal* 39 (1995): 182–92.

———. "Politics and Space/time." In *Space, Place, Gender*, 249–72. Minneapolis: University of Minnesota Press, 1994.

Matsuda, Matt K. "Doctor, Judge, Vagabond: Identity, Identification, and Other Memories of the State." *History and Memory* 6 (1994): 73–94.

McGrew, Anthony. "A Global Society?" In *Modernity and Its Futures*, ed. Tony McGrew, Stuart Hall, and David Held, 61–116. Cambridge: Open University Press, 1992.

McKeown, Adam. *Chinese Migrant Networks and Cultural Change: Peru, Chicago, Hawaii, 1900–1936*. Chicago: University of Chicago Press, 2001.

McMichael, Philip. *Development and Social Change*. Thousand Oaks, Calif.: Sage, 1996.

Melman, Billie. *Women's Orients: English Women and the Middle East, 1718–1918: Sexuality, Religion and Work*. Ann Arbor: University of Michigan Press, 1992.

Meyer, John. "The Changing Cultural Content of the Nation-State: A World Society

Perspective." In *State/Culture: State Formation after the Cultural Turn*, ed. George Steinmetz. Ithaca: Cornell University Press, 1999.

Milton, Giles. *Nathaniel's Nutmeg, or, The True and Incredible Adventures of the Spice Trader Who Changed the Course of History*. New York: Penguin Books, 1999.

Mittleman, James. *The Globalization Syndrome*. Princeton: Princeton University Press, 2000.

Moretti, Franco. *Atlas of the European Novel 1800–1900*. London: Verso, 1998.

———. "Conjectures on World Literature." *New Left Review* 1 (January/February 2000): 54–68.

———. "Graphs, Maps, Trees. Abstract Models for Literary History III." *New Left Review* 28 (2004): 43–63.

———. *Graphs, Maps, Trees: Abstract Models for a Literary History*. London: Verso, 2005.

———. *Modern Epic: The World System from Goethe to Garcia Marquez*. Trans. Quintin Hoare. London: Verso, 1996.

———. "More Conjectures." *New Left Review* 20 (2003): 73–81.

———. "The Slaughterhouse of Literature." *Modern Language Quarterly* 61, no. 1 (2000): 207–27.

Morgan, Lewis H. *Ancient Society* [1877]. Cambridge: Harvard University Press, 1964.

Morris-Suzuki, Tessa. *Reinventing Japan: Time Space Nation*. Armonk, N.Y.: M. E. Sharpe, 1998.

Newman, David, and Anssi Paasi. "Fences and Neighbors in the Postmodern World." *Progress in Human Geography* 22, no. 2 (1998): 186–207.

O'Brien, Richard. *Global Financial Integration: The End of Geography*. London: Pinter, 1991.

Ohmae, Kenchi. *The Borderless World*. New York: Harper, 1990.

Orsini, Francesca. "Maps of Indian Writing." *New Left Review* 13 (2002): 75–88.

Orwell, George. *The Road to Wigan Pier*. New York: Harcourt Brace, 1958.

Panitch, Leo. "Globalization and the State." In *Socialist Register*, ed. Ralph Miliband and Leo Panitch, 60–93. London: Merlin Press, 1994.

Panofsky, Erwin. *Perspective as Symbolic Form* [1927]. Trans. C. S. Wood. New York: Zone Books, 1992.

Parla, Jale. "The Object of Comparison." *Comparative Literature Studies* 41, no. 1 (January 2004): 116–25.

Perdue, Peter C. *China Marches West: The Qing Conquest of Central Eurasia*. Cambridge: Harvard University Press, 2005.

Pieterse, Jan Nederveen. *Empire and Emancipation: Power and Liberation on a World Scale*. London: Pluto Press, 1990.

Pomeranz, Kenneth. "Beyond the East-West Binary: Resituating Development Paths in the Eighteenth-Century World." *The Journal of Asian Studies* 61, no. 2 (May 2002): 539–88.

Poovey, Mary. *A History of the Modern Fact: Problems of Knowledge in the Sciences of Wealth and Society*. Chicago: University of Chicago Press, 1998.

Prendergast, Christopher, ed. *Debating World Literature*. London: Verso, 2004.

———. "Negotiating World Literature." *New Left Review* 8 (2001): 100–22.

———. "The World Republic of Letters." In *Debating World Literature*, ed. Christopher Prendergast, 1–25. London: Verso, 2004.

Prigogine, Ilya. *The End of Certainty: Time, Chaos, and the New Laws of Nature*. New York: Free Press, 1997.

Radice, Hugo. "The National Economy: A Keynesian Myth?" *Capital and Class* 22 (1984): 111–40.

Rafael, Vicente. "The Cultures of Area Studies in the United States." *Social Text* 41 (winter 1994): 91–111.

Ralph, Jason G. *Defending the Society of States: Why America Opposes the International Criminal Court and Its Vision of World Society*. Oxford: Oxford University Press, 2007.

Rapp, Stephen H. Jr. . "Chronology, Crossroads, and Commonwealths: World-Regional Schemes and the Lessons of Caucasia." In *Interactions: Transregional Perspectives on World History*, ed. Jerry H. Bentley, Renate Bridenthal, and Anand A. Yang, 167–201. Honolulu: University of Hawaii Press, 2005.

Reich, Robert. *The Work of Nations*. New York: Knopf, 1991.

Robertson, Roland. "Globalisation or Glocalisation." *The Journal of International Communication* 1, no. 1 (1994): 33–51.

———. *Globalization*. London: Sage, 1992.

Rosenberg, Justin. *The Follies of Globalisation Theory*. London: Verso, 2000.

Ruggie, John. "Territoriality and Beyond: Problematizing Modernity in International Relations." *International Organization* 47, no. 1 (1993): 139–74.

Sack, Robert. *Human Territoriality: Its Theory and History*. New York: Cambridge University Press, 1986.

Sahlins, Marshall. "Cosmologies of Capitalism: The Trans-Pacific Sector of 'the World System.'" *Proceedings of the British Academy* 74 (1988): 1–51.

Sahlins, Peter. *Boundaries: The Making of France and Spain in the Pyrenees*. Berkeley: University of California Press, 1989.

Said, Edward W. *Orientalism*. New York: Pantheon, 1978.

———. "Criticism between Culture and System." In *The World, the Text, and the Critic*, Edward W. Said, 178–225. Cambridge: Harvard University Press, 1983.

———. *Edward Said: Criticism and Society*. London: Verso, 2002.

———. *Humanism and Democratic Criticism*. New York: Columbia University Press, 2004.

Sassen, Saskia. *Losing Control? Sovereignty in an Age of Globalization*. New York: Columbia University Press, 1996.

Schmidt, Andre. "Colonialism and the 'Korea Problem' in the Historiography of Modern Japan." *Journal of Asian Studies* 59, no. 4 (November 2000): 951–75.

Schmitt, Carl. *The Concept of the Political*. Chicago: University of Chicago Press, 2007.

Scholte, Jan Aart. *Globalization: A Critical Introduction*. London: Palgrave, 2000.

Schwarz, Roberto. *Misplaced Ideas*. London: Verso, 1992.

Scott, Allen J. *Regions and the World Economy*. London: Pion, 1998.

Shaw, Martin. "Global Society and Global Responsibility: The Theoretical, Historical and Political Limits of International Society." *Millennium* 21 (1992): 421–34.

Shea, Christopher. "A Blacker Shade of Yale: African-American Studies Takes a New Direction." *Lingua Franca* 11, no. 2 (March 2001): 42–49.

Sheppard, Eric. "The Spaces and Times of Globalization: Place, Scale, Networks and Positionality." *Economic Geography* (2002): 307–30.

Sheppard, Eric, and Robert McMaster. *Scale and Geographic Inquiry*. Oxford: Blackwell, 2003.

Smith, Neil. "Contours of a Spatialized Politics: Homeless Vehicles and the Production of Geographical Scale." *Social Text* 33 (1992): 54–81.

———. "Remaking Scale: Competition and Cooperation in Prenational and Postnational Europe." In *Competitive European Peripheries*, ed. Heikki Eskelinen and Folke Snickars, 59–74. Berlin: Springer, 1995.

———. "Spaces of Vulnerability: The Space of Flows and the Politics of Scale." *Critique of Anthropology* 16, no. 1 (1996): 63–77.

———. *Uneven Development: Nature, Capital, and the Production of Space*. London: Blackwell, 1984.

Snow, C. P. *The Two Cultures* [1959]. New York: Cambridge University Press, 1993.

Soja, Edward. *Postmetropolis*. Cambridge: Blackwell, 2000.

Spivak, Gayatri C. *Death of a Discipline*. New York: Columbia University Press.

———. *In Other Worlds: Essays in Cultural Politics*. New York: Methuen, 1987.

———. "World-Systems and the Creole." *Narrative* 14, no. 1 (2006): 102–12.

Spruyt, Hendrik. *The Sovereign State and Its Competitors*. Princeton: Princeton University Press, 1994.

Spybey, Tony. *Globalization and World Society*. Oxford: Polity, 1996.

Stedman, Henry. *Palestine with Jerusalem: The Bradt Travel Guide*. Old Saybrook: Globe Pequot Press, 2000.

Stein, Gertrude. *The Making of Americans* [1925]. Champaign, Ill.: Dalkey Archive Press, 1995.

Stern, Steve J. "Feudalism, Capitalism, and the World-System in the Perspective of Latin America and Africa." In *Confronting Historical Paradigms: Peasants, Labor, and the Capitalist World System in Africa and Latin America*, ed. Frederick Cooper, Allen Isaacman, Florencia Mallon, William Roseberry, Steve Stern, 23–83. Madison: University of Wisconsin Press, 1993.

———. "Feudalism, Capitalism, and the World-System in the Perspective of Latin America and the Caribbean." *The American Historical Review* 93, no. 4 (October 1988): 829–72.

Storper, Michael. *The Regional World*. New York: Guilford, 1996.

Swyngedouw, Eric. "Elite Power, Global Forces and the Political Economy of 'Glocal' Development." In *The Oxford Handbook of Economic Geography*, ed. Gordon Clark, Maryann Feldman, and Meric Gertler, 541–58. New York: Oxford University Press, 2000.

———. "The Heart of the Place: The Resurrection of Locality in an Age of Hyperspace." *Geografiska Annaler* B 71, no. 1 (1989): 31–42.

———. "The Mammon Quest: 'Glocalisation,' Interspatial Competition and the Monetary Order: The Construction of New Scales." In *Cities and Regions in the New Europe*, ed. Mick Dunford and Grigoris Kafkalas, 39–68. London: Belhaven Press, 1992.

———. "Neither Global Nor Local: 'Glocalization' and the Politics of Scale." In *Spaces of Globalization*, ed. Kevin Cox, 137–66. New York: Guilford, 1997.

Taylor, Charles. *Modern Social Imaginaries*. Durham: Duke University Press, 2004.

Taylor, Peter J. "Embedded Statism and the Social Sciences: Opening Up to New Spaces." *Environment and Planning* A 28, no. 11 (1996): 1917–28.

———. *Metageographical Moments*. Research Bulletin 33, Globalization and World Cities Study Group and Network, University of Loughborough, 2000.

———. "The State as Container: Territoriality in the Modern World-System." *Progress in Human Geography* 18, no. 2 (1994): 151–62.

Tomashevsky, Boris. "Thematics [1925]." In *Russian Formalist Criticism: Four Essays*, ed. Lee T. Lemon and Marion J. Reis, 61–95. Lincoln: Nebraska University Press, 1965.

Trilling, Lionel. "The Leavis-Snow Controversy." In *Beyond Culture: Essays on Literature and Learning*, 133–58. New York: Viking Press, 1965.

Tsing, Anna. "The Global Situation." *Cultural Anthropology* 15, no. 3 (200): 327–60.

Virilio, Paul. *Speed and Politics*. New York: Semiotexte, 1984.

Walker, R. B. J. *Inside/Outside: International Relations as Political Theory*. New York: Cambridge University Press, 1993.

Wallerstein, Immanuel, ed. *Open the Social Sciences: Report of the Gulbenkian Commission on the Restructuring of the Social Sciences*. Stanford: Stanford University Press, 1996.

Wallerstein, Immanuel. *After Liberalism*. New York: New Press, 1995.

———. "An American Dilemma of the 21st Century." *Societies without Borders* 1, no. 1 (2006): 7–20.

———. "Call for a Debate about the Paradigm." In Wallerstein, *Unthinking Social Science*, 237–56.

———. *The Capitalist World-Economy*. New York: Cambridge University Press, 1979.

———. "Class Conflict in the Capitalist World-Economy." In Balibar and Wallerstein, *Race, Nation, Class*, 115–24.

———. "The Creation of a Geoculture." In *World-System Analysis*, 97–119.

———. "The Curve of US Power," *New Left Review* 2, no. 40 (July/August 2006): 77–94.

——. *The Decline of American Power*. New York: W. W. Norton, 2003.

——. *The End of the World as We Know It: Social Science for the Twenty-First Century*. Minneapolis: University of Minnesota Press, 1999.

——. *The Essential Wallerstein*. New York: New Press, 2000.

——. *European Universalism: The Rhetoric of Power*. New York: New Press, 2006.

——. "Fanon: Reason and Violence." *Berkeley Journal of Sociology* 15 (1970): 222–31.

——. "Globalization or the Age of Transition?" *International Sociology* 15, no. 2 (2000): 249–65.

——. "The Heritage of Sociology, The Promise of Social Science." Presidential Address, XIV World Congress of Sociology, Montreal, July 26, 1998. *Current Sociology* 47, no. 1 (1999): 1–37.

——. *Historical Capitalism*. London: Verso, 1983.

——. *Historical Capitalism with Capitalist Civilization*. London: Verso, 1996.

——. "Inventions of Time Space Realities." *Geography* 73, no. 4 (1988): 289–97.

——. *The Modern World-System I: Capitalist Agriculture and the Origins of the European World-Economy in the Sixteenth Century*. New York: Academic Press, 1974.

——. *The Modern World-System II: Merchantilism and the Consolidation of the European World-Economy, 1600–1750*. New York: Academic Press, 1980.

——. *The Modern World-System III: The Second Era of Great Expansion of the Capitalist World-Economy, 1730–1840s*. New York: Academic Press, 1989.

——. "The Modern World-System in Crisis." In *World-Systems Analysis: An Introduction*, 121–41. Durham: Duke University Press, 2004.

——. "L'organization des sciences humaines et l'objectivité." *Cahiers Internationaux de Sociologie*, Nouvelle Série, L (1971): 41–48.

——. *The Politics of the World-Economy*. New York: Cambridge University Press, 1984.

——. "Restructuration capitaliste et système-monde." *Agone* 16 (October 1996): 207–33.

——. "The Rise and Future Demise of the World Capitalist System: Concepts for Comparative Analysis [1974]." In *The Essential Wallerstein*, 71–105. New York: The New Press, 2000.

——. "The Rise and Future Demise of the World Capitalist System." In Wallerstein, *The Capitalist World-Economy*, 7–19.

——. "Social Science and Contemporary Society: The Vanishing Guarantees of Rationality." Inaugural address, Convegno Internazionale di Studi dell'Associazione Italiana di Sociologia, Palermo, 26–28 October 1995. *International Sociology* 11, no. 1 (March 1996): 7–26.

——. "There is No Such Thing as Sociology." *The American Sociologist* 6, no. 4 (November 1971): 328.

——. *Uncertainties of Knowledge*. Philadelphia: Temple University Press, 2004.

——. *Unthinking Social Science: The Limits of Nineteenth-Century Paradigms*. Cambridge, U.K.: Polity Press, 1991.

————. *Utopistics: Or Historical Choices of the Twenty-First Century*. New York: New Press, 1998.

————. "The World-System." In *The Blackwell Dictionary of Twentieth-Century Social Thought*, ed. William Outhwaite and Tom Bottomore. Cambridge: Blackwell, 1993.

————. *World-Systems Analysis: An Introduction*. Durham: Duke University Press, 2004.

Wapner, Paul. "Politics beyond the State: Environmental Activism and World Civic Politics." *World Politics* 47 (1995): 311–40.

Wasserstrom, Jeffrey. *Perspectives Online*. January 2001, online at www.theaha.org.

Waters, Malcolm. *Globalization*. New York: Routledge, 1995.

Weber, Max. *Economy and Society*. Vol. 1. Ed. Guenther Roth and Claus Wittich. Berkeley: University of California Press, 1978.

Weinbaum, Alys, Lynn Thomas, Priti Ramamurthy, Uta Poiger, Madeleine Dong, and Tani Barlow, eds. *The Modern Girl Around the World*. Durham: Duke University Press, 2008.

Weiss, Linda. *The Myth of the Powerless State*. New York: Polity, 1998.

White, Richard. *The Middle Ground: Indians, Empires, and Republics in the Great Lakes Region, 1650–1815*. Cambridge: Cambridge University Press, 1991.

Wigen, Kären. "Culture, Power, and Place: The New Landscapes of East Asian Regionalism." *American Historical Review* 104, no. 1 (October 1999): 1183–201.

————. "Japanese Perspectives on the Time/Space of Early Modernity." Paper presented at the XIX International Congress of Historical Sciences, Oslo, Norway, 7 August 2000. The paper can be accessed at www.oslo2000.uio.no/english/index.htm (under Major Themes 1a, "Is Universal History Possible?").

Wilk, Richard. "The Local and the Global in the Political Economy of Beauty: From Miss Belize to Miss World." *Review of International Political Economy* 2 (2005): 117–34.

Williams, Raymond. *Culture and Society, 1780–1950*. New York: Harper and Row, 1958.

Wills, John E., Jr. *1688: A Global History*. New York: Norton, 2001.

Wolf, Eric R. *Europe and the People Without History*. Berkeley: University of California Press, 1982.

Wolff, Christian von. *The Law of Nations Treated According to a Scientific Method* [1758]. Trans. Joseph H. Drake. Oxford: Clarendon Press, 1934.

Yeung, H. W. C. "Capital, State and Space: Contesting the Borderless World," *Transactions, Institute of British Geographers* 23 (1998): 291–309.

Yue Meng, and Dai Jinhua. Surfacing onto the Horizon of History: A Study in Modern Women's Literature (*Fuchu lishi dibiao: xiandai funü wenxue yanjiu*). Zhengzhou: Henan Renmin Chubanshe, 1980.

Žižek, Slavoj. "Psychoanalysis in Post-Marxism: The Case of Alain Badiou." *South Atlantic Quarterly* (spring 1998): 235–61.

Contributors

Gopal Balakrishnan is an associate professor in the History of Consciousness Department, University of California, Santa Cruz, and the author of *The Enemy: An Intellectual Portrait of Carl Schmitt* and *Antagonistics: Capital and Power in an Age of War*. He is on the editorial board of the *New Left Review*.

Tani Barlow teaches in the History Department at Rice University where she also directs the Chao Center for Asian Studies, a research-oriented institute for advanced study. The center also offers an undergraduate major in globalized Asian studies. Barlow is completing a monograph focused on advertising art and social science in the Chinese twentieth-century interwar years.

Neil Brenner is a professor of sociology and metropolitan studies at New York University and is the author of *New State Spaces: Urban Governance and the Rescaling of Statehood* (2004). His research and teaching focus on critical urban theory, sociospatial theory, comparative geopolitical economy, and urban and regional development.

Richard E. Lee is a professor of sociology and the director of the Fernand Braudel Center at Binghamton University. He teaches the theory and methodology of historical social science; his research agenda focuses on the long-term intellectual and disciplinary structures of knowledge formation in writings that range across the sciences, social sciences, and humanities.

Franco Moretti teaches literature at Stanford and writes often for *New Left Review*. His recent books include *Signs Taken for Wonders: Essays in the Sociology of Literary Forms* (1997), *Atlas of the European Novel 1800–1900* (1998), and *Graphs, Maps, Trees: Abstract Models for a Literary History* (2005).

David Palumbo-Liu is a professor of comparative literature, and, by courtesy, English, at Stanford University. He is editor of the electronic journal *Occasion: Interdisciplinary Studies in the Humanities*. He is completing a book on narrative, ethics, and globalization, *The Deliverance of Others: Literature in a Global Age*, forthcoming from Duke University Press.

Bruce Robbins is the Old Dominion Foundation Professor in the Humanities at Columbia University. His books include *Upward Mobility and the Common Good*

(2007) and *Feeling Global: Internationalism in Distress* (1999). He is co-editor of *The Longman Anthology of World Literature* (2003) and *Cosmopolitics* (1998).

Helen Stacy, a senior fellow at the Center on Democracy, Development, and the Rule of Law at Stanford University's Freeman Spogli Institute for International Studies and a senior lecturer at Stanford Law School, is a scholar of international and comparative law, human rights, and legal philosophy. Her latest work, *Human Rights for the Twenty-First Century: Sovereignty, Civil Society, Culture* (2009), analyzes the burgeoning role of regional courts in promoting human rights while also honoring social, cultural, and religious values.

Nirvana Tanoukhi is Sheila Biddle Fellow at the W. E. B. Du Bois Institute for African and African American Studies at Harvard University in 2010–2011, where she is at work on a book on the place of the African novel in World Literature. Tanoukhi's articles have appeared in *Research in African Literatures*, *New Literary History*, and *The Routledge Companion to World Literature*. She is translator of two novels and short fiction from Arabic.

Immanuel Wallerstein is a senior research scholar at Yale University. He is the author of *The Modern World-System* (four volumes), and recently *After Liberalism* (1995), *Utopistics: Or Historical Choices of the Twenty-First Century* (1998), *The End of the World as We Know It: Social Science for the Twenty-First Century* (1999), *The Decline of American Power* (2003), *Uncertainties of Knowledge* (2004), *World-Systems Analysis: An Introduction* (2004), and *European Universalism: The Rhetoric of Power* (2006).

Kären Wigen is a professor of history at Stanford University, where she teaches courses on early modern Japan and on the history of cartography. Author with Martin Lewis of *The Myth of Continents: A Critique of Meta-Geography* (1997), she recently co-edited a collection of essays titled *Seascapes: Maritime Histories, Littoral Cultures, and Trans-Oceanic Exchanges* (2007). Her latest book is *A Malleable Map: Geographies of Restoration in Central Japan, 1600–1912* (2010).

Index

Italicized page numbers refer to illustrations, figures (f), and tables (t)

For more information on the editors, see the list of contributors.

David Palumbo-Liu is a professor of comparative literature
at Stanford University.

Bruce Robbins is the Old Dominion Foundation Professor
in the Humanities at Columbia University.

Nirvana Tanoukhi is Sheila Biddle Fellow at the W. E. B. Du Bois Institute
for African and African American Studies at Harvard University.

Chapter 3 originally appeared as "World Systems Analysis, Evolutionary Theory, *Weltliteratur*," in *Review: A Journal of the Fernand Braudel Center* 28, no. 3 (2005). Chapter 4 originally appeared as "The Scale of World Literature," in *New Literary History* 39, no. 3 (2008), 599–617. © 2008 New Literary History, The University of Virginia. Reprinted with permission of The Johns Hopkins University Press. Chapter 5 originally appeared as "Beyond State-Centrism? Space, Territoriality and Geographical Scale in Globalization Studies," in *Theory and Society* 28, no. 2 (1999): 39–78. Chapter 6 originally appeared as "Cartographies of Connection: Ocean Maps as Metaphors for Inter-Area History" in Hanna Schissler and Yasemin Soysal, eds., *The Nation, Europe, the World: Textbooks and Curricula in Transition* (New York: St. Martin's Press / Berlin: Berghahn Books, 2002). Portions of chapter 7 are adapted from Tani Barlow's article, "History and the Border," which first appeared in *Journal of Women's History* 18, no. 2 (2006), 8–32. © 2006 *Journal of Women's History*. Reprinted with permission by The Johns Hopkins University Press.

Library of Congress Cataloging-in-Publication Data
Immanuel Wallerstein and the problem of the world :
system, scale, culture / David Palumbo-Liu, Bruce Robbins,
and Nirvana Tanoukhi, eds.
p. cm.
Includes bibliographical references and index.
ISBN 978-0-8223-4834-4 (cloth : alk. paper)
ISBN 978-0-8223-4848-1 (pbk. : alk. paper)
1. Wallerstein, Immanuel Maurice, 1930– 2. Social sciences—
Philosophy. 3. Sociology—Philosophy. 4. History—Philosophy.
5. Literature—History and criticism. I. Palumbo-Liu, David.
II. Robbins, Bruce. III. Tanoukhi, Nirvana.
H61.I443 2011   300.1—dc22   2010038079